George Washington Greene

A Short History of Rhode Island

George Washington Greene

A Short History of Rhode Island

ISBN/EAN: 9783743320352

Manufactured in Europe, USA, Canada, Australia, Japa

Cover: Foto ©ninafisch / pixelio.de

Manufactured and distributed by brebook publishing software (www.brebook.com)

George Washington Greene

A Short History of Rhode Island

A

SHORT HISTORY

OF

RHODE ISLAND,

BY

GEORGE WASHINGTON GREENE, LL.D.,

LATE NON-RESIDENT PROFESSOR OF AMERICAN HISTORY IN CORNELL
UNIVERSITY; AUTHOR OF "THE LIFE OF MAJOR-GENERAL
NATHANAEL GREENE;" "HISTORICAL VIEW OF THE
AMERICAN REVOLUTION," ETC., ETC.

PROVIDENCE:
J. A. & R. A. REID, PUBLISHERS,
1877.

Entered according to Act of Congress, in the year 1877, by

ANNA MARIA GREENE,

in the office of the Librarian of Congress, at Washington, D. C.

TO
Anna Maria Greene,

My Dear Mother:

You bear your ninety-three years so lightly that I invite your attention to a new volume of mine with as much assurance of your sympathy as when I crowed and wondered over my first picture book an infant on your knee. For your sympathy is as quick and as warm as it was then, and your memory goes back with unerring certainty to the men and the scenes of almost a century ago. Your eyes have looked upon Washington, and your tenacious memory can still recall the outline of his majestic form.

The first time that I ventured to send forth a volume to the world, I set upon the dedication page the name of my father. He has been dead many years. You still linger behind, and long may you linger. Long may those fresh memories which give such a charm to your daily life continue to cheer you and instruct those who have the privilege of living with you. They have seen life imperfectly who have not seen what a charm it wears when the heart that has beat so long still lends its genial warmth to the still inquiring mind.

Reverentially and affectionately your son,

GEORGE W. GREENE.

Preface.

THERE are two classes of history, each of which has claims upon our attention peculiarly its own. One is a sober teacher, the other a pleasant companion. One opens new paths of thought, the other throws new light upon the old, and both agree in making man the chief object of their meditations.

Nearly two thousand years ago a Roman historian likened the life of his country to the life of man. Time has confirmed the parallel. Nations, like men, have their infancy and their youth, their robust manhood and their garrulous old age. Their lives like the lives of men are full of encouragement and of warning. Interpret them aright and they become trusty guides. Misapply their lessons and you grope in the dark and stumble at every step.

And both states and men have their special duties and were created for special ends. The God that made them assigned to each its problem, and to work this out is to work out His will. Of this problem history is the record and the interpreter. It tells us what man has been, and thereby aids us to divine what he yet may be.

If with the philosopher history reveals the laws of life, with the poet she recalls the past and stirs human sympathies in their profoundest depths. Man follows man on her checkered stage; nations rise and fall; mysteries enchain us; imagination controls us; reason guides us; conscience admonishes and warns; and first and foremost of all our stimulants to action is our sympathy with our fellow-man.

I have attempted in the following pages to tell what the part of Rhode Island has been in this great drama. A talent was entrusted to her. Did she wrap it in a napkin?

To those who are familiar with the accurate and exhaustive work of Governor Arnold, it will be needless to say that but for the aid of his volumes, mine would never have been written.

GEORGE W. GREENE.

WINDMILL COTTAGE,
East Greenwich, R. I., April 8th, 1877.

Analytical Table.

CHAPTER I.

CONDITION OF AFFAIRS IN MASSACHUSETTS BAY AND PLYMOUTH COLONIES.—ARRIVAL AND BANISHMENT OF ROGER WILLIAMS.

		Page.
	The religious sentiment connected with the foundation of states,	1
	Resistance to the doctrine of theocracy occasioned the settlement of Rhode Island,	2
1631.	Ship Lyon arrived at Boston, bringing Roger Williams,	2
	Early life of Williams,	2
	Massachusetts in possession of two distinct colonies,	3
	In Massachusetts Colony the clergy were virtually rulers, and they were extremely rigid,	3
	Disputes between Williams and the authorities of Massachusetts Bay Colony,	4
	Removal of Williams to Plymouth,	4
	Williams makes friendship with Massasoit and Miantonomi,	5
	Learns the Indian language,	5
	Williams returns to Salem,	5
1635.	He is persecuted and finally banished,	6
	Articles of banishment,	6

CHAPTER II.

SUFFERINGS OF ROGER WILLIAMS IN THE WILDERNESS.—FOUNDS A SETTLEMENT ON THE SEEKONK RIVER.—IS ADVISED TO DEPART.—SEEKS OUT A NEW PLACE WHICH HE CALLS PROVIDENCE.

Attempt to send Williams to England,	7
His flight,	8
He is fed by the Indians,	8

ANALYTICAL TABLE.

	Page.
He is given land on the Seekonk River by Massoit and starts a settlement,	8
He receives a friendly letter from the Governor of Plymouth asking him to remove,	9
He starts with five companions in a canoe to find a place for a settlement, and finally lands at Providence,	9

CHAPTER III.

WILLIAMS OBTAINS A GRANT OF LAND AND FOUNDS A COLONY.—FORM OF GOVERNMENT IN THE COLONY.—WILLIAMS GOES TO ENGLAND TO OBTAIN A ROYAL CHARTER.

		Page.
	Early inhabitants of Rhode Island,	11
	Williams makes peace between Canonicus and Massasoit,	12
	He receives a grant of land from Canonicus and begins a settlement,	12
	Compact of the colonists at Providence,	13
	Experiment of separation of church from state tried in the new Colony.	13
	The right of suffrage not regarded as a natural right. Illustrated by Joshua Verin and his wife,	14
1639.	The first church founded in Providence,	15
	Five select men appointed to govern the Colony, subject to the action of the Monthly Town Meeting,	15
	Massachusetts Colony applied for a new charter to cover the land occupied by Providence,	15
1643.	Providence in connection with Aquidneck and Warwick sent Williams to England to obtain a Royal charter,	15
1644.	Williams returns in 1644 successsful, and is received with exultation,	16

CHAPTER IV.

SETTLEMENT OF AQUIDNECK AND WARWICK.—PEQUOT WAR.—DEATH OF MIANTONOMI.

| 1637. | Anna Hutchinson arrived in Massachusetts and banished, | 17 |

Nineteen of her followers under William Coddington and John Clarke, purchased the Island of Aquidneck and formed settlements at Pocasset and Newport, . . 17
Roger Williams proclaimed the right of religious liberty to every human being, . 18
Samuel Gorton banished from Pocasset, . 19
He denied the authority of all government except that authorized by the King and Parliament, ... 19
He, with eleven others, bought Shawomet and settled there, . . . 19
He is besieged by troops from Massachusetts, is captured, imprisoned, and afterwards released, ... 19
He is appointed to a magistracy in Aquidneck, 19
Roger Williams prevented the alliance| of the Pequots and Narragansetts, and formed one between the English and the Narragansetts, 21
Pequots rooted out and crushed, . 21
Miantonomi treacherously put to death,| . 22
The Narragansetts put themselves under the protection of the English, . . 22

CHAPTER V.

CHARTER GRANTED TO PROVIDENCE PLANTATIONS.—ORGANIZATION UNDER IT.—THE LAWS ADOPTED.

1643. The charter granted to Providence Plantations, 23
Provisions of the charter, . . . 23
1647. The corporators met at Portsmouth and in a general assembly accepted the charter, and proceeded to organize under it, . 24
The government declared to be democratical, . 24
President and other officers chosen, . 25
Description of the code of laws, . . 25
Design for a seal adopted, . . 26
Roger Williams presented with one hundred pounds for services in obtaining the charter, 26
Spirit of the law, ... 27

CHAPTER VI.

FOREIGN AND DOMESTIC TROUBLES.—UNSUCCESSFUL ATTEMPT AT USURPATION BY CODDINGTON.

		Page.
	Death of Canonicus,	28
	Possibility of the doctrine of soul liberty demonstrated,	28
	Dissensions among the colonists,	29
	Troubles with Massachusetts,	29
	Baptists persecuted in Massachusetts,	30
1651.	Coddington obtained a royal commission as Governor of Rhode Island and Connecticut for life, which virtually dissolved the first charter,	30
	Roger Williams sent to England to ask for a confirmation of the charter,	31
	John Clarke, also, sent to ask for a revocation of Coddington's commission,	31
1652.	Slaves not allowed to be held in bondage longer than ten years.	32
	Commerce with the Dutch of Manhattan interrupted by war between England and Holland.	32
	Coddington's commission revoked and the first charter restored,	32

CHAPTER VII.

MORE FOREIGN AND DOMESTIC TROUBLES. — CIVIL AND CRIMINAL REGULATIONS OF THE COLONY.—ARRIVAL OF QUAKERS.

	Conscience claimed as the rule of action in civil as well as religious matters,	33
	Contentions between the Island and the mainland towns,	34
1654.	Court of Commissioners met and effected a reunion in the Colony,	34
	Attempts of the United Colonies to make war on the Narragansetts, but they failed, as Williams had influenced Massasoit not to sanction it,	35
	Qualification of citizenship,	36

ANALYTICAL TABLE. xi

		Page.
	Duties of citizenship ascendant over dignity of office,	37
	Protection of marriage,	38
	The Pawtuxet controversy settled by acknowledgement of the claims of Rhode Island,	38
	Fort built for protection against Indians,	39
	Quakers arrived. Difference of treatment of them between Rhode Island and Massachusetts,	39
1663.	A new charter granted by Charles II. and accepted by the colonists,	40

CHAPTER VIII.

TROUBLES IN OBTAINING A NEW CHARTER.—PROVISIONS OF THE CHARTER.—DIFFICULTIES CONCERNING THE NARRAGANSETT PURCHASE.—CURRENCY.—SCHOOLS.

	The new charter gave a democratic government,	41
	Some of its provisions,	41
	Religious liberty recognized by it,	42
	Assembly and courts reörganized,	43
	State magistrates chosen by the freemen,	44
	Jealousy of Massachusetts,	44
	Trouble concerning the ownership of Narragansett,	45
	Attempt to dispossess Rhode Island of part of her territory,	46
	The Narragansetts compelled to mortgage their lands to the United Colonies,	47
	New charter obtained by Connecticut extending its bounds to the Narragansett River,	48
1663.	The boundary line left to arbitrators who fix it at the Pawcatuck River,	49
	The intrigues of John Scott for the purchase of the Narragansett tract,	49
	Letter obtained from the King, putting the Narragansett purchase under protection of Massachusetts and Connecticut,	50
	This was rendered null by the second charter of Rhode Island grant soon afterward,	51
	Wampum used as money in the Colony,	52

xii ANALYTICAL TABLE.

Page.

	Also used as an article of ornament by the natives, ...	52
1652.	Massachusetts began to coin silver in 1652,	53
	Rhode Island abolished the use of wampum ten years later, ...	53
1662.	New England shilling made legal tender in Rhode Island, ...	53
1640–1663.	First schools established at Providence and Newport, ...	53
	Affirmation is declared to be equal to an oath,	54

CHAPTER IX.

TERRITORY OF RHODE ISLAND IS INCREASED BY THE ADDITION OF BLOCK ISLAND.—DISPUTES BETWEEN RHODE ISLAND AND THE OTHER COLONIES SETTLED BY ROYAL COMMAND.—STATE OF AFFAIRS IN THE COLONY IN 1667.|

1663.	Block Island added to Rhode Island, . .	55
	[Regulations concerning its admission, .	56
	It is incorporated under the name of New Shoreham, ...	56
	Four Commissioners sent to America to reduce the Dutch and settle all questions of appeal between the colonies, . . .	57
	The vexed questions of boundary line between Rhode Island and Plymouth; the Narragansett question and Warwick difficulties referred to the Commissioners, who referred the first to the King and decided the second in favor of Rhode Island, . . .	57
	The Indians removed from King's Province,	59
	Five propositions submitted by the Commissioners to the Rhode Island Assembly, .	59
	1st. All householders should take the oath of allegiance to the King, . .	59
	2d. Mode of admitting freemen, . .	59
	3d. Admission to the sacrament open to all well disposed persons, . . .	60
	4th. All laws and resolves derogatory to the King repealed, ...	60
	5th. Provisions for self-defence, . .	60

ANALYTICAL TABLE. xiii

Page.

1672.	Trouble with John Paine concerning Prudence Island,	62
	Members of the Assembly to be paid for their services,	63
	Financial difficulties in the Colony,	64
1667.	Preparations for defence against the French,	64
1672.	Act passed to facilitate the collection of taxes,	65

CHAPTER X.

KING PHILIP'S WAR.

Wamsutta summoned before the General Court at Plymouth,	67
His death,	67
Indignation of the Indians, especially King Philip,	68
Condition of the Indians,	68
Attack on Swanzey,	69
The Indians pursued by the English,	69
Philip and his allies beseiged in a swamp at Pocasset,	71
His escape,	71
The Indian attack on Hadley,	71
Goffe, the regicide,	72
Philip joined the Narragansetts,	72
Battle in the swamp,	73
Indians defeated, and their village destroyed,	74
Depredations in Rhode Island,	75
Death of Canonchet,	76
Death of Philip and end of the war,	77
Condition of the country after the war,	77

CHAPTER XI.

INDIANS STILL TROUBLESOME.—CONDITION OF THE PEOPLE.—
TROUBLES CONCERNING THE BOUNDARY LINES.

Precautions against the Indians,	78
Troubles with Connecticut concerning Narragansett,	79
Two agents sent to England,	80

xiv   ANALYTICAL TABLE.

		Page.
	War party obtains power,	80
	Foundation of East Greenwich,	82
	Bitter controversy concerning the limits and extent of the Providence and Pawtuxet purchase,	82
1696–1712.	Settled in 1696 and 1712,	83

CHAPTER XII.

DEATH OF SEVERAL OF THE MOST PROMINENT MEN.—CHANGES IN LEGISLATION.

	The United Colonies still encroached upon Rhode Island,	84
	Deaths of John Clarke, Roger Williams, Samuel Gorton, William Harris, and William Coddington,	85
1678.	Financial condition of the Colony in 1678,	88
	Changes in the usages of election,	89
	Bankrupt law passed and afterwards repealed,	89
	Law concerning disputed titles to lands,	90
1679.	Law for the protection of servants,	91
	Law for the protection of sailors,	91
	John Clawson's curse,	92

CHAPTER XIII.

COURTS AND ARMY STRENGTHENED.—COMMISSIONERS SENT FROM ENGLAND.—CHARTER REVOKED.

	Disputes concerning the title of Potowomut,	93
1680.	Power of the town to reject or accept new citizens,	93
	Efficiency of the courts increased,	94
	English navigation act injures the commercial interests of the Colony.	95
	Commissioners appointed to settle the vexed question of the King's Province,	96
	Rhode Island's position in New England in regard to the other colonies,	96
	Trouble with the Commissioners,	97
	Charter revoked,	98
	Rhode Island returned to its original form of government,	98

ANALYTICAL TABLE. XV

CHAPTER XIV.

CHANGES IN FORM OF GOVERNMENT.—SIR EDMOND ANDROS APPOINTED GOVERNOR.—HE OPPRESSES THE COLONISTS AND IS FINALLY DEPOSED.

                                            Page.

John Greene sent to England with an address to the King for the preservation of the charter, 100
Changes in the names and boundaries of Kingston, Westerly and East Greenwich, . 101

1687. Arrival of Sir Edmond Andros, . . 101
Taxes farmed out, ... 102
Marriages made illegal unless performed by the rites of the English Church, . . 103
Passport system introduced, . . 103
Composition of the council, . . . 103
Andros's commission enlarged, . . 105
The press subjected to the will of the Governor, 105
Title of Rhode Island to King's Province again confirmed, ... 106
Persecution of the Huguenots, . . 107
Andros deposed, ... 107

CHAPTER XV.

CHARTER GOVERNMENT AGAIN RESUMED.—FRENCH WAR.—INTERNAL IMPROVEMENTS.—CHARGES AGAINST THE COLONIES.

Chief-Justice Dudley attempted to open his court, he is seized and imprisoned, . . 108
Return of the old form of government, . 108
Legality of resumption confirmed by the King, 109

1690. The Assembly reörganized, . . 110
Town house built, ... 111
The colonists taxed to sustain the French and Indian war, ... 112
Coast invaded by French privateers, . 112
New taxes levied, ... 113
Small-pox broke out in the Colony, . 113

1691. Sir William Phipps appointed Governor of Massachusetts with command over all the forces of New England, . . . 114

xvi   ANALYTICAL TABLE.

		Page.
	This command over the forces of Rhode Island restricted to time of war,	115
1693.	First mail line established between Boston and Virginia,	116
	State officers to be paid a regular salary,	116
	Assembly divided into two houses,	116
	Indians still troublesome,	117
	Courts of Admiralty established in the Colony,	117
1697–1698.	Trouble from enemies to the charter government,	117
	Interests of trade fostered,	118
	Smuggling common,	118
	Charges made against the Colony by the Royal Governor,	119
	Captain Kidd,	119

CHAPTER XVI.

COLONIAL PROSPERITY.—DIFFICULTIES OCCASIONED BY THE WAR WITH THE FRENCH.—DOMESTIC AFFAIRS OF THE COLONY.

1702.	Prosperity of the Colony,	120
	Providence the second town in the Colony,	120
	Religious freedom,	120
	Attempt to establish a Vice-Royalty over the Colonies,	122
1701.	Better Laws enacted,	123
1702.	Preparations for defence,	123
1703.	Boundary line between Rhode Island and Connecticut finally settled,	124
	The character and interest of the Colony misunderstood by England.	124
	French privateer captured,	125
	Further acts of the Assembly,	126
	Slave trade.	127
1708.	First census taken,	127
	Public auctions first held.	128
	Commercial and agricultural progress,	128
1709.	First printing press set up at Newport,	129
	Internal improvements,	130

CHAPTER XVII.

PAPER MONEY TROUBLES.—ESTABLISHMENT OF BANKS.—PROTECTION OF HOME INDUSTRIES.—PROPERTY QUALIFICATIONS FOR SUFFRAGE.

		Page.
	Issue of paper money,	131
	Clerk of the Assembly first elected from outside the House,	131
	Arts of peace resumed,	132
	New militia laws enacted,	132
	Laws concerning trade,	133
	Troubles occasioned by paper money,	134
1715.	Banks established in Massachusetts and Rhode Island,	134
	Paper money question carried into election,	134
	Improvements in Newport,	136
	Criminal code,	136
1716.	School-houses built in Portsmouth,	136
	Punishment of slander,	137
	Indian lands taken under the protection of the Colony,	137
	Law concerning intestates,	137
1719.	First edition of the laws printed,	138
	Boundary troubles,	138
	Industry of the Colony protected by loans and bounties,	138
1724.	Freehold act passed,	139
1723.	Pirate captured,	139
	Evidences of the progress of the Colony,	139
	Death of Governor Cranston,	141

CHAPTER XVIII.

CHANGE OF THE EXECUTIVE.—ACTS OF THE ASSEMBLY.—GEORGE BERKELEY'S RESIDENCE IN NEWPORT.—FRIENDLY FEELING BETWEEN THE COLONISTS AND THE MOTHER COUNTRY.

	New Governor elected,	142
	State of affairs in England,	142
1728.	Revision of the criminal code,	143

		Page.
	Laws for the encouragement and regulation of trade,	144
1727.	Earthquake,	145
1723-1724.	Division of the Colony into counties.	146
	George Berkeley,	146
	Establishment of Redwood Library,	147
	Laws concerning charitable institutions, Quakers and Indians,	147
1730.	New census taken.	148
1731.	New bank voted.	149
	Commercial prosperity,	149
	New edition of the laws published.	149
	Fisheries encouraged,	150
	Regulation concerning election,	150
	William Wanton chosen Governor,	152
	Depreciation of paper money,	152
1733.	Marriage laws.	152
	John Wanton chosen Governor,	153
	Watchfulness of the Board of Trade,	153
1735-1736.	Throat distemper,	154
	Law against bribery at elections,	154
	Arrival of his Majesty's ship Tartar,	155
	Means of protection against fire,	155

CHAPTER XIX.

WAR WITH SPAIN.—NEW TAXES LEVIED BY ENGLAND.—RELIGIOUS AWAKENING AMONG THE BAPTISTS.

	Preparation for war against the Spaniards,	156
	Great expedition against the Spanish West Indies,	157
	New taxes levied on importations by England,	157
	Death of Governor Wanton, who is succeeded by Richard Ward,	158
	Arrival of Whitefield and Fothergill,	159
	Further provisions for the defence of the Colony.	159
	Report of the Governor concerning paper money.	160
1741.	Boundary line between Rhode Island and Massachusetts settled,	161

CHAPTER XX.

PROGRESS OF THE WAR WITH THE FRENCH.—CHANGE IN THE JURISDICTION OF THE COURTS.—SENSE OF COMMON INTEREST DEVELOPING AMONG THE COLONISTS.—LOUISBURG CAPTURED.

		Page.
	Privateers fitted out,	162
1741.	James Greene started an iron works,	162
	Changes of the jurisdictions of the courts,	163
	Encroachments of Connecticut,	163
1741.	Newport Artillery chartered,	165
	Counterfeit bills troublesome,	164
1744.	Lotteries legalized,	165
	Rhode Island's part in the capture of Louisburg,	165
	Death of Colonel John Cranston,	166
	Two privateers and two hundred men lost,	166
	Sense of common interest and mutual dependence gaining ground,	166
	Caution against fraudulent voting,	167
	Disaster to the French armada,	168
1746.	Close of the campaign,	168
	Accession of territory,	168

CHAPTER XXI.

ATTEMPT TO RETURN TO SPECIE PAYMENTS.—CHANGES IN THE REQUIREMENTS OF CITIZENSHIP.—NEW COUNTIES AND TOWNS FORMED.—FRENCH AND INDIAN WAR.—WARD AND HOPKINS CONTEST.—ESTABLISHMENT OF NEWSPAPERS.

1748.	Peace of Aix-la-Chapelle,	170
	Hutchinson's scheme for returning to specie payment rejected by Rhode Island,	171
	Act against swearing revised,	172
	Provisions concerning legal residence,	172
	New census taken,	172
1748–1749.	Death of John Callender,	173
	Beaver Tail Light built,	173
	Troubles from depreciation of currency,	173
1754.	First divorce granted,	174
	Kent County formed.	174

ANALYTICAL TABLE.

		Page.
1752.	Gregorian calendar adopted,	175
	Troubles concerning the Narragansett land settled,	175
1753.	First patent granted in the Colony for making potash,	175
	Fellowship Club founded—afterwards the Newport Marine Society,	176
1754.	Commissioners sent to the Albany Congress,	176
	French and Indian war,	177
	French settlers imprisoned,	178
	Ward and Hopkins contest,	178
	Providence court house and library burned,	179
	David Douglass built a theatre at Providence,	180
1758.	Newport Mercury established,	180
1762.	Providence Gazette established,	180
	Writs of assistance first called for,	181
1759.	Death of Richard Partridge,	181
	Freemasonry first introduced into the Colony,	181
	Regulations concerning fires,	181
	Towns of Hopkinton and Johnston formed,	182

CHAPTER XXII.

RETROSPECT.—ENCROACHMENTS OF ENGLAND.—RESISTANCE TO THE REVENUE LAWS.—STAMP ACT.—SECOND CONGRESS OF COLONIES MET AT NEW YORK.—EDUCATIONAL INTEREST.

	Resumé of the progress of the Colony,	183
	Reason for the enactment of the laws,	184
	Rhode Island's solution of the problem of self-government and soul-liberty,	185
	Encroachments of England on the liberties of the colonies,	186
	War had taught the colonies a much needed lesson,	187
	Harbor improvements,	188
	Parliament votes men and money for the defence of the American colonies,	188
	Restrictions of commerce,	189
1764.	Molasses and sugar act renewed and extended,	189
	Resistance to the enforcement of the obnoxious revenue laws,	190
	Action of the colonies in regard to the stamp act,	191

ANALYTICAL TABLE.

		Page.
	England is obliged to repeal the stamp act,	193
	Resistance to impressment,	193
1765.	Second Colonial Congress met at New York and issued addresses to the people, Parliament, and to the King,	194
	New digest of the laws completed and printed,	195
1766.	Free schools established at Providence,	196
	Brown University founded,	196
	Iron mine discovered,	197

CHAPTER XXIII.

TRANSIT OF VENUS.—A STRONG DISLIKE TO ENGLAND MORE OPENLY EXPRESSED.—NON-IMPORTATION AGREEMENT.—INTRODUCTION OF SLAVES PROHIBITED.—CAPTURE OF THE GASPEE.

	Collision between British officers and citizens,	199
	Dedication of liberty trees,	199
	Laws concerning domestic interests,	199
	Transit of Venus,	200
	Armed resistance to England more openly talked of,	201
	Scuttling of the sloop-of-war Liberty,	202
	Non-importation of tea agreed to,	203
	Prosperity of Newport,	203
	First Commencement at Rhode Island College,	204
1770.	Further introduction of slaves prohibited,	204
	Governor Hutchinson advanced a claim for the command of the Rhode Island militia,	205
	Evidence of justice in Rhode Island,	206
	Capture and destruction of the schooner Gaspee,	207

CHAPTER XXIV.

PROPOSITION FOR THE UNION OF THE COLONIES.—ACTIVE MEASURES TAKEN LOOKING TOWARDS INDEPENDENCE.—DELEGATES ELECTED TO CONGRESS.—DESTRUCTION OF TEA AT PROVIDENCE.—TROOPS RAISED.—POSTAL SYSTEM ESTABLISHED.—DEPREDATIONS OF THE BRITISH.—"GOD SAVE THE UNITED COLONIES."

1774.	Limitation of negro slavery,	210
	Resolution recommending the union of the colonies passed at Providence town meeting,	210

ANALYTICAL TABLE.

		Page.
1774.	Boston port bill passed, . .	211
	Small-pox at Newport, . .	211
	Indication of popular indignation, .	212
	Activity of Committees of Correspondence, .	212
	Publishment of the Hutchinson letters. .	213
	Franklin removed from his position as superintendent of American post-offices, .	214
1774.	General Gage entered Boston as Governor,	·215
	Sympathy of Rhode Island for Boston; East Greenwich the first to open a subscription, .	215
	Hopkins and Ward elected delegates to Congress, ...	216
1774.	Congress met in Philadelphia; adopted a declaration of rights; recommended the formation of an American Association, . . .	217
	Distribution of arms, . . .	218
	Exportation of sheep stopped; manufacture of fire-arms begun, ...	219
	Tea burnt at Providence, .	219
	Troops started for Boston, . .	219
	Army of Observation formed with Nathanael Greene, commander, . .	220
	Rhode Island troops on Jamaica Plains,	221
	Articles of war passed, . .	221
	Capture of a British vessel by Captain Abraham Whipple, ...	221
	Rhode Island Navy founded, . .	222
	William Goddard's postal system went into operation, . . .	222
	Colony put upon a war footing, .	223
	Bristol bombarded and the coast of Rhode Island plundered.	224
	Part of the debt of Rhode Island assumed by Congress as a war debt, . .	225
	Rhode Island in the expedition against Quebec,	226
	Depredation of the British squadron, .	226
	Battle on Prudence Island, .	227
	Evacuation of Boston, . .	228
	Death of Samuel Ward. . .	228
	The Assembly of Rhode Island renounced their allegiance to the British Crown, .	228

CHAPTER XXV.

RHODE ISLAND BLOCKADED.—DECLARATION OF INDEPENDENCE INDORSED BY THE ASSEMBLY. — NEW TROOPS RAISED.— FRENCH ALLIANCE.—UNSUCCESSFUL ATTEMPT TO DRIVE THE BRITISH FROM RHODE ISLAND.

		Page.
	Islands and waters of Rhode Island taken possession of by the British,	229
	Quota of Rhode Island,	230
	Inoculation introduced,	231
	Treatment of Tories	231
	Declaration of Independence indorsed by the Assembly,	232
	Rhode Island's part in the Continental Navy,	232
	Convention of Eastern States to form a concerted plan of action,	233
	Financial troubles,	234
	Regiment of negroes raised,	234
1778.	Tidings of the French alliance received,	235
	Expedition against Bristol and Warren,	235
	Attempt to drive the British from Rhode Island rendered unsuccessful by a terrible storm, and jealousy among the officers of the French fleet,	236

CHAPTER XXVI.

ACTS OF THE BRITISH TROOPS.—DISTRESS IN RHODE ISLAND.— EVACUATION OF NEWPORT.—REPUDIATION.—END OF THE WAR.

Disappointment of the Americans,		241
Wanton destruction of life and property by the British,		241
Pigot galley captured by Talbot,		242
Scarcity of food in Rhode Island,		242
Steuben's tactics introduced into the army,		244
Difficulty in raising money,		244
British left Newport.		245
Town records carried off by the British,		246
Repudiation of debt,		247
Rhode Island's quota.		248

xxiv ANALYTICAL TABLE.

		Page.
	Preparations for quartering and feeding the troops,	249
	An English fleet of sixteen ships menaced the Rhode Island coast,	250
	Assembly met at Newport; the first time in four years,	250
1781.	End of the war,	251
	The federation completed,	251

CHAPTER XXVII.

ARTS OF PEACE RESUMED.—DOCTRINE OF STATE RIGHTS.

	Name of King's County changed to Washington,	252
	New census taken.	253
	Question of State Rights raised,	253
1782.	Nicholas Cooke died,	254
	Armed resistance to the collection of taxes,	254
	Troubles arising from financial embarrassment,	255
1783.	Acts of the Assembly,	256

CHAPTER XXVIII.

DEPRECIATION OF THE CURRENCY.—INTRODUCTION OF THE SPINNING-JENNY. — BITTER OPPOSITION TO THE FEDERAL UNION. — RHODE ISLAND FINALLY ACCEPTS THE CONSTITUTION.

	Desperate attempt to float a new issue of paper money,	257
	Forcing acts declared unconstitutional,	258
	First spinning-jenny made in the United States,	259
	Bill passed to pay five shillings in the pound for paper money,	260
	Refusal of Rhode Island to send delegates to the Federal Convention,	261
	Proposed United States Constitution printed,	261
	Acceptance of the Constitution by various states,	261
	State of manufactures,	262
1790.	Rhode Island declared her adhesion to the Union,	264

CHAPTER XXIX.

MODE OF LIFE IN OUR FOREFATHERS' DAYS.

	Page.
Early condition of the land,	265
Agriculture the principal pursuit of the early settlers,	266
Early traveling,	267
Early means of education,	267
Amusements,	268

CHAPTER XXX.

COMMERCIAL GROWTH AND PROSPERITY OF RHODE ISLAND.

	Rhode Island wiser on account of her previous struggles for self-government,	270
	Commercial condition of Rhode Island,	271
	Trade with East Indies commenced,	271
1790.	First cotton factory went into operation,	273
1799.	Free school system established,	273
1819.	Providence Institution for Savings founded,	274
	Canal from the Providence River to the north line of the state projected and failed,	274
1801.	Great fire in Providence,	274
	Visit of Washington to Rhode Island,	275
1832.	Providence made a city,	275
	Rhode Island in the War of 1812,	276

CHAPTER XXXI.

THE DORR REBELLION.

	The Right of Suffrage becomes the question of Rhode Island's politics,	277
	Inequality of representation,	278
	No relief obtainable from the Assembly,	278
	Formation of Suffrage Associations,	279
	Peoples' Constitution, so called, voted for,	279
1842.	Thomas Wilson Dorr elected Governor under it,	280
	Conflict between the old and new government,	280
	Attempt of the Dorr government to organize and seize the arsenal both failures,	281

ANALYTICAL TABLE

	Page.
End of the War,	281
Dorr tried for treason and sentenced to imprisonment for life; afterwards restored to his political and civil rights,	281
New Constitution adopted,	282
Freedom of thought and speech the foundation of Rhode Island's prosperity,	228

CHAPTER XXXII.

LIFE UNDER THE CONSTITUTION.—THE WAR OF THE REBELLION.—THE CENTENARY.

Life under the Constitution,	283
The War of the Rebellion,	283
Rhode Island's quota,	284
The Centennial Exposition,	285

APPENDIX.

King Charles' Charter,	291
Present State Constitution,	301
Copy of the Dorr Constitution,	317
State seal,	333
Governors of Rhode Island,	334
Deputy-Governors of Rhode Island,	337
Members of the Continental Congress,	339
Towns, date of incorporation, &c.,	340
Population from 1708 to 1875,	345
State valuation,	348
The Corliss Engine at the Centennial Exposition,	349

A Short History of Rhode Island.

CHAPTER I.

CONDITION OF AFFAIRS IN MASSACHUSETTS BAY AND PLYMOUTH COLONIES.—ARRIVAL AND BANISHMENT OF ROGER WILLIAMS.

The nations of antiquity, unable to discover their real origin, found a secret gratification in tracing it to the Gods. Thus a religious sentiment was connected with the foundation of states, and the building of the city walls was consecrated by religious rites. The Christian middle ages preserved the spirit of Pagan antiquity, and every city celebrated with solemn rites the day of its patron saint. The colonies, which, in the natural progress of their development, became the United States of America, traced their history, by authentic documents, to the first Christian cultivators of the soil; and in New England the religious idea lay at the root of their foundation and development. In Plymouth it took the form of separatism, or a simple severance from the Church of England. In Massachusetts Bay it aimed at the establishment of a theocracy, and the enforcement of a rigorous uniformity of creed and discipline.

From the resistance to this uniformity came Rhode Island and the doctrine of soul liberty.

On the 5th of February, 1631, the ship Lyon, with twenty passengers and a large cargo of provisions, came to anchor in Nantaskett roads. On the 8th she reached Boston, and the 9th, which had been set apart as a day of fasting and prayer for the little Colony, sorely stricken by famine, was made a day of thanksgiving and praise for its sudden deliverance. Among those who, on that day, first united their prayers with the prayers of the elder colonists, was the young colonist, Roger Williams.

Little is known of the early history of Roger Williams, except that he was born in Wales, about 1606; attracted, early in life, the attention of Sir Edward Coke by his skill in taking down in short hand, sermons, and speeches in the Star Chamber; was sent by the great lawyer to Sutton Hospital, now known as the Charter House, with its fresh memories of Coleridge and Charles Lamb: went thence in the regular time to Oxford; took orders in the Church of England, and finally embraced the doctrine of the Puritans. Besides Latin and Greek, which formed the principal objects of an University course, he acquired a competent knowledge of Hebrew and several modern languages, for the study of which he seemed to have had a peculiar facility. His industry and attainments soon won him a high place in the esteem of his religious brethren, and although described by one who knew him as "passionate and precipitate," he gained and preserved the respect of some of the most eminent among his theological opponents. The key to his life may be found in the simple fact that he possessed an active and progressive mind in an age wherein thought instantly became profession, and profession passed promptly into action.

When this "godly and zealous young minister" landed in Boston, he found the territory which has long been known as Massachusetts in the possession of two distinct colonies, the Colony of Plymouth, founded in 1620, by the followers of John Robinson, of Leyden, and known as the colony of separatists, or men who had separated from the Church of England, but were willing to grant to others the same freedom of opinion which they claimed for themselves; and the Colony of Massachusetts Bay, founded ten years later by a band of intelligent Puritans, many of them men of position and fortune, who, alarmed by the variety of new opinions and doctrines which seemed to menace a total subversion of what they regarded as religion, had resolved to establish a new dwelling place in a new world, with the Old and New Testament for statute book and constitution. Building upon this foundation the clergy naturally became their guides and counselors in all things, and the control of the law, which was but another name for the control of the Bible, extended to all the acts of life, penetrating to the domestic fireside, and holding every member of the community to a rigid accountability for speech as well as action. Asking for no exemption from the rigorous application of Bible precept for themselves, they granted none to others, and looked upon the advocate of any interpretation but theirs as a rebel to God and an enemy to their peace.

It was to this iron-bound colony that Roger Williams brought his restless, vigorous and fearless spirit. Disagreements soon arose and suspicions were awakened. He claimed a freedom of speech irreconcilable with the fundamental principles of their government; and they a power over opinion irreconcilable with freedom of thought. Neither of them could look upon his own position from the other's point of view. Both were equally sincere. And much as we may now condemn the treatment which Williams received at the hands of the colonial government of Massachusetts Bay, its charter and its religious tenets justified it in treating him as an intruder.

The first public expression of the hostility he was to encounter came from the magistrates of Boston within two months after his arrival, and, on the very day on which the church of Salem had installed him as assistant to their aged pastor, Mr. Skelton. The magistrates were a powerful body, and before autumn he found his situation so uncomfortable that he removed to Plymouth, where the rights of individual opinion were held in respect, if not fully acknowledged. Here, while assiduously engaged in the functions of his holy office, he was brought into direct contact with several of the most powerful chiefs of the neighboring tribes of Indians, and among them of Massasoit and Miantonomi, who were to exercise so controlling an influence over his fortunes. His fervent spirit caught eagerly at the prospect of bringing them under Christian influences, and his natural taste for the study of languages served to lighten the labor of preparation. "God was pleased," he wrote many years afterwards, "to give me a painful, patient spirit to lodge with them in their filthy holes, even while I lived at Plymouth and Salem, to gain their tongue; my soul's desire was to do the natives good."

This was apparently the calmest period of his stormy career. It was at Plymouth that his first child, a daughter, was born. But although he soon made many friends, and had the satisfaction of knowing that his labors were successful, his thoughts still turned towards Salem, and, receiving an invitation to resume his place as assistant of Mr. Skelton, whose health was on the wane, he returned thither after an absence of two years. Some of the members of his church had become so attached to him that they followed him to the sister colony.

And now came suspicions which quickly ripened into controversies, and before another two years were over led to what he regarded as persecution, but what the rulers of the Bay Colony held to be the fulfillment of the obligation which they had assumed in adopting the whole Bible as their rule of life. In 1635 he was banished from the colony by a solemn sentence of the General Court, for teaching :

"1st. That we have not our land by Pattent from the King, but that the natives are the true owners of it, and that we ought to repent of such receiving it by Pattent.

2d. That it is not lawful to call a wicked person to swear, to pray, as being actions of God's worship.

3d. That it is not lawful to heare any of the Ministers of the Parish Assemblies in England.

4th. That the civil magistrates power extends only to the Bodies and Goods and outward state of man."

For us who read these charges with the light of two more centuries of progress upon them, it seems strange that neither the General Court nor Williams himself should have perceived that the only one wherein civilization was interested was that to which they have assigned the least conspicuous place.

CHAPTER II.

SUFFERINGS OF ROGER WILLIAMS IN THE WILDERNESS.—FOUNDS A SETTLEMENT ON THE SEEKONK RIVER.—IS ADVISED TO DEPART.—SEEKS OUT A NEW PLACE, WHICH HE CALLS PROVIDENCE.

WHEN the sentence of banishment was first pronounced against the future founder of Rhode Island, his health was so feeble that it was resolved to suspend the execution of it till spring. This, however, was soon found to be impracticable, for the affection and confidence which he had inspired presently found open expression, and friends began to gather around him in his own house to listen to his teaching. Lack of energy was not a defect of the government of the Colony of Massachusetts Bay, and learning that rumors of a new colony to be founded on Narragansett Bay were already afloat, it resolved to send the supposed leader of the unwelcome enterprise back to England. A warrant, therefore, was given to Captain Underhill, a man of doubtful character in the employment of the Colony, with orders to proceed directly to Salem, put the offender on board his pinnace, and convey him to a ship that lay in Boston harbor ready to sail for England with the first fair wind. When the pinnace reached Salem, he found only the wife and infant children of the banished man, and a people deeply grieved for the loss of their pastor. Williams was gone, and whither no one could say.

And whither, indeed, could he go? The thin and scattered settlements of the northern colonies were bounded seaward by a tempestuous ocean, and inland by a thick belt of primeval forest, whose depths civilized man had never penetrated. If he escaped the wild beasts that prowled in their recesses, could he hope to escape the wilder savage, who claimed the forest for his hunting grounds? "I was sorely tossed," Williams writes in after years, "for fourteen weeks in a bitter winter-season, not knowing what bread or bed did mean." The brave man's earnest mind bore up the frail and suffering body.

And now he began to reap the fruit of his kind treatment of the natives, and the pains which he had taken to learn their language. "These ravens fed me in the wilderness," he wrote, with a touching application of Scripture narrative. They gave him the shelter of their squalid wigwams, and shared with him their winter store. The great chief Massasoit opened his door to him, and, when spring came, gave him a tract of land on the Seekonk River, where he "pitched and began to build and plant." Here he was soon joined by some friends from Salem, who had resolved to cast in their lot with his. But the seed which they planted had already begun to send up its early shoots, when a letter from his "ancient friend, the Governor of Plymouth," came, to "lovingly advise him" that he was "fallen into the edge of their bounds;" that they were "loth to displease the Bay," and that if he would "remove but to the other side of the water," he would have "the country before [him] and might be as free as themselves," and they "should be loving neighbors together." Williams accepted the friendly counsel, and, taking five companions with him, set out in a canoe to follow the downward course of the Seekonk and find a spot whereon he might plant and build in safety. As the little boat came under the shade of the western bank of the pleasant stream, a small party of Indians was seen watching them from a large flat rock that rose a few feet above the water's edge. "Wha-cheer, netop?—Wha-cheer?—how are you, friend?" they cried; and Williams accepting the friendly salutation as a favorable omen, turned the prow of his canoe to the shore. Tradition calls the spot where he landed, Slate Rock, and the name of Wha-cheer square has been given in advance to the land around it. What was said or done at that first interview has not been recorded, but the parting was as friendly as the meeting, and Williams resuming his course, soon found himself at the junction of the Seekonk and Mooshausick. Two points mark the intermingling of the two streams, and in those days the waters must have spread their broad bosom like a lake, and gleamed and danced within their fringe of primeval forest. Williams, following, perhaps, the counsel of the Indians, turned northward and held his way between the narrowing banks of the Mooshausick, till he espied, at the foot of a hill which rose shaggy with trees and precipitate from its eastern shore, the flash and sparkling of a spring. Here he landed, and, recalling his trials and the mighty hand that had sustained him through them all, called the place Providence.

CHAPTER III.

WILLIAMS OBTAINS A GRANT OF LAND AND FOUNDS A COLONY.—FORM OF GOVERNMENT IN THE COLONY.—WILLIAMS GOES TO ENGLAND TO OBTAIN A ROYAL CHARTER.

THE territory which now forms the State of Rhode Island, with the exception of Bristol County, in which lay Mount Hope, the seat of Massasoit, chief of the Wamponoags, was held by the Narragansetts, a tribe skilled in the Indian art of making wampum, the Indian money, and the art common to most barbarous nations of making rude vessels in clay and stone. They had once been very powerful, and could still bring four or five thousand braves to the warpath. Their language was substantially the same with that of the other New England tribes, and was understood by the natives of New York, New Jersey and Delaware. With this language Roger Williams had early made himself familiar.

It was labor well bestowed, and he was to reap the reward of it in his day of tribulation. The chiefs of the Narragansetts when he came among them were Canonicus, an "old prince, most, shy of the English to his latest breath," and his nephew, Miantonomi. Their usual residence was on the beautiful Island of Conanicut; and when Williams first came he found them at feud with his other friend, Ossameguin, or Massasoit, Sachem of the Wamponoags. His first care was to reconcile these chiefs, "traveling between them three to pacify, to satisfy all these and their dependent spirits of (his) honest intention to live peaceably by them." The well founded distrust of the English which Canonicus cherished to the end of his life did not extend to Williams, to whom he made a grant of land between the Mooshausick and the Wanasquatucket; confirming it two years later by a deed bearing the marks of the two Narragansett chiefs. This land Williams divided with twelve of his companions, reserving for them and himself the right of extending the grant "to such others as the major part of us shall admit to the same fellowship of vote with us." It was a broad foundation, and he soon found himself in the midst of a flourishing colony.

The proprietors, dividing their lands into two parts, "the grand purchase of Providence," and the "Pawtuxet purchase," made an assignment of lots to other colonists, and entered resolutely upon the task of bringing the soil under cultivation. The possession of property naturally leads to the making of laws, and the new colonists had not been together long before they felt the want of a government. The form which it first assumed amongst them was that of a democratic municipality, wherein the "masters of families" incorporated themselves into a town, and transacted their public business in town meeting. The colonists of Plymouth had formed their social compact in the cabin of the Mayflower. The colonists of Providence formed theirs on the banks of the Mooshausick. "We, whose names are hereunder," it reads, "desirous to inhabit in the town of Providence,. do promise to subject ourselves in active or passive obedience to all such orders or agreements as shall be made for public good for the body, in an orderly way, by the major assent of the present inhabitants, masters of families, incorporated together into a town fellowship, and such others as they shall admit unto them only in civil things."

Never before, since the establishment of Christianity, has the separation of Church from State been definitely marked out by this limitation of the authority of the magistrate to civil things; and never, perhaps, in the whole course of history, was a fundamental principle so vigorously observed. Massachusetts looked upon the experiment with jealousy and distrust, and when ignorant or restless men confounded the right of individual opinion in religious matters with a right of independent action in civil matters, those who had condemned Roger Williams to banishment, eagerly proclaimed that no well ordered government could exist in connection with liberty of conscience. Many grave discussions were held, and many curious questions arose before the distinction between liberty and license became thoroughly interwoven with daily life; but only one passage of this singular chapter has been preserved, and, as if to leave no doubt concerning the spirit which led to its preservation, the narrator begins with these ominous words: "At Providence, also, the Devil was not idle."

The wife of Joshua Verin was a great admirer of Williams's preaching, and claimed the right of going to hear him oftener than suited the wishes of her husband. Did she, in following the dictates of her conscience, which bade her go to a meeting which harmonized with her feelings, violate the injunction of Scripture which bids wives obey their husbands? Or did he, in exercising his acknowledged control as a husband, trench upon her right of conscience in religious concerns? It was a delicate question; but after long deliberation and many prayers, the claims of conscience prevailed, and "it was agreed that Joshua Verin, upon the breach of a covenant for restraining of the libertie of conscience, shall be withheld from the libertie of voting till he shall declare the contrarie"—a sentence from which it appears that the right of suffrage was regarded as a conceded privilege, not a natural right.

Questions of jurisdiction also arose. Massachusetts could not bring herself to look upon her sister with a friendly eye, and Plymouth was soon to be merged in Massachusetts. It was easy to foresee that there would be bickerings and jealousies, if not open contention between them. Still the little Colony grew apace. The first church was founded in 1639. To meet the wants of an increased population the government was changed, and five disposers or selectmen charged with the principal functions of administration, subject, however, to the superior authority of monthly town meetings ; so early and so naturally did municipal institutions take root in English colonies. A vital point was yet untouched. Williams, indeed, held that the Indians, as original occupants of the soil, were the only legal owners of it, and carrying his principle into all his dealings with the natives, bought of them the land on which he planted his Colony. The Plymouth and Massachusetts colonists, also, bought their land of the natives, but in their intercourse with the whites founded their claim upon royal charter. They even went so far as to apply for a charter covering all the territory of the new Colony.

Meanwhile two other colonies had been planted on the shores of Narragansett Bay: the Colony of Aquidnick, on the Island of Rhode Island, and the Colony of Warwick. The sense of a common danger united them, and, in 1643, they appointed Roger Williams their agent to repair to England and apply for a royal charter. It has been treasured up as a bitter memory that he was compelled to seek a conveyance in New York, for Massachusetts would not allow him to pass through her territories. His negotiations were crowned with full success. In 1644 he was again in the colonies, and the inhabitants of Providence, advised of his success, met him at Seekonk and escorted him across the river with an exultant procession of fourteen canoes.

To defray the expenses of his mission he taught Latin, Greek and Hebrew—counting "two sons of Parliament men" among his pupils—and read Dutch to Milton.

CHAPTER IV.

SETTLEMENT OF AQUIDNECK AND WARWICK.—PEQUOT WAR.—DEATH OF MIANTONOMI.

I HAVE said that two other colonies had been founded in Rhode Island. Like Providence, they both had their origin in religious controversy. Not long after the return of Roger Williams there came to Boston a woman of high and subtle spirit, deeply imbued with the controversial temper of her age. Her name was Anna Hutchinson, and she taught that salvation was the fruit of grace, not of works. It is easy to conceive how such a doctrine might be perverted by logical interpretation, and religious standing made independent of moral character. This was presently done, and Massachusetts, true to her theoretic system, banished Anna Hutchinson and her followers as she had banished Roger Williams. In the autumn of 1637, nineteen of these Antinomians, as they were called to distinguish them from the legalists or adherents of the law, took refuge in Rhode Island, where they were kindly welcomed; and, soon after, purchasing the Island of Aquidneck, through the intervention of Williams and Sir Henry Vane, laid the foundation of a new town at Pocasset, near the north end of the Island.

Their leaders were William Coddington and John Clarke, under whose wise guidance the little Colony made rapid progress, and soon began another settlement at Newport, in the southern part of the island. Here, breaking roads, clearing up woods, exterminating wolves and foxes, opening a trade in lumber, engaging boldly in building ships, and above all forming a free and simple government, with careful regard to religion and education, they soon found themselves in advance of their elder sister, Providence. In both colonies the principle of religious liberty formed the basis of civil organization. On Rhode Island, however, it was confined to Christians—a step greatly in advance of the general intelligence of the age. But in Providence Roger Williams went still further, and, meeting the wants of all future ages, proclaimed it the right of every human being.

The other Colony, as if to illustrate the varieties of human opinion, was founded by Samuel Gorton, one of those bold but restless men who leave doubtful names in history because few see their character from the same point of view. In Gorton's religious sentiments there seems to have been a large leaven of mysticism, and the writings that he has left us are not pleasant reading. But the practical danger of his teaching lay in his denial of all government not founded upon the authority of the King or of Parliament. Massachusetts was a legitimate government within her own bounds. But unchartered Rhode Island had no legal existence. At Pocasset Gorton soon came into collision with the civil authorities and was banished. In Providence he presently raised such dissensions that Williams almost lost heart, and began to think seriously of withdrawing to his little Island of Patience, in Narragansett Bay. At last Gorton with eleven companions bought Shawomet of its Indian owners and established himself there. This brought him into open hostility with Massachusetts, which having already cast longing eyes upon the commercial advantages of Narragansett Bay, was secretly endeavoring to establish a claim to all the land on its shores.

Hostile words were soon followed by hostile acts. Gorton and his companions were besieged in their house by an armed band, compelled to surrender, carried by force to Massachusetts, tried for heresy, and barely escaping the gibbet, condemned to imprisonment and irons. A reaction soon followed. Public sentiment came to their relief. They were banished indeed from Massachusetts, but they were set at liberty and allowed to return to Rhode Island. At Aquidneck they were received with the sympathy which generous natures ever feel for the victims of persecution, and Gorton was raised to an honorable magistracy in the very colony wherein he had been openly whipped as a disturber of the public peace. It was not till the claims of Massachusetts had been virtually set aside by the charter which Roger Williams obtained for his Colony that Gorton returned to Shawomet, and set himself to rebuild the Colony of Warwick.

Meanwhile great changes had taken place in the relations of the white man 'to the red. I have told how kindly the natives received Roger Williams, and how justly he dealt by them. I will now tell, though briefly, with what a Christian spirit he used the influence over the Indians, which his justice had won for him, to protect the white men who had driven him from amongst them. On the western border of the territory of the Massachusetts dwelt the fierce and powerful Pequots. No Indian had ever hated the whites with a hatred more intense than they, or watched the growth of the white settlements with a truer perception of the danger with which they menaced the original owners of the soil. They resolved upon war, and to make their triumph sure, resolved also to win over the Narragansetts as active allies. Tidings of the danger soon reached the Bay Colony, and Governor Vane appealed to Roger Williams to interpose and prevent the fatal alliance. Not a moment was to be lost. The Pequot embassadors were already in conference with Canonicus and Miantonomi on Conanicut. Forgetting his personal wrongs, and barely taking time to tell his wife whither he was going, he set forth alone in his canoe, "cutting through a stormy wind and great seas, every minute in hazard of life."

Greater hazard awaited him on shore. English blood had already been shed by the Pequots, and knowing their fierce nature, he "nightly looked for their bloody knives at his own throat also." For three days and three nights he confronted them face to face, and so great was the control which he had gained over the Narragansett chiefs that he succeeded in "breaking in pieces the Pequot negotiation and design, and made and finished by many travels and charges the English league with the Narragansetts and Mohegans against the Pequots." The war came. The Narragansetts were on the side of the English; fearful massacres were committed; the Pequots were rooted out from their native soil forever; Massachusetts was saved; but the Christian, forgetting of injuries wherewith Williams had come to her aid in the critical moment of her fortunes, was not deemed of sufficient virtue to wash out the stain of heresy, and the sentence of banishment was left unrepealed on the darker page of her colonial records.

The Pequots were crushed. The turn of the Narragansetts came next. It was the fate of the red man to everywhere give way as a civilization irreconcilable with his habits and his beliefs advanced, and it is for the good of humanity that it is so. But it is sad to remember that the Christian, with the Bible in his hand, should have sought his examples in the stern denunciations of the Old Testament, rather than in the injunctions to love and mercy of the New. Six years after the formation of the league against the Pequots, a war broke out between Sequasson, an ally of Miantonomi and the Mohegans. The Narragansett Sachem, trusting to the good faith of his adversary, the powerful Uncas, was betrayed in a conference, and his followers, taken by surprise in open violation of the laws of even Indian warfare, were put to flight. The unfortunate chief fell into the hands of his enemy, who, fearing the English too much to put an ally of theirs to death, referred the question of his fate to the Commissioners of the United Colonies—Massachusetts, Plymouth, Connecticut and New Haven—who were about to hold a conference in Boston. Rhode Island, which had been excluded from the league, had no voice in this outrage, and Williams, whose remonstrances might have been of some avail, was in England. To give greater solemnity to their deliberations the Commissioners called to their aid "five of the most judicious elders," and by their united voices Miantonomi was condemned to die. The execution of the sentence was entrusted to Uncas, and the only condition attached to the shameful act was that the generous friend of the white man should not be tortured. His people never recovered from the blow. In the very next year they placed themselves by a solemn resolution under the protection of the King, and appointed four commissioners, one of whom was Gorton, to carry their submission to England.

CHAPTER V.

CHARTER GRANTED TO PROVIDENCE PLANTATIONS.—ORGANIZATION UNDER IT.—THE LAWS ADOPTED.

We have seen that in 1643 Roger Williams had been sent to England as agent to solicit a charter for the three colonies of Narragansett Bay. He found the King at open war with the Parliament, and the administration of the colonies entrusted to the Earl of Warwick and a joint committee of the two Houses. Of the details of the negotiation little is known, but on the 14th of March of the following year, a "free and absolute charter was granted as the Incorporation of Providence Plantations in Narragansett Bay in New England." It was not such as Charles would have given. But one fetter was placed upon the free action of the people—"that the laws, constitutions, punishments for the civil government of the said plantation be conformable to the laws of England"—and that was made powerless by the qualifying condition that the conformity should extend only "so far as the nature and constitution of that place will admit." Civil government and civil laws were the only government and laws which it recognized; and the absence of any allusion to religious freedom in it shows how firmly and wisely Williams avoided every form of expression which might seem to recognize the power to grant or to deny that inalienable right. The regulation of the "general government" in its "relation to the rest of the plantations in America," was reserved "to the Earl and Commissioners."

Yet more than three years were allowed to pass before it went into full force as a bond of union for the four towns. Then, in May, 1647, the corporators met at Portsmouth in General Court of Election, and, accepting the charter, proceeded to organize a government in harmony with its provisions. Warwick, although not named in the charter, was admitted to the same privileges with her larger and more flourishing sisters.

This new government was in reality a government of the people, to whose final decision in their General Assembly all questions were submitted. "And now," says the preamble to the code, "sith our charter gives us powere to governe ourselves and such other as come among us, and by such a forme of Civill Government as by the voluntairie consent, &c., shall be found most suitable to our estate and condition:

"It is agreed by this present Assembly thus incorporate and by this present act declared, that the form of Government established in *Providence Plantations*, is Democratical; that is to say, a Government held by ye free and voluntairie consent of all or the greater part of the free Inhabitants."

In accordance with this fundamental principle all laws were first discussed in Town Meeting, then submitted to the General Court, a committee of six men from each town freely chosen, and finally referred to the General Assembly. The General Court possessed, also, the power of originating laws, by recommending a draft of law to the towns, upon whose approval the draft obtained the force of law till the next meeting of the General Assembly.

The first act of this first Colonial Assembly was to organize by electing John Coggeshall Moderator, and secure an acting quorum by fixing it at forty. It was next "agreed that all should set their hands to an engagement to the Charter." Then, after some provision for the union of the towns, the formation of the General Court and the adoption of the laws "as they are contracted in the bulk," Mr. John Coggeshall was chosen "President of this Province or Colonie; Wm. Dyer, General Recorder; Mr. Jeremy Clarke, Treasurer, and Mr. Roger Williams, Mr. John Sanford, Mr. Wm. Coddington and Mr. Randall Holden, Assistants for Providence, Portsmouth, Newport and Warwick" respectively. Then, entering boldly upon its independent existence, the little Colony—a State in all but the name—proceeded to examine the body of laws which had been prepared for its acceptance. One of the most significant of them, as indicating their commercial aspirations, was their adoption of the laws of Oleron for a maritime code; and another, as illustrating their consciousness of their perilous position in the midst of savages, still able to strike sudden blows, though no longer strong enough to wage long wars, the revival and extension of "the Statute touching Archerie," and the enactment of a stringent militia law. The laws against parricide, murder, arson, robbery and stealing, show that there were men in the community who were believed to be capable of these crimes. The law against suicide, and still more the law against witchcraft, are too much in harmony with the general spirit of the age to warrant a severe condemnation. The punishment provided against drunkenness reads as though it were not an infrequent offence. Marriage was regarded as a civil contract. The law of debt was wise and humane, forbidding the sending of the debtor to prison, "there," it says with simplicity and force, "to lie languishing to no man's advantage, unless he refuse to stand to their order." The character of the whole code was just and benevolent, breathing a gentle spirit of practical Christianity and a calm consciousness of high destinies. "These," it says, "are the laws that concern all men, and these are the Penalties for the transgression thereof; which by common consent are Ratified and Established throughout this whole Colonie; and otherwise than thus what is herein forbidden, all men may walk as their consciences persuade them, every one in the name of his God."

By the same Assembly it was ordered, "that the seale of the Providence shall be an anchor." A free gift, also, of one hundred pounds was made to Roger Williams, "in regarde to his so great travaile, charges, and good endeavors in the obtaining of the Charter for this Province." This sum was "to be levied out of the three towns;" and how far the island was in advance of the main-land may be seen by the distribution of the levy which assigns fifty pounds to Newport and thirty to Portsmouth, while Providence was held at twenty. Of Warwick, still poor and weak, nothing was asked.

The spirit of this first legislation may be comprised in four articles: the first of which provides for the protection of the citizen against the government by guaranteeing liberty of property and person, and restricting criminal suits to the violation of the letter of the law. The second forbids the assumption of office by any who are not legally chosen, and the extension of official action beyond its prescribed bounds. The third by making the charter and acts of the Assembly the sources of law, secures the rights of minorities. And the fourth, displaying a comprehension of the true principles of public service which succeeding generations would do well to study, required that every citizen should serve when chosen to office or pay a fine, and that his service should receive an adequate compensation. The engagement of state and officer was reciprocal—the officer binding himself to serve the state faithfully, and the state to stand by her officers in the legitimate exercise of their functions.

CHAPTER VI.

FOREIGN AND DOMESTIC TROUBLES.—UNSUCCESSFUL ATTEMPT AT USURPATION BY CODDINGTON.

AND now, just as the new Province was entering upon that chartered existence which was to lead to such brilliant results, the wise and peaceable Canonicus died, closing in humiliation and sorrow a life which had begun in strength and hope. He had seen the first foot-prints of the stranger; had aided him in his weakness; had resisted him in his strength; had lived to see his destined successor fall victim to an unholy policy, and his people, impoverished and enfeebled, vainly strive to avenge the murder on their adversaries; and thus with a heavy heart he passed away from the scene of his early glory and his long humiliation. We shall see bye and bye the miserable end of the great Narragansetts.

The new Colony entered upon its career with two great problems before it. The first was almost solved. An experience of eleven years' had demonstrated the possibility of soul liberty, which had taken a hold upon the hearts of the colonists too strong to be shaken. But did it leave the needed strength in the civil organization to bear "a government held by the free and voluntary consent of all, or the greater part, of the free inhabitants?" Thus the reconciliation of liberty and law formed from the beginning the fundamental problem of Rhode Island history.

At first there were great and frequent dissensions. There were dissensions between Newport and Portsmouth. There were still greater dissensions in Providence. Enemies exulted, foretelling an early dissolution of the feeble bands which held the dangerous Colony together. Friends trembled lest their last hope of the reconciliation of liberty and law should fail them. But still the great work of solution went on, each new dissension revealing some new error, or aiding in the demonstration of some new truth. It would take us far beyond our limits were we to attempt to follow up the history of these dissensions in detail, even if the materials for a full narrative of them had been preserved. There were other difficulties, also, which demand more than a passing allusion.

Massachusetts had not yet renounced her designs upon the territories of the heretical Colony. A party in Pawtuxet which had put itself under the protection of the Bay Colony had opened the way for action, and the dispute with Shawomet had enlarged it. Gorton was in England in 1647, exerting himself to answer the assertions of the Massachusetts agent, Winslow. Three years later the question became so complicated and the danger so imminent that Roger Williams was asked to go again to England on behalf of the Colony.

Meanwhile there were menacing indications of an Indian war, and a serious effort was made on the part of the Island towns to obtain admission to the New England confederation. The application was refused unless on terms equivalent to the surrender of all right to independent existence. The time for justice and a clear comprehension of the common interest was not yet come. Especially strong was Massachusetts' dread of the Baptists, who were becoming a powerful body in Rhode Island, and three of the prominent members of that communion, among whom was John Clarke, one of the most illustrious of the colonists, were siezed at Lynn—whither they had been summoned to give comfort and counsel to an aged brother—cast into prison, fined, and one of their number, Obadiah Holmes, ·cruelly scourged with a three-corded whip.

Another danger menaced the Colony. William Coddington, who had been chosen President, but had never taken the legal engagement, had gone to England, and, as was soon ascertained, with the design of applying for a commission as Governor of the Island. For two years he was unable to obtain a hearing. The new government of England was too busy with its own concerns to lend an ear to the agent of a distant and humble Colony. At last the favorable moment came, and, on the 3d of April, 1651, he received a commission from the Council of State, appointing him Governor for life of Rhode Island and Connecticut. By what representations or misrepresentations he obtained the object of his ambition, history does not tell us. A council of six, nominated by the people and approved by him, were to assist him in the government. The charter government was apparently dissolved.

But the men of Providence and Warwick did not lose heart. Roger Williams, who had already given proof of his diplomatic skill at home by his successful negotiations with the native chiefs, and in England by obtaining a charter, was still with them, and to him all turned their eyes in this hour of supreme danger. It was resolved that he should repair to England without delay, and ask for a confirmation of the charter in the name of Providence and Warwick. To provide money for the support of his family during his absence he sold his trading-house in Narragansett, and, obtaining a hard-wrung leave to embark at Boston, set forth in October, 1651, upon his memorable mission. In the same ship went John Clarke, as agent for the Island towns, to ask for the revocation of Coddington's commission. On the success of their application hung the fate of the Colony. Meanwhile the Island towns submitted silently to Coddington's usurpation, and the main-land towns continued to govern themselves by their old laws, and meet and deliberate as they had done before in their General Assembly.

It was in the midst of these dangers and dissensions that on the 19th of May, in the session of 1652, it was "enacted and ordered .... that no black mankind or white being forced by covenant, bond or other wise shall be held to service longer than ten years," and that "that man that will not let them go free, or shall sell them any else where to that end that they may be enslaved to others for a longer time, hee or they shall forfeit to the Colonie forty pounds." This was the first legislation concerning slavery on this continent. If forty pounds should seem a small penalty, let us remember that the price of a slave was but twenty. If it should be objected that the act was imperfectly enforced, let us remember how honorable a thing it is to have been the first to solemnly recognize a great principle. Soul liberty had borne her first fruits.

In the same month of May the embarrassments of the Colony were increased by the breaking out of a war between England and Holland, which interrupted the profitable commerce between Rhode Island and the Dutch of Manhattan. But welcome tidings came in September, and still more welcome in October. Williams and Clarke, who went hand in hand in their mission, had obtained, first, permission for the Colony to act under the charter until the final decision of the controversy, and a few weeks later the revocation of Coddington's commission. The charter was fully restored. Williams had again proved himself a consummate diplomatist, and Clarke had proved himself worthy to be his colleague. We shall soon see him using his newly acquired skill under more difficult circumstances.

CHAPTER VII.

MORE FOREIGN AND DOMESTIC TROUBLES. — CIVIL AND CRIMINAL REGULATIONS OF THE COLONY.—ARRIVAL OF QUAKERS.

AND now it seemed as though the little Colony might peaceably return to its original organization and devote itself to the development of its natural resources. But the spirit of dissension had struck deep. The absolute independence which was claimed for religious opinion, led some to claim an equal independence for civil action. If conscience was to be the supreme test in the relations between man and God, why should not conscience decide between man and man? Roger Williams addressed a letter full of calm wisdom to the Town of Providence, explaining, under the figure of a ship, the distinction between civil obedience and soul liberty. A few years later an able advocate of the opposite opinion was found in William Harris; and for a long while an unhealthy agitation pervaded the community, justifying, in appearance, the unfriendly prophecies of the early enemies of Williams and his doctrines.

There was still another ground of contention. Who should take the lead in restoring the charter government? The Island towns claimed it on the ground of superior wealth and population, the main-land towns because they had always held fast to their charter. There were double elections and two Assemblies, and the dispute grew so warm as to threaten a permanent division. At the same time the Island towns entered zealously into the Dutch war, issuing letters of marque and making captures which led to new controversies with the United Colonies. Williams became alarmed, and leaving Mr. Clarke in charge of their common business hurried back from England to meet the danger. Sir Henry Vane, who had already been a firm friend of Rhode Island, wrote in a public letter, "Are there no wise men among you? no public, self-denying spirits who can find some way of union before you become a prey to your enemies?"

At last, in August, 1654, a full Court of Commissioners met at Warwick, and on the 31st set their hands to articles of reunion. To meet the difficulties that arose from the different acts of independent assemblies, it was agreed that all such acts should be held good for the towns and persons who originally took part in them. Then the charter was once more made the fundamental law of the land, and finally the General Assembly recognized by fixing the number of delegates from each town at six for all purposes except the election of officers. Two days were then devoted to general legislation, and among other acts the delicate question of a Sunday law was reconciled with the distinguishing principle of the Colony, by referring the matter to the several towns under the head of a day "for servants and children to recreate themselves."

As the danger of civil commotions passed away, came the danger of an Indian war. The Narragansetts had old quarrels with the Indians of Long Island, and in 1654 a new quarrel broke out between them. For the Colony itself there was nothing to fear from the Narragansetts with whom it had always maintained friendly relations. But should the Long Island Indians prevail, an inroad upon the main would bring them dangerously near to the new towns. The United Colonies, proceeding as usual with a high hand, summoned Ninigret, the chief sachem of the Narragansetts, to Hartford. He refused to go, saying that the enemy had slain a sachem's son and sixty of his people—all he asked of the English was that they would let him alone. "If your Governor's son were slain," he said, "and several other men, would you ask counsel of another nation how and when to right yourselves?" The spirit of the Narragansetts was not yet broken. Williams, who was then President, wrote to the government of Massachusetts defending the Indians, asserting that the war was a war of self-defence, and that the Narragansetts had always been true to the English. But the Commissioners were resolved upon war, and without listening to his remonstrances sent Captain Willard with a body of troops to seize the refractory chief. The wily Indian took post in a swamp where the troops were unable to reach him. The Commissioners were sorely annoyed, but Massachusetts, listening, perhaps, to the energetic representations of Williams, refused to sanction the war, and without her coöperation it could not be carried on.

There were still dissensions and jars, but the Colony throve and grew in industry and strength. Newport above all increased in wealth and population. In estimating the population, however, we must bear in mind that not every inhabitant was a freeman, nor every resident a legal inhabitant. A probationary residence was required before the second step was reached and the resident became an inhabitant with certain rights to the common lands, the right of sitting on the jury and of being chosen to some of the lower offices. This, also, was a period of probation, and it was only after it had been passed to the satisfaction of the freemen that the name of the new candidate could be proposed in town meeting for full citizenship. Even then he had to wait for a second meeting before he could be admitted to all the rights and distinctions of that honorable grade.

As a picture of the times it deserves notice that there was still a struggle with crime which called for stocks and a jail; that the sale of liquors was regulated by a license, and the number of taverns that could be licensed in a single town limited to three; that the bars were closed at nine in the evening; that a fine of ten pounds or whipping, "accordinge as ye court shall see meete," was the penalty of giving a blow in court; that malicious language was treated as slander and made ground for legal prosecution. The Assembly seldom sat beyond three or four days, and six in the morning was the usual hour of entering upon the business of the day. Absence from roll call was punished by a fine of a shilling. As an illustration of the degree in which the idea of the duties of citizenship prevailed over the idea of the dignity of office, it deserves to be recorded that when the first justices' court was established in Providence for the hearing of cases under forty shillings, Roger Williams though President of the Colony was appointed one of the justices, and of the other two Thomas Olney was assistant for Providence, and Thomas Harris a member of the Assembly. The principle of the reciprocal obligation of citizen and state seems, as we have already observed, to have found early acceptance. High treason was recognized as a great crime and provision made for sending the accused to England for trial—a dangerous measure even in that early day, and which in the following century became a just ground of alarm. But now, even Coddington not only came off unharmed from his daring usurpation, but appears again in 1656 as member of the Court of Trials. A written submission and a fine for refusing to give up the public records were the only penalties that he paid for his offence. Early provision was made for the protection of marriage, and to give it that publicity which is essential to security the bans were announced in town meeting, or at the head of a company on training days, or by a written declaration signed by a magistrate and set up in some place of common resort. If objections were made the parties were heard by a tribunal of two magistrates, or for final decision by the Court of Trials. Freedom in the young society was always connected with morality.

There were still questions to arrange with Massachusetts, which had not yet given up the hope of enlarging her territory at the expense of her diminutive neighbors. The Pawtuxet controversy which began almost with the beginning of the Colony, was a fruitful source of anxiety till 1658, when it was finally settled by the acknowledgment of the claims of Rhode Island, Roger Williams again appearing in his favorite character of mediator. Hog Island, at the mouth of Bristol harbor, gave rise to other disputes which extended through several years. In the original purchase of Aquidneck the grass only had been bought. To secure the fee of the land itself a second purchase was required. Other purchases also were made, which gave rise to long and vexatious disputes. Small as it was, it was almost inch by inch that Rhode Island won its narrow territory.

From time to time, also, there were alarms of Indians. In 1656 their movements excited so much apprehension in Providence, that a fort was built on Stamper's Hill for the protection of the town. In this same year the fundamental principles of the governments of Rhode Island and of Massachusetts were brought into striking contrast by the arrival of the Quakers. In Massachusetts they were imprisoned, scourged, mutilated, put to death, and with the increase of persecution increased in numbers. In Rhode Island they were allowed to follow their own convictions and became useful and industrious citizens. And when the United Colonies urged the General Assembly, not without threats, to join in the persecution, it appealed to Cromwell, asking "that it might not be compelled to exercise any civil power over men's consciences so long as human orders, in point of civility, are not corrupted or violated."

In these days great changes were taking place in England. Cromwell was dead. Richard Cromwell soon resigned the Protectorate. A general reaction for royalty followed, and Charles II. was received as King with general satisfaction. How would the young and dissolute monarch look upon the claims of Rhode Island? It was well for her that at this perilous moment she was represented at the new court by so earnest, clear-headed and dexterous a diplomatist as John Clarke. By his exertions a new charter was obtained, and, on the 24th of November, 1663, accepted "at a very great meeting and assembly of the Colony of Providence Plantations, at Newport, in Rhode Island, in New England." With the adoption of this charter begins a new period in the history of Rhode Island.

CHAPTER VIII.

TROUBLES IN OBTAINING A NEW CHARTER.—PROVISIONS OF THE CHARTER.—DIFFICULTIES CONCERNING THE NARRAGANSETT PURCHASE.—CURRENCY.—SCHOOLS.

The charter of Charles II. was a practical recognition of the right of self-government. The government which it established, like that instituted by the colonists in their first organization, was a pure democracy, emanating from the people and framed for their good. In form it consisted of a Governor, a Deputy-Governor, ten assistants, and a House of Deputies, six of whom represented Newport, four Providence, four Portsmouth, four Warwick, and two each other towns. The first appointments of Governor, Deputy-Governor, and assistants, as preparatory to a permanent organization, were made by the King. The organization once effected, they were chosen annually at Newport, on the first Wednesday in May. The deputies were elected by the people in their respective towns. Thus election day became the great civil festival of the year, bringing the inhabitants of the towns together to interchange thoughts and feelings, and make merry with their wives and children in the chief town of the Colony.

Although the new charter was negotiated by John Clarke, it is impossible not to recognize in it the spirit of Roger Williams. The original right of the natives to the soil was acknowledged, practically, in other colonies; but it was acknowledged as subordinate to the right of the King. The royal grant preceded the actual purchase. But in Rhode Island the royal grant followed the Indian title-deed, and was never accepted as sufficient of itself to justify the occupation of Indian territory. This doctrine, so widely at variance with the received doctrine of the age, stood first in the list of heresies for which Massachusetts had driven Roger Williams into exile.

No less prominent in the second charter was that great principle which had formed the leading characteristic of the first. "Noe person," it says, "within the sayd colonye, at any tyme hereafter, shall be any wise molested, punished, disquieted, or called in question, for any difference of opinion in matters of religion which doe not actually disturb the civill peace of our sayd colonye; but that all and everye person may, from tyme to tyme and at all tymes hereafter, freelye and fullye have and enjoy his and their own judgments and consciences, in matters of religious concernments, through the tract of lande hereafter mentioned, they behaving themselves peaceablie and quietlie, and not using this libertye to licentiousness, and profaneness, nor to the civill injurye or outward disturbance of others."

There was much work for the new Assembly to do, and it addressed itself promptly to the task. The statute book contained laws which, arising from circumstances no longer existing, were "inconsistent with the present government." To weed these out and replace them by others better suited to the new order of things, was an early object of attention. Hitherto the assistants had not been vested with legislative authority. They now held it by the charter, and henceforth acted in conjunction with the deputies, a change which at a later day led to the division into two houses. The increase of population brought with it an increase of litigation. The original courts were not sufficient to meet the demand for legal protection. They were reorganized.

There were two general courts of trials, composed of the Governor, with or without the aid of the Deputy-Governor, and of a body of assistants whose number was never less than six. Their place of meeting was Newport, the seat of government and largest town, and their regular sessions were held in May and October. Providence and Warwick had each a court of trials— Providence in September and Warwick in March. But in these, as if in indication of their subordinate authority, neither the Governor nor the Deputy-Governer had a seat, and the number of assistants absolutely required to give validity to its acts was reduced from six to three. To complete their organization twelve jurors were added, six from each town. Their decision, however, was not final, and the cases which they had tried could be carried by appeal to the General Court. To quicken the tardy steps of justice any litigant who was willing to bear the expense, might, with the sanction of the Governor or Deputy-Governor, have a special court convened for the immediate decision of his cause.

The grand and petty jurors were chosen from the four towns, five of each from Newport, three from Portsmouth, and two from Providence and Warwick respectively. The same superiority was accorded to Newport in the apportionment of state officers, five of whom were required to live there. In this, however, Providence outranks Portsmouth, having three allotted to her for her portion, while Portsmouth had but two. The duties of coroner were performed by the assistant "nearest the place occasion shall present."

Another grave question met them on the threshold of their work of organization. The charter left a doubt concerning the manner of choosing the state magistrates. Should they be elected by the freemen in town meeting, or by the General Assembly? The democratic instinct prevailed, and the choice was left to the freemen.

There was a still graver question to be decided, requiring firmness, self-control and skilled diplomacy. Rhode Island had never been looked upon by Massachusetts with friendly eyes. That a banished man should have become the founder of a new colony close upon her borders was irritating to her pride. That his success as a colonizer should have cut her off from the beautiful Narragansett Bay was humiliating to her ambition of territorial aggrandizement. That a freedom of conscience subversive of her theological dogmas should have been the fundamental principle of the new government was irritating to her bigotry. Thus, although she did not hesitate to avail herself of the good offices of Roger Williams to avert a dangerous war, she did not scruple to forbid the sale to citizens of Rhode Island of the powder and arms which they needed for their own protection, and exclude them from the league which the other colonies of New England had formed for their common defence. When, in 1642, four of the principal inhabitants of Pawtuxet factiously put themselves under her protection, she greedily seized the opportunity of securing for herself a foothold in the coveted territory. It was not till 1658 that this dangerous dispute was settled and the perpetual menace of mutilation removed from the northern district of the Colony soon to reappear in the southern. Amid the fresh recollections of this contest, the General Assembly passed a law forbidding, under the penalty of confiscation, the introduction of a foreign authority within the limits of the Colony. Both Massachusetts and Connecticut laid claim to Narragansett, a valuable tract in the southern part of the Colony and controlling the communication with the bay of that name. The claim of Rhode Island was founded upon purchase, and although her physical inferiority left her no hope of success except through an appeal to the King, she was none the less vigilant in defending her rights. The necessity of this watchfulness was soon made manifest, for scarce a year had passed from the passage of the prohibitory law, when, in direct violation of its provisions, a company of aliens purchased Quidneset and Namcook, two large and valuable tracts on Narragansett Bay. It was like throwing down the gauntlet to the little Colony, for it was only by supporting the pretensions of Massachusetts or Connecticut that the purchasers could hope to make their title good. An artful attempt was made to obtain the sanction of Roger Williams's name by offering him, under the title of interpreter, a liberal grant of land. But the loyal old man refused to connect himself in any way with the illegal act, and warned the company of the dangerous ground whereon they were treading.

The warning was not heeded, and Humphrey Atherton, John Winthrop and their associates, completing their bargain with the Indians, claimed the tracts as theirs by lawful purchase. New complications followed. The very next year the Commissioners of the United Colonies, following up their aggressive policy towards the Narragansetts, imposed upon the feeble remnant of the once powerful tribe a heavy fine for alleged injuries to the Mohegans, and compelled them to mortgage their whole territory for the payment of it. Atherton paid the fine, and held that his claim was strengthened by this act of unjustifiable violence.

For a time hopes were entertained of inducing the company to accept the jurisdiction of Rhode Island, but they were futile. The attempt of either party to exercise legal authority in the disputed territory was a signal for the active intervention of the other. It was soon evident that the decision must be referred to England. Fortunately for Rhode Island, John Clarke was still there.

Agents from Connecticut, also, were there petitioning for a new charter, and their petition was enforced by the wise and virtuous John Winthrop. Court favor came to his aid, and he used it judiciously. The venerable Lord Say and Seal lent him the influence of his name, and the skillful negotiator dexterously reviving the memory of the intercourse between his father and Charles the First, succeeded in touching for a moment the callous heart of Charles II. In the season of that intercourse Charles had given Winthrop a curious and valuable ring, and now when the son of the subject came before the son of the King as a suppliant for a charter for his distant home, he bore that ring in his hand as a record of kind feelings on one side and reverential observance on the other. The plea was successful, and, on the

30th of May, 1662, a charter was granted. In this charter the eastern boundary of Connecticut was extended to Narragansett River, and Narragansett River it was claimed was Narragansett Bay.

Great was the indignation of Rhode Island when the tidings of this arbitrary mutilation of her territory reached her. It was like introducing a foreign jurisdiction into the heart of the Colony, and stripping it by a stroke of the pen of some of the chief advantages which it had promised itself from its long and painful labor of colonization. There was but one hope left, and that lay in the wisdom and firmness of John Clarke. The trust was well placed. Not for a moment did the brave man lose heart or suffer himself to grow weary in his difficult task. Of the details of his negotiations no accurate record has been preserved, but we know that, possessing no means of corruption, even if his noble nature could have stooped to it, he placed his confidence in the justice of his cause. In negotiating for a charter he had presented two elaborate petitions to the King, giving a rapid sketch of the origin and principles of the Colony, and asking for "a more absolute, ample, and free charter of civill incorporation," as for men who "had it much on their hearts (if they may be permitted) to hold a lively experiment, that a flourishing free state may stand, yea, and best be maintained, and that among English spirits, with a full liberty in religious concernments."

The question of a charter was for the King to decide, and we have already seen how he decided it. But the question of boundaries was within the competence of the agents of the two colonies. After much discussion it was decided to refer it to arbitration. Four arbitrators were chosen, and on the 7th of April, 1663, they rendered their award in four articles, by one of which the Pawcatuck River was made the eastern boundary of Connecticut. The Atherton company was left free to decide under which of the two jurisdictions it would live.

As long as Winthrop remained, although Clarke had much to apprehend from his open opposition, he had nothing to fear from secret intrigues or willful misinterpretation. But not all the advocates of the Atherton purchase were like John Winthrop. False claims will always find base agents, and no sooner was Winthrop gone than one of these willing instruments of wrong pressed eagerly forward to his loathsome office. His name was John Scott, and the record of his meanness has been preserved in his own hand. "Mr. Winthrop," begins his confidential correspondence with Captain Hutchinson, the corresponding agent of the company, "was very averse to my prosecuting your affairs, he having had much trouble with Mr. Clarke whiles he remained in England; but as soon as I received intelligence of his departure from the Downes, I took into the society a Potent Gentleman and

4

prepared a Petition against Clarke, &c., as enemyes to the peace and well being of his Majestye's good subjects, and doubt not effecting the premises in convenient tyme, and in order to accomplish y^r businesse, I have bought of Mr. Edwards a parcel of curiosityes to ye value of sixty pounds; to gratifye persons that are powerfull, that there may be a Letter filled with Awthorising Expressions to the Collonyes of the Massachusetts and Connecticut, that the proprietors of the Narraganset countrye, shall not only live peaceably, but have satisfaction for Injuryes already received by some of the saide Proprietors and the power y^t shall be soe invested (viz) the Massachusetts and Connecticut by virtue of the saide letter will joyntlye and severallye, have full power to do us justice to all intents, as to our Narraganset concernes."

For a moment it seemed as though this vile intrigue were about to succeed. A letter from the King to the United Colonies was obtained, recommending the interests of the Atherton company to their protection. John Scott's "curiosityes" had done their work. The "Potent Gentleman" had not failed him. The little Colony lay unarmed at the feet of its powerful enemies. But the triumph was short. John Clarke was carefully bringing his negotiations for a new charter to a close. Surrounded by bitter and unscrupulous adversaries he still kept his own counsel, kept the object of his mission constantly in view, and, after much weary waiting and watching, came out triumphant. The charter of Charles the Second, as I have already stated, which so long served the Colony as a constitution and exercised such a controlling influence upon her development, passed the seals on the 8th of July, 1663. By this charter the western boundary line was fixed at Pawcatuck River, "any Grant or Claim in a late Grant to the Governor and Company of *Connecticut* Colony in *America* to the contrary thereof in any wise notwithstanding." Thus the Pawcatuck River was henceforth to be held as the same with the Narragansett River, and the question of western boundary decided in accordance with the agreement, which, "after much debate," Clarke and Winthrop had both signed in the names of their respective colonies. It is evident that there was much ignorance, and no very firm principle of action with regard to the colonies in the cabinet of the second Charles.

While these events were passing an important change took place in the commercial medium of the country. When the colonists first began to trade with the natives, they found them already advanced in their buyings and sellings from the primitive barter of product for product to the use of a fixed medium of exchange. This medium, indeed, was of a purely conventional character. There were neither mines of gold, nor mines of silver, nor mines of copper to perform the office of money. But the waters of their rivers and bays yielded an abundant supply of shells, and these they wrought with much ingenuity into beads; the periwinkle furnishing the material for the lower values, six of its white shells being held at an English penny, while the dark eye of the quahog or round clam, smoothed by grinding, and polished and drilled, was rated at twice the value of the white shell. Both were known as wampum or peage. As money belts of wampum were counted by the fathom, three hundred and sixty of the white passing for five shillings sterling, and a fathom of the black being worth twice as much as a fathom of the white. Like the metallic medium of other countries they served also for personal decoration, supplying the Indian belles and beaux with their necklaces and bracelets, and princes with the most valued ornaments of their regalia. When used for this purpose they were wrought into girdles, or worn as a scarf about the shoulders, great pains being taken and not a little skill displayed in arranging the colors in various figures. The mints in which this primitive money was coined were on the sea-shore, where shells were found in great abundance, and so well was this simple article adapted to the wants and the tastes of the aborigines that it passed current six hundred miles from the coast, and was used by the colonists in all their bargains with the natives. But shells like metals and paper are subject to the same inexorable laws of trade. When beaver skins became plenty in the colonial market and wampum was made in larger quantities, it fell from ten shillings a fathom to five, and the Indian hunter thought it hard that an equal number of furs should bring him but half as much wampum as before. Like all money, also, wampum was liable to be counterfeited, and even in that rude commerce there were men who preferred the ill-gotten gain of the counterfeiter to the fruit of honest industry. Fortunately for the native he was quick in detecting the fraud, and never failed to exact full compensation. But wampum, like the race for whom it was made, was unable to hold its ground against the advancing civilization. We have seen it reduced to half its original value by overissues and the increasing supply of furs in the colonial market. Gradually it began to disappear. Rhode Island continued to use it long after it had ceased to be current in colonies where the intercourse with Europe was more direct. Massachusetts had begun to coin silver in 1652, but Rhode Island continued to accept wampum as a legal tender for ten years longer, when it reached its lowest point, and, like the Continental money of a century later, was abolished by statute. Thenceforth all taxes and costs of court were exacted in "current pay" in sterling that is, or in New England coin of thirty shillings New England to twenty-two shillings sixpence sterling.

Nothing has been said thus far of the measures taken by the young Colony for the establishment of schools. Newport, though only in the second year of her settlement, took the lead in 1640, by "calling Mr. Robert Lenthall to keep a school for the learning of youth, and for his encouragement there was granted to him and his heirs one hundred acres of land, and four more for a house lot." In the same meeting it was voted: "That one hundred acres should be laid forth and appropriated for a school, for the encouragement of the poorer sort, to train up their youth in learning, and Mr. Robert Lenthall, while he continues to keep school, is to have the benefit thereof." The wise example was followed by Providence in 1663, and at May town meeting a hundred acres of upland and six acres of meadow were reserved for the support of a school.

But in nothing perhaps does the character of the Colony appear to more advantage than in the law of oaths. "Forasmuch," reads the statute, "as the consciences of sundry men, truly conscionable, may scruple the giving or the taking of an oath, and it would be no wise suitable to the nature and constitution of our place, who profess ourselves to be men of different consciences, and not one willing to force another, to debar such as cannot do so, either from bearing office among us, or from giving in testimony in a case depending; be it enacted by the authority of this present Assembly, that a solemn profession or testimony in a court of record, or before a judge of record, shall be accounted throughout the whole colony, of as full force as an oath." So strong was the hold which the principle of soul liberty had taken of the public mind.

CHAPTER IX.

TERRITORY OF RHODE ISLAND IS INCREASED BY THE ADDITION OF BLOCK ISLAND.—DISPUTES BETWEEN BLOCK ISLAND AND THE OTHER COLONIES SETTLED BY ROYAL COMMAND.—STATE OF AFFAIRS IN THE COLONY IN 1667.

THE charter came at a fortunate moment, for petition and remonstrance had reached their utmost, and it is difficult to see how the little Colony could have preserved the integrity of its territory much longer against two such powerful neighbors but for the intervention of an authority that was recognized by all. The services of John Clarke must be estimated by the imminence of the danger, and his skill by the difficulty of the negotiation. Meanwhile the territories of Rhode Island were enlarged in another direction.

Block Island has already been mentioned in connection with the Pequot war. In 1658 it was granted by Massachusetts, in whose hands the war had left it, to Governor John Endicott and three others, as a reward for their public services. Endicott and his associates sold it to Simon Ray and eight associates, who, in 1661, entered upon their work of colonization by liquidating the Indian title with a reservation in favor of the natives, and setting apart one-sixteenth of the lands for the support of a minister forever. The new settlement had not yet reached its third year when it passed under the jurisdiction of Rhode Island, and, in the May session of the General Assembly for 1663, was summoned to appear at the bar of the house and be regularly received into the Colony. At the appointed time three messengers presented themselves, bringing the submission of the inhabitants to "his Majesty's will," and a petition of householders for the freedom of the island. Three select men were chosen to govern it with power to "call town meetings," hear causes under forty shillings, and where a greater amount was involved, grant appeals to the General Court of Trials, and "issue warrants in criminal cases." Their representation in the Assembly was fixed at two, and their attention was called to the clause in the charter declaring freedom of conscience. The question of a harbor for the encouragement of the fisheries soon attracted the attention of the Assembly, and, as early as 1665, we find John Clarke with the Governor and Deputy-Governor examining this important subject on the spot. But it was no work for a feeble Colony, and it was not till two hundred years later and under a rich and powerful national government that it was begun. Meanwhile the population grew and throve under colonial protection. Nine years after its first civil organization Block Island was incorporated under the name of New Shoreham, "as sign," say the petitioners, "of our unity and likeness to many parts of our native country."

The conflict of patents did not end with the promulgation of the second charter. Massachusetts and Connecticut still persisted in their claims, and Rhode Island in her resistance. Fortunately for her the final decision lay with the Crown, and, although both of the intruding colonies made repeated attempts to set up governments of their own within the limits of the disputed territory, they were restrained from persistent violence by the knowledge that Rhode Island claimed and was prepared to exercise the right of appeal. An opportunity soon offered of making an important step towards decision. Four Commissioners—Colonel Richard Nichols, Sir Robert Carr, George Cartwright and Samuel Maverick—were ordered to proceed to America, reduce the Dutch provinces, and decide all questions of appeal, jurisdiction and boundary between the colonies. On their arrival in New York harbor, where they made the British fleet their headquarters, Rhode Island sent a deputation of three, with John Clarke at their head, to welcome the Royal Commissioners in the name of the Colony.

They set themselves promptly to their work. The first question that came up for decision was the boundary line between Rhode Island and Plymouth. This they were unable to settle, and reserved it for reference to the King. Next came the vexed question of Narragansett. The submission of the sachems was confirmed, an annual tribute of two wolf-skins imposed, and the right to make war and sell land reserved to the authorities set over them by the Crown. A new division of the territory followed, all of the land west of the Bay, the southern half of the present Kent County, being set apart as King's Province, under the administration of the Governor and Council of Rhode Island, as magistrates of King's Province. Last came the bitter Warwick question, which had almost led to bloodshed. This was decided in favor of Rhode Island, upon the ground that no colony had a right to exercise jurisdiction beyond its chartered limits. It would have been well for the three colonies if the dispute had ended here. But neither Massachusetts nor Connecticut was satisfied. It was hard to give up the beautiful Narragansett Bay, "the largest," say the Commissioners, "and safest port in New England, nearest the sea and fittest for trade."

The Indian was fast disappearing, and sometimes under circumstances which awaken a natural regret that where adverse civilizations met so little could be done for the individual. The old Sachem Pumham still clung to his home in the woodlands of Warwick Neck, encouraged, it was believed, by the hope of support from Massachusetts. John Eliot, the translator of the Bible interceded for him. Roger Williams asked for a little delay till the harvest was in. But twenty years experience had shown that his residence there was incompatible with the peace of the Colony. Sir Robert Carr, the Royal Commissioner, met Eliot's intercession by sending him copies of all the papers relating to the question, and so far satisfied the scruples of Williams as to secure his hearty coöperation in the removal of this thorn from the side of the struggling Colony. Thirty pounds were paid into the hands of the old chief, a large sum for those days of general poverty, and he removed forever beyond the limits of King's Province.

The Royal Commissioners on their arrival in Rhode Island had laid before the Assembly five propositions as "the will and pleasure of the King:"

"1st. That all householders inhabiting the Colony take the oath of allegiance, and that the administration of justice be in his Majesty's name."

This brought up the delicate question of oaths, which, recurring from time to time, was gradually shaped by successive modifications so as to meet the demands of government without infringing upon the principle of soul-liberty.

"2d. That all men of competent estates and of civil conversation, who acknowledge and are obedient to the civil magistrate, though of different judgments, may be admitted to be freemen and have liberty to chose and to be chosen, officers, both military and civil."

This was accepted and the mode of admitting freemen prescribed.

"3d. That all men and women of orthodox opinion, competent knowledge and civil lives, who acknowledge and are obedient to the civil magistrate and are not scandalous, may be admitted to the Sacrament of the Lord's Supper, and their children to Baptism, if they desire it, either by admitting them into the congregations already gathered, or permitting them to gather themselves into such congregations where they may enjoy the benefit of the Sacraments, and that difference of opinion may not break the bonds of peace and charity."

If we interpret the word orthodox according to the Rhode Island standard of theological interpretation, this was already Rhode Island doctrine and required no deliberation.

"4th. That all laws and expressions in laws derogatory to his Majesty, if any such have been made in these late and troublesome times, may be repealed, altered and taken off the files."

This, also, was accepted, and a revision of the laws ordered for that purpose.

"5th. That the Colony be put in such a posture of defence that if there should be any invasion upon this island, or elsewhere in this Colony (which God forbid) you might in some measure be in readiness to defend yourselves, or if need be to relieve your neighbors, according to the power given you by the King in your charter and to us in the King's commission and instructions."

This, also, struck a familiar cord. Provisions for self-defence had already been made as circumstances called for them. A new militia law was now passed, requiring six trainings a year under heavy penalties, and allowing nine shillings a year for each enlisted soldier. Every man was to keep on hand two pounds of powder and four of lead, and each town was required to maintain a public magazine. To defray the expenses of these magazines Newport was taxed fifty pounds, and the other three towns twenty pounds each.

The Royal Commissioners were well satisfied with the conduct of Rhode Island, and Rhode Island, surrounded by powerful enemies, had every reason to be well satisfied with the Commissioners. Still the encroachments and aggressions of Massachusetts and Connecticut continued. As a prospective means of defence against them John Clarke was again asked to carry the complaints of the suffering Colony to England, and John Greene was chosen to accompany him. In 1672 a new claimant appeared in the lists.

The Council of Plymouth had been lavish of its gifts of land, and in its ignorance of American geography had formed a perplexing map of conflicting claims. In one of its grants it had given the greater part of Maine, together with

Nantucket, Martha's Vineyard, Long Island and the adjacent islands, to the Earl of Stirling. The Earl of Stirling sold his grant to the Duke of York, already proprietor by royal gift of the recently conquered province of New Netherlands. The term adjacent islands would have included Acquidneck and the other islands of Narragansett Bay. Prudence, one of the pleasantest and most valuable of them, had been bought of the Indian proprietors by Roger Williams and John Winthrop. In the course of time it passed by regular sale to John Paine, a Boston merchant, who had won the favor of the Duke of York by contributing liberally to the rebuilding of Fort James, in New York harbor. Governor Lovelace, the Duke's attorney, felt that such liberality was deserving of a signal reward. Paine was already the owner of Prudence. Lovelace resolved to make it a free-manor by the name of Toply manor, and confer the governership for life on Paine. By a second grant the original quit-rent of two barrels of cider and six pairs of capons was remitted, and this territory of seven miles in length became an untaxed and independent government.

But Rhode Island was an uncongenial soil for feudal tenures. Paine was arrested, indicted and convicted under the law of 1658 against the introduction of a foreign jurisdiction, and Prudence without any formal act of adjustment returned to its original position as a part of Portsmouth.

Thus the Rhode Island Colony grew apace. From time to time questions of practical government arose, to be worked out and solved by experience. It was not easy to make citizens feel their duty to the State. More than once the Assembly failed in attendance, to the serious detriment of the public. Fines were imposed, and that some inducement to greater regularity might be held out, a small pay of three shillings a day, which was soon reduced to two, was attached to the function of delegate. To facilitate the expression of opinion voting by proxy was permitted, and to secure the election of the most acceptable candidate it was enacted, "that whereas there may happen a division in the vote soe that the greater half may not pitch decidedly on one certaine person, yett the person which hath the most votes shall be deemed lawfully chosen." The laws of the Colony had been the growth of circumstances, expressing new wants and representing a progressive society. Committees were appointed on several occasions to revise and harmonize them. On the committee of October, 1664, we find Roger Williams and John Clarke.

The progress of society has established a fundamental distinction between legislative, executive and judicial powers, which was not known to ancient publicists. The Court of Trials was composed of members of the Assembly, and thus the whole body of law-makers was gradually led to exercise judicial authority.

The Colony was poor, and the persecutions of Massachusetts and Connecticut compelled it to incur expenses greatly beyond its means. When Roger Williams went on his second mission to England he sold part of his estates in order to raise the money for his expenses. When John Clarke was sent to negotiate the second charter he was obliged to burthen his estate with a mortgage. The whole sum due him by the Colony was but three hundred and forty-three pounds, and yet so hard was it to collect the tax by which this sum was to be paid that it was not until twenty years after his death that the mortgage was lifted.

Internal dissensions and the alarm of foreign war troubled the Colony in 1667. Two names long prominent in Rhode Island, Harris and Fenner, appear at the head of two hostile factions in Providence and continue for a while to disturb the public peace. England, whose wars now found a reëcho in the colonies, was again at war with France and Holland. Efficient measures were taken to put the Colony in a state of defence, and thus new burthens were imposed. A council of war was organized in each town. Ammunition was collected. Officers were commissioned. Cannon were mounted at Newport. Cavalry corps were formed in the towns. The Governor and Council met in frequent deliberations. The Indians were disarmed and sent off the Island. A line of beacons was established from Wonumytomoni Hill, near Newport, to Mooshausick Hill, in Providence. Abundant proof was given of the energy and good statesmanship of the Colony. But the day of real trial was not yet come.

The question of taxation was an early cause of difficulty. The poorer towns felt themselves aggrieved, and often put insuperable obstacles in the way of the collector. Even the tax for the payment of John Clarke was disputed, and Roger Williams drew upon himself a severe condemnation from Warwick by a letter wherein he urged its payment. At last, in 1672, the Assembly took the matter seriously in hand and passed a bill declaring, "that whoever opposed by word or deed, in town meeting or elsewhere, any rate laid, or any other of the acts or orders of the General Assembly should be bound over to the Court of Trials, or imprisoned till it meet, at the discretion of the justice, for high contempt and sedition ; and if found guilty, should be fined, imprisoned or whipped, as the court might adjudge."

It was not altogether without reason that this stringent act was passed, for the aggressions of Connecticut and the alarm of an Indian war made it necessary to strengthen as far as possible the hands of government. But there was a danger in this legislative omnipotence which the people quickly perceived, and the new Assembly of May undid by a comprehensive repeal the work of its predecessor of April.

CHAPTER X.

KING PHILIP'S WAR.

I HAVE now reached the story of the longest and bloodiest war which the colonists had yet waged with the Indian. It is known in colonial history as King Philip's war, and belongs more to the histories of Massachusetts and Connecticut than to that of Rhode Island, although two of its bloodiest battles were fought on Rhode Island soil. Like all wars with barbarians it is filled with strange mixtures of barbarism and heroism, the savage warrior often rising in the pursuit of his ideal to a moral grandeur which his civilized antagonist failed to attain. And although like the war with the Pequots it was fatal to those who began it, it has left one of great names of Indian history, and brought into play some of the greatest traits of Indian character.

First and most faithful of the allies of the English was Massasoit, Sachem of the Wamponoags. A pestilence too malignant to be controlled by the medical science of the natives had decimated his tribe and exposed him to the ambition of the Narragansetts, his immediate neighbors, a little before the arrival of the Pilgrims. Perceiving only the present danger, he looked upon the advent of the white man as a means of preserving his independence, and eagerly made a covenant with him which he faithfully kept to the end of his life, (1661). At his death his eldest son, Wamsutta, or Alexander as he was called by the English, succeeded to his authority, but not to the confidence of his allies. Suspicion arose; he was accused of plotting against the colonists, and though an independent chief, summoned to appear at the General Court at Plymouth. Disobeying the summons, he was threatened with personal violence, and reluctantly yielding set forth with his warriors and women, some eighty in all, under the escort of a small body of troops commanded by Major Winslow. The indignity was too great for the unfortunate chief. Winslow saw that he was sinking under fatigue—for the weather was very hot—and wounded pride, for wrong was hard to bear. "Take my horse," he said, touched with compassion. "No!" replied the chief with a last touch of pride, "there are no horses for my wife and the other women." When they reached Winslow's house, which was on the way he sickened, and though allowed to turn back, quickly died. Deep was the indignation of the Indians at this treatment of their sachem, and even some of the colonists felt that they had gone too far.

But there was one among them into whose breast the wrong sank deepest, for it called him to avenge not only a chief but a brother. That brother was known in colonial history as Philip of Pocanoket. The story of Philip has been variously told, some looking upon him as a crafty savage loving the wiles and cruelty of Indian warfare and fighting with no other object than immediate success; others as an Indian patriot contending for the independence of his country. In either case, if we judge him by the standard of his own people, he was a great ruler in peace and a valiant leader in war.

We are told that it was a sore grief to the young sachem to see the white man daily taking a firmer hold of the soil, and the red man melting before him. But how could the march of the invader be stayed? The arrow was a feeble weapon with which to oppose the firelock, the tomahawk even in the strongest hand was no match for the sabre. The foresight, judgment, method and power of combination of the white man enabled him to provide for the future while making wise provision for the present. While he was well supplied with food, the Indian was starving. While he was warmly clad, the Indian was exposed almost naked to the rudest blasts of winter. Philip saw the danger and resolved to face it.

His first step was to secure allies by winning over the neighboring tribes. It was a broad field for diplomacy, wherein Indian not Christian ethics prevailed, and was well suited to his bold and wily nature. Yet with all his wiles he could not so completely cover his track as not to excite the suspicions of the English. He was summoned to Plymouth and closely questioned. But the hour for action was not yet come and he succeeded in allaying suspicions by giving up his arms.

But treason beset his path. A "praying Indian," as the converts of Eliot were called, who had lived some years with Philip as secretary and counselor, betrayed the secret of the sachem's preparations. The betrayal cost him his life but saved the Colony by compelling Philip to begin his outbreak before his preparations were completed. It is said that when he saw the necessity he cast himself upon the ground and wept bitterly.

But there was no escaping it, and collecting his forces he fell upon the settlements with fire and sword, and what was still more dreaded, the scalping knife and tomahawk. The first to feel his fury was the border town of Swanzey, where houses and barns were burnt and nine of the inhabitants put to death and seven wounded. Succor came promptly from Plymouth and Boston. The Indians fell back upon Mount Hope, Philip's favorite seat. Mutilated corpses and burning dwellings marked the track of the pursued. The pursuer looked round him in vain for an enemy. A few dogs prowled round the deserted wigwams, but not an Indian was to be seen.

And here comes into view one of the boldest leaders of the colonists in their wars with the natives, Benjamin Church, of Plymouth, a man skilled in all the arts of Indian warfare, and in whose ardent nature a sound judgment and self-control were combined with intrepidity and enterprise. He pressed close upon the track of the enemy, crossed the bay to Aquidneck, and after a six hours' fight with a superior force was compelled to take refuge on board a sloop just as his ammunition began to fail.

The war was fairly begun, and for over a twelvemonth raged with various fortunes but unabated fury. Plymouth and Massachusetts suffered most, but it left bloody traces in Rhode Island also.

For unfortunately for Rhode Island, Philip's favorite seat was that beautiful range of hills, some twelve miles long, which separates the Taunton River and Mount Hope Bay from Narragansett Bay, thus bringing him within the limits of the present Town of Bristol. Tradition still points to a rock on the southernmost hill where the "noble savage" loved to sit and gaze on the waters as they held their way to the Atlantic, revolving, perhaps, in his embittered mind, a bloody vengeance upon his arrogant foe. It was from Mount Hope that he set forth to strike his first blow, and thither that he returned to fall by the hand of a traitor. "But a small part of the domain of my ancestors is left," he said to his friend, John Borden. "I am determined not to live till I have no country."

Part only of the bloody record as I have

already said belongs to Rhode Island. In the modern Town of Tiverton, known in those earlier colonial days as Pocasset, there was a swamp—seven miles in length—one of those difficult spots wherein Indian warriors love to concentrate their forces in the hour of danger. Here, amidst intricate paths and trembling morasses Philip first awaited the assault of the enemy. The colonists came up bravely to the charge, but were bravely repulsed with the loss of sixteen men. Then they resolved to take possession of the avenues to the swamp and starve the Indians into surrender. But the wily Philip after standing a siege of thirteen days made good his escape by night and took refuge on the Connecticut River, where he was joined by the Nipmucks, a Massachusetts tribe which he had won over to his fortunes. Surprises, pursuits, gallant stands, fearful massacres follow. At Brookfield it is an ambush followed by a siege. At Deerfield there was a battle in which the Indians were worsted, then a second trial of strength in which the town was burnt. At Hadley the enemy came while the inhabitants were in the meeting-house engaged in their devotions. For a while the men, who had brought their arms with them and were well trained to the use of them, thus held their ground firmly. But the surprise had shaken their nerves, and they were beginning to cast anxious glances around them, when suddenly in their midst appeared a venerable man clad in the habiliments of another age and with a sword in his hand. With a clear, firm voice he roused the flagging courage of the villagers, reformed their ranks and led them to the charge. A Roman would have taken him for one of the Dioscuri—a Spaniard for St. Jago. What wonder that the Hadleyites thought him a divine messenger, and if with such a proof of God's favor to inspirit them, they sprang forward with dauntless hearts and drove their enemy before them. When the victory was won, the same clear voice bade them bow their heads in prayer, and when they raised them again the mysterious speaker was gone. None but the village preacher knew that it was Goffe, the regicide.

A surprise and massacre have left their name to Bloody Brook. Springfield was burned. But at Hatfield Philip received a check, and having laid waste the western frontier of Massachusetts, turned his steps toward the land of the Narragansetts. For the success of the war depended mainly upon the decision of that still powerful tribe. In the beginning a doubtful treaty had been patched up between them and the English. But their hearts were with their own race, and when Philip came they resolved to cast in their fortunes with his. The colonists prepared themselves sternly for the contest. Fifteen hundred men were enlisted in Massachusetts, Plymouth and Connecticut; a body of friendly Indians joined them, and though it was mid-winter, thinking only of the necessity of striking a decisive blow they began their march. Volunteers from Rhode Island joined them on the way, but Rhode Island as a colony was not consulted.

The Narragansetts were on their own ground and had chosen the strongest point for their winter quarters. It was an island of between three and four acres in the midst of a vast swamp in the southwestern part of the State, three or four miles from the present village of Kingston. To the trees and other natural defences the Indian chief had added palisades and such appliances as his rude engineering suggested. Here he had built his wigwams and stored his provisions, and prepared to pass the winter.

Towards this fated spot at the dawn of a December Sabbath the little army of Puritans took their way. The snow was falling fast and the wind dashed it in their faces, but bated not their speed. By one they were in front of the stronghold, and though weary with the long march and faint with hunger they pressed eagerly forward. The only entrance was over the trunk of a tree. The Indian guns and arrows covered every foot of the way. The colonists undaunted rushed on—officers in the van. First to feel the murderous Indian aim was Captain Johnson, of Roxbury. Captain Davenport, of Boston, fell next, but before he fell penetrated the enclosure. More than two hours the battle raged with unabated fury. At one time the English made their way into the fort, but the Indians rallied and forced them back again. But over-confident in the natural strength of their fortress they had neglected to secure with palisades a strip which they had thought sufficiently guarded by a sheet of water. The English discovered it, and crossing took the astonished natives in the rear. At the same time some one shouted, "Fire their wigwams." The fatal flame caught eagerly the light boughs and branches of which the frail tenements were made, and in a few moments the fort was all ablaze. Imagination shrinks appalled from the scene that followed. Night was coming on. The snow storm had set in with fresh violence. A thousand Indian warriors lay dead or wounded within the fort. Five hundred wigwams were burning within the same narrow compass—consuming alike the bodies of the wounded and the dead. The women and children, like their protectors, perished in the flames. Eighty of the English, too, were killed—a hundred and fifty were wounded. Had the wigwams been spared there would have been food and shelter for the victors. But victors and vanquisher were driven out into the bleak night, weary and spent with long marching and fasting—the Indian to crouch in an open cedar swamp not far from the fort—the English to return to the spot from whence they had set out in the morning for this dreadful victory—Smith's plantation, near the present village of Wickford. Several of the wounded died by the way.

Even after this blow Philip succeeded in arousing the Maine and New Hampshire tribes to his support, and the war still raged for a while through the New England settlements. Rhode Island suffered severely. Warwick was burned, and the cattle driven off. Tradition says that when the enemy approached Providence, Roger Williams, now a very old man, went out to meet them. "Massachusetts," he said, "can raise thousands of men at this moment, and if you kill them, the King of England will supply their places as fast as they fall." "Let them come," was the reply, "we are ready for them. But as for you, brother Williams, you are a good man; you have been kind to us many years; not a hair of your head shall be touched." Fifty-four houses in the northern part of the town were burned, but the fearless old man was not harmed.

Many of the colonists took refuge on Aquidneck, where the inhabitants of Newport and Portsmouth received them with great kindness. To protect the island a little flotilla of four boats, manned each by five or six men, was kept sailing around it day and night. There was no rest for old or young. April opened a brighter prospect. Canonchet, chief of the Narragansetts was taken prisoner. A young Englishman attempted to examine him. "You much child; no understand matters of war. Let your brother or your chief come. Him I will answer," was his haughty reply. He was offered his life if his tribe would submit, but refused it. The offer was renewed and he calmly said, "Let me hear no more about it." He was sent to Stonington, where a council of war condemned him to death. "I like it well," said he; "I shall die before my heart is soft, or I have said anything unworthy of myself." That as many as possible of his own race should take part in his execution Pequots were employed to shoot him, Mohegans to cut off his head and quarter him, and the Niantics to burn his body. When all this had been done, his head was sent to the Commissioners at Hartford as "a taken of love and loyalty."

Throughout the spring and early summer the war still raged with unabated violence. The Rhode Island Assembly was so hard pushed that it was compelled to repeal the law exempting Quakers from military service. A few days before the capture of Canonchet he had surprised a party of Plymouth men near Pawtuxet. A battle was fought in an open cedar swamp in Warwick. But at last fortune seemed to turn towards the English. Philip's allies began to fall from him. His wife and children were taken prisoners. Captain Church with a chosen band was on his trail. Hunted from lair to lair he sought refuge at Mount Hope. A few followers still clung to his fortunes. His mind was harassed by unpropitious dreams, and in his weariness his pursuers came upon him unawares. As he rose to flee he was shot down by a renegade Indian. The victors drew his body out of the swamp, cut off his head, and dividing the trunk and limbs into four parts hung them upon four trees. The head was sent to Plymouth where it was hung upon a gibbet. One hand was sent to Boston where it was welcomed as a trophy, and the other was given to the renegade who shot him, by whom it was exhibited for money. His son was sold into West India servitude.

With the death of Philip the war ended, although there were occasional collisions and bloodshed. For two members of the New England confederacy it had been a war of desolation. Connecticut, the third, escaped unharmed. Rhode Island, which had never been a member of it and had never been consulted concerning the war, although some of its leading incidents occurred within her borders, suffered most. Her second town was burned, her plantations laid waste and the inhabitants of her main-land driven for shelter to the island.

With the vanquished it went hard. Many were killed in battle, some were shot in cold blood by the sentence of an English court-martial. Many were sold into slavery—with this distinction in favor of Rhode Island, that while the other colonies sold their prisoners into unqualified servitude, she established for hers a system of apprenticeship by which the prospect of ultimate freedom was opened to all.

CHAPTER XI.

INDIANS STILL TROUBLESOME.—CONDITION OF THE PEOPLE.—TROUBLES CONCERNING THE BOUNDARY LINES.

WAR was followed by pestilence, which moves so fatally in her train. Of this pestilence we only know that it ran its deadly course in two or three days, and left its traces in almost every family. Meanwhile the legislature was sedulously repairing the breaches of the war. Laws passed in order to meet an urgent want were repealed, and chief among them as most repugnant to the tolerant spirit of the Colony the law of military service. The farmers returned to their desolate fields—citizens to the ruins of their hamlets. "Give us peace," they may have said, "and we will efface the traces of these ruins."

But it was long before real peace returned. The Indians though subdued were still turbulent. Active measures were required to prevent them from passing on and off the Island at will, and building their wigwams and mat-sheds on the commons and even on private lands. Rumsellers were found ready to sell them rum, and at Providence parties were sent out to scour the woods and guard against surprises. As an encouragement to the men engaged in these duties their wounded were nursed at public expense.

There was more serious danger from another quarter. Connecticut had not renounced her designs against Rhode Island territory, nor was she slow in declaring her intentions. The first step was an order of the Council at Hartford forbidding every one, whether white man or Indian, to occupy any lands in Narragansett without its consent. The Assembly met this order by a counter prohibition. No jurisdiction was to be exercised there but that of Rhode Island. This declaration of claims was promptly followed by action. Three planters who had returned to their plantations in Warwick were siezed by the Connecticut authorities and sent to Hartford. They appealed to their own Governor, Governor Clarke for protection. One of the most important measures of the Rhode Island government was the reëstablishment of King's Province. Full power of protection was conferred upon a court of justices to be held in Narragansett. No one was allowed to enter the Province without permission from the Assembly. Ten thousand acres of land were set apart for new settlers at the rate of a hundred acres to each man—the new settlers to be approved by the Assembly. Rhode Island threatened to appeal to the King. Connecticut declared that she was ready to meet the appeal. Attempts at compromise were made by both parties. Connecticut proposed to fix the line at Coweset, the modern East Greenwich. Rhode Island offered to allow Connecticut to dispose of half the unpurchased lands in the Province if the settlers would accept the jurisdiction of Rhode Island. The loss of King's Province would have imperilled the future independence of Rhode Island, and therewith the great principle on which it was founded. Connecticut could not renounce her last hope of securing a part of Narragansett Bay. Neither offer was accepted, and it soon became evident that no decision could be reached except by appeal to the King. Peleg Sandford and Richard Bailey were chosen agents, and two hundred and fifty pounds voted for their expenses. The money was to be raised by the sale of ten thousand acres of lands in Narragansett at the rate of a shilling an acre.

Meanwhile the Assembly was very active. A party change took place at the election of 1677—Governor Arnold was chosen in place of Governor Clarke. This was equivalent to a triumph of the war party. The militia law was again revised, care still being taken to protect the rights of conscience. How jealously these were guarded appears also in the unwillingness to multiply oaths of office. Five years before an act had been passed requiring deputies to take an engagement on entering upon the duties of their office. This law met with great opposition at its original passage, and its repeal was hailed with general satisfaction. Every freeman, it was said, made an engagement of allegiance on receiving the rights of citizenship. An oath is too solemn a thing to be lightly taken—why should we use it? So reasoned those concientious men. By another act, also, they showed how fast they held to this fundamental principle.

Another sect, the Sabbatarians or Seventh-Day Baptists, had taken root and begun to flourish in the free air of Rhode Island. In 1667 they were sufficiently numerous to justify them in asking that market day might be changed from Saturday, their Sabbath, to some other day. Without breaking in upon an old custom by changing the day, the Assembly added Thursday as another market day and thus quieted the scruples of honest and useful citizens.

We have seen how promptly and firmly the Assembly met the encroachments of Connecticut. Their remonstrances were followed up by spirited and judicious action. The surest way to strengthen their hold upon the disputed territory was by peopling it. Among the coves and inlets which give such quiet beauty to Narragansett Bay there is none more beautiful than that broad sheet of navigable water which still retains in part its original name of Coweset. Here it was resolved to plant a colony and build a town. Five hundred acres were set apart in lots on the bay for house lots—four thousand five hundred in farms of ninety acres, which were distributed among fifty men on condition of building within a year and opening roads from the bay into the country. To guard against rash speculation no colonist was to sell his land within twenty-one years unless with the consent of the Assembly. Thus on the verdant hill-side at whose foot a ripple from the Atlantic mingles with the inland murmur of Mascachugh was built the pleasant hamlet of East Greenwich.

Another bitter controversy arose concerning the limits and extent of the original Providence and Pawtuxet purchase — a question of great local interest, and which lost none of its heat from having for opposite leaders Roger Williams and William Harris. Several difficult questions were mixed up with it, greatly disturbing the harmony of the northern section of the Colony. Williams had shown himself to be an inaccurate conveyancer in the drafting of the original deed. This was purely a question of title. A still more difficult one arose when Warwick was colonized. Agents were sent to England to ask for the appointment of commissioners to decide the controversies which the local tribunals were unable to decide effectually. John Greene and Randall Holden were the agents for Warwick; William Harris for Pawtuxet. This William Harris, as we have already seen, was a bold thinker and an energetic actor. He made several voyages to England in defence of his party, and followed up with great energy every advantage that he gained before the tribunals at home. On his last voyage he fell into the hands of Barbary corsairs, and though ransomed after a year of captivity died soon after his redemption. The controversy did not cease with his death. Other voyages were made to England and other decisions obtained. But it was not till many years later that the unwise contest was settled. Then, in 1696, the line between Providence and Warwick was settled by the Assembly, with the Pawtuxet River for boundary. That between Providence and Pawtuxet was continued till 1712 and then settled by compromise.

CHAPTER XII.

DEATH OF SEVERAL OF THE MOST PROMINENT MEN.—CHANGES IN LEGISLATION.

THE woes of Rhode Island begin anew. Scarcely had the war ceased when Connecticut as we have already seen renewed her claim to Narragansett. Massachusetts soon followed in the name of the Atherton company. And presently Plymouth joined herself to the roll of Rhode Island's enemies by advancing a claim to Aquidneck itself. Connecticut sought to strengthen her pretensions by asserting that the disputed territory was now hers by right of conquest. Thus far the sturdy little colony had held its ground and grown and prospered in the midst of enemies. Would she continue to hold it? Humanity itself was concerned in the answer, for of all the powers and kingdoms of the earth she alone was founded upon the principle of perfect toleration. The contest was a long and a weary one, too long for the purpose of this volume, for it is a history of seventy years of discussion and aggression, of bitter attack and firm resistance, terminating at last in the triumph of the weak and single-handed. Rhode Island not only preserved her original territory but added to it from that of two of her enemies. I shall select a few incidents to illustrate the progress of the contest.

It was to be waged for the most part by a new generation. The great men of the foundation were passing away. John Clarke, who had thrown the mild lustre of his purity over the first half of the life of the Colony, died in 1676, leaving a deep longing, or rather a sore need of his civil virtues and diplomatic skill. Samuel Gorton, whose tenacious convictions made him stern and intolerant in public life though gentle and attractive in private intercourse, and whose vigorous and subtle intellect led him to rejoice in the bitterness of controversy as the swift horse rejoices in the dust of the race-course, died the year after. Roger Williams was spared a few years longer—bold, ardent, disputatious, resolute, sincere and earnest to the last. But the young of his middle age were growing old, and the companions of his active years were falling around him. His colony had thriven and flourished. The five men who followed him from Salem had become "a thousand or twelve hundred men able to bear arms." In spite of the threatening of the political horizon his strong faith told him that the being in whom he had put his trust thus far would stand by him still. And thus he laid his head upon his last pillow, a satisfied and happy man.

Another man of bold, original type—William Harris—had run his active career, and died with his hands and heart still full of unfinished work. We have seen to what length he carried his doctrine of individual right to free action. We have seen him wage a bitter controversy with Roger Williams. Time after time he crossed the Atlantic as agent of the great boundary questions which fill so large a space in the Rhode Island history of this period; the last time, and from which he was never to return, as agent for Connecticut. A deep presentiment of disaster seems to have filled his mind as he was preparing himself for this voyage, and not satisfied with making his will he presented it for probate with his own hands. The presentiment was well founded. On the outward passage he was taken by a Barbary corsair and sold into slavery. By the exertion of friends he was ransomed after a year's captivity and made his way through Spain and France to England. But the year of slavery had told hard upon him, and three days after his arrival he died. It has been remarked by a profound thinker that while Williams's more comprehensive mind could embrace both the practical and ideal in their mutual relations, the moment that Harris touched the ideal he became a radical. It does not seem to have struck his cotemporaries as it does us to see him accepting the agency of Connecticut in her controversy with Rhode Island. But he has a definite place in Rhode Island history and did her good service through his long and somewhat turbulent career.

William Coddington, who had been an eminent man in Massachusetts before he became a very eminent man in Rhode Island, lived to take an active part in the controversy, and died in 1678, while holding for the time the office of Governor. His temporary usurpation had been forgiven and forgotten, and men remembered only that he had sincerely renounced his hostile designs and become a loyal and useful citizen.

Such were some of the men who bore the largest part in moulding the original character of Rhode Island. Talent and character like theirs was required to guide the little Colony through the dangers that surrounded it. But before we return to the external history of these days we will gather from the acts of the Assembly a few records of the moral and intellectual life of the Colony and its progress to a higher civilization.

The publicity of the laws is a question of deep interest in every stage of society, but particularly interesting in small communities. In the early days of Rhode Island they were published by beat of drum under the seal of the Colony. The violation of a law found no excuse in the plea of ignorance.

The sessions of the Assembly were held in a tavern or sometimes in a private house, always beginning, as the Roman assemblies did, at a very early hour. We have already seen that early attempts were made to allure the members to their duty by payment. It was still some time before this became a fixed law. In 1679 a resolution was passed for paying the board and lodging of the members of the Assembly and of the Court of Trials. In the May session of 1680 a definite sum was fixed upon—seven shillings a week. The true nature of the reciprocal obligation of the citizen and the State was not yet fully understood.

The frequent appeals to England which the aggressions of the other New England colonies made necessary, made it also necessary to keep resident agents at the English court. Thus the increased expenditure of the Colony kept pace with the increase of her resources.

In 1678 a tax was laid which enables us to form a tolerably accurate idea of the financial condition of the Colony. Its full amount was three hundred pounds. "Of this sum Newport was assessed one hundred and thirty-six pounds, Portsmouth sixty-eight, New Shoreham and Jamestown twenty-nine each, Providence ten, Warwick eight, Kingston sixteen, afterwards reduced to eight, East Greenwich and Westerly two each." As the greater part of this tax was commutable, we are enabled to form a pretty accurate idea of the price of living just after the war. "Fresh pork was valued at twopence a pound, salted and well packed pork at fifty shillings a barrel, fresh beef at twelve shillings a hundred weight, packed beef in barrels thirty shillings a hundred, peas and barley malt two and sixpence a bushel, corn and barley, two shillings, washed wool sixpence a pound, and good firkin butter fivepence. The quarter part of this tax was paid in wool at the rate of fivepence a pound." If we compare these prices with those of 1670, we shall see that war had proved here as everywhere a great scourge.

In the law by which this tax was levied we find a practical illustration of the principle which less than a century later became the fundamental principle of colonial resistance to the mother country. None but a complete representation of all the towns could levy a tax, or as it was formulated by James Otis—taxation without representation is tyranny.

It is also worthy of observation that there was a tendency to extend the usage of election to direct choice by vote of the freemen. The office of major which at its first institution during Philip's war was filled by vote of the militia, passed, in 1678, to the whole body of freemen. The necessity of a distinction between martial and civil law seems, also, to have made itself more sensibly felt at the same period, and a permanent court-martial was formed for the trial of delinquent soldiers. As the commercial spirit of the Colony increased the necessity of a bankrupt law was felt, but on trial it was found to be premature and repealed. An attempt was also made to avoid the conflict of land titles in Narragansett, where the interest of townships as well as of private individuals was involved. To correct this evil which struck at the root of social organization the Assembly ordered that the disputed tracts should be surveyed and plats made of them. For the more efficacious protection of this fundamental interest it was ordered that all who held by Indian titles "should present their deeds to be passed on by the Assembly." Descending to minuter particulars, we find a law against fast riding—first, in "the compact parts of Newport," and not long after, of Providence, also. We find it also ordered that a bell be provided and set up in some convenient place for calling the Assembly and courts and council together. Of deeper interest was the act appointing a committee to make a digest of the laws, "that they may be putt in print." Only part, however, of this resolution was carried out, and it was not till 1719 that the laws were put into a permanent form.

Not the laws only but the language in which they were expressed attracted attention. We now meet for the first time in the enacting clause of a law, "and by the authority thereof be it ordained, enacted and declared." Instead of executor administrator was written, "it being in that case the more proper and usual term in the law." In one act we find an instance of grim humor. The accounts of a general sergeant were found to be in inextricable confusion. The auditing committee resolved to call them square "and voted that by this act there is a full and fynal issue of all differences relative to said accounts from the beginninge of the world unto this present Assembly."

In some instances the public mind was not made up concerning a law, and one Assembly would undo the work of its predecessor. One of the most important acts of this class was an act denying the revisory power of the Assembly over decisions of courts of trials. In the August session of 1680, after two years of experiment, the act was repealed.

The existence of a law proves, also, the existence of an evil. In the May session of 1679, we find an act for the protection of servants, whom "sundry persons being evil-minded" were in the habit of overtasking at home, and then hiring others to let out for work on Sunday—thus infringing the law which practically made Sunday a holiday. This is not a pleasant picture, but the action of the Assembly forbidding the abuse shows that public opinion was sound. We find, also, that then as now sailors were more or less at the mercy of sailor landlords. The Assembly took up their defence. Those who trusted a sailor for more than five shillings without an order from his captain forfeited their claim. Another law bearing directly upon navigation was passed in the May session of 1679. "The master of every vessel of over twenty tons burthen was required to report himself to the head officer of the town upon arrival and departure, and if over ten days in port, then to set up notice in two public places in the town three days before sailing." In this last act we see the influence of the navigation act which was so long held to be the guardian genius of England's commercial prosperity, and which was communicated to all the colonies by royal edict in 1680.

And here, as illustrative of border life when Rhode Island was a border colony, comes the story of John Clawson's curse. This John Clawson was a hired servant of Roger Williams, who, at the instigation of a desperate fellow by the name of Herendeen, was attacked in the night from behind a thicket of barberry bushes, near the old north burial ground by an Indian named Waumaion. The Indian, who was armed with a broad axe, split open Clawson's chin at the first blow. The wound was mortal, but the wounded man lived long enough to utter his curse—that "Herendeen and his posterity might be marked with split chins and haunted with barberry bushes" forever. The malediction, legend says, was fulfilled, and the descendants of the murderer were still distinguished in the last century by a furrowed chin, and fired up with indignation at the mention of a barberry bush.

CHAPTER XIII.

COURTS AND ARMY STRENGTHENED.—COMMISSIONERS SENT FROM ENGLAND.—CHARTER REVOKED.

DISPUTES of title fill, as we have seen, a full but monotonous chapter in this part of our history. Among them was the dispute for Potowomut, a neck of land on Coweset Bay which had been purchased of the Indians by order of the Assembly as early as 1659. Bitter disputes soon followed, Warwick claiming it, and individuals both English and Indians disputing the claim. At last the question was disposed of, as was supposed, finally, at a town meeting in 1680, in which it was divided "into fifty equal lots or rights, and the names of the proprietors were inserted on the records." But the very next year we meet it again as a contest between Warwick and Kingston. At last the Assembly interposed, forbidding all occupancy of the land till further orders, warning off intruders, but permitting the Warwick men to mow and improve the meadows as heretofore.

Among the questions brought before the Assembly in the time of these disputes, was the question of the power of the Town Council to reject or accept new citizens. The question was brought up by Providence and decided in the affirmative. The form of application for leave to reside has been preserved: "To ye Towne mett this 15th of December 1680. My request to ye Towne is; that they woold grant the liberty to reside in ye Towne during the Townes Approbation, behaving myselfe as a civill man ought to doe, Desireing not to putt ye Towne to any charge by my residing here; and for what ye Towne shall cause farther to enquire of me, I shall see I hope to give them a true and sober Answer thereunto. Y^{or} friend and servant Tho. Waters."

One of the lessons of the war had been the importance of cavalry, and in 1682 a company was raised in the main-land towns consisting of thirty-six men, exclusive of officers. To put them on the same footing with the infantry they were allowed the same privileges, and held to the same obligation of exercising six days in the year. Not long after the number of majors was doubled, and John Greene appointed for the main-land and John Coggeshall for the island. Measures were also taken to give greater efficiency to the courts, and it was decided that the October sessions should be held in Providence and Warwick annually. That there might be no delay in the execution of sentences, each of these towns was required to furnish a cage and stocks. Thus surely but gradually the resolute Colony went on in its work of organization. But perilous days were at hand.

The appeals of the colonies to England had attracted her attention to these distant domains, which but for that might long have continued to grow and prosper in obscurity. But when called upon to grant privileges she naturally began to examine into the nature of her rights, and interpreted them not by the genius of the colonies, but by the commercial interests of the mother country. The act of navigation, which had its origin in English jealousy of Holland, bore hard from the beginning on the commercial industry of the colonies. Although first passed by the republican Parliament of 1651, it did not become an efficient act until the first Parliament of Charles II. in 1660, when it was formally proclaimed in all the colonies by beat of drum. Custom-houses with all their parapheranalia followed close in its track. The burthen was soon felt, and smuggling, the natural relief of overtaxed commerce, became general. The bays and inlets of New England afforded great facilities for illicit trade, and the public conscience could not long resist the temptation. We shall see before another century is over to what England's narrow policy led.

Questions relating to the colonies were generally referred to the Board of Trade. In 1680 came a letter from the board containing twenty-seven queries concerning Rhode Island. The agents in England also went prepared to give all the information that was required for the understanding of the claims and condition of the Colony. As long as Charles, the grantor of the charter lived, there was nothing done to excite alarm. But no sooner did his bigoted brother ascend the throne, than it became evident that an entire change was to be made in colonial policy. Rhode Island was quick to feel the blow. A commission of nine was appointed to settle the vexed question of King's Province. Head of the commission was the notorious Cranfield, who had made himself a bad name by his tyrannical government of New Hampshire. Next came Randolph, detested in Massachusetts for his oppressive administration of the acts of trade. These names excited gloomy anticipations which were presently fulfilled.

And here let us pause a moment to observe the exact situation of Rhode Island at this critical emergency. Having had her origin in a practical appeal from the intolerance of Massachusetts, she had never been admitted to the confederation which gave unity and strength to the other New England colonies. Her doctrine of soul-liberty was a stench in their nostrils, and her possession of the broad and beautiful Narragansett Bay so favorable for maritime and internal commerce, was, as we have seen, a constant subject of bickering and envy. Massachusetts laid claim to Pawtuxet and Warwick, and a Massachusetts company to part of Narragansett; Connecticut to a large portion of the remainder of Narragansett,

Plymouth to Aquidneck and other islands of the Bay. Little was left to Rhode Island but the plantations on the Mooshausick. All of these claims were enforced by all the means and arts within the command of the stronger colonies except actual war, and resisted with admirable resolution and perseverance by the weaker colony. We have seen how agents were sent to plead her cause at the court of their common sovereign, how every attempt to establish jurisdiction had been promptly resisted and every intrusion instantly repelled. In the darkest hour she never lost heart nor bated one jot her rights. But the darkest hour of all was at hand.

Cranfield and Randolph set themselves zealously to their congenial task. The Assembly met for theirs. The Commissioners refused to establish their position by showing their credentials. The Assembly refused to recognize them officially without credentials. The rupture was open and violent. The Assembly appointed new agents to repair to court and lay the evidence in behalf of the Colony before the King. A tax of four hundred pounds was imposed to meet their expenses. Much importance was attached to an address to the King drawn up by Randall Holden and John Greene. Meanwhile the Commissioners on their part were not idle. Cranfield wrote to the Board of Trade that the colonies were disloyal. "It never will be otherwise," he added, "till their charters are broke and the college at

Cambridge utterly extirpated, for from thence these half-witted philosophers turn either Atheists or seditious preachers." He was right, for it was at Cambridge that Otis and Quincy and Warren and the two Adamses imbibed the principles which led to independence.

It was in 1684, in the midst of these struggles, that a petition of the Jews for protection was presented to the Assembly and granted—Rhode Island remaining true to the last to the principle of her origin.

The decision of the Royal Commissioners was unfavorable to Rhode Island, and it is hard to see how she could have escaped mutilation. But she was menaced by a still greater danger. In 1684 Charles the Second died, and his brother James ascended the throne, bringing with him a narrow mind and a bad heart. To establish an arbitrary government and restore the supremacy of the Romish Church were the cardinal points of his policy. The American colonies afforded a favorable field for the trial. It began by the revocation of their charters, and was speedily followed up by putting the government of the New England colonies under one head.

Rhode Island found herself where she stood at the beginning, a government of towns. Her original four towns had united under one government for self-defence, and now that they were arbitrarily separated by a power too great to be resisted they naturally fell back upon their original municipal institutions. This closing scene is not without its dignity. The Assembly met at its accustomed time. The Governor, Walter Clarke, solemnly called upon the freemen for counsel. The whole question of dangers and difficulties was discussed, and wisely preferring petition to resistance, it was resolved to address a solemn appeal to the King for the preservation of their charter. Then all returned to its original order. The freemen met and discussed their town interests in their town meetings. Town officers elected by their townsmen performed their accustomed duties. The tradesman and the farmer went on in his chosen calling and the towns throve and prospered, still looking with unwavering trust to a day of redemption.

CHAPTER XIV.

CHANGES IN FORM OF GOVERNMENT.—SIR EDMOND ANDROS APPOINTED GOVERNOR.—HE OPPRESSES THE COLONISTS AND IS FINALLY DEPOSED.

Thus a provisional government took the place of the charter government under which New England had grown so rapidly. A great and successful experiment in political science was suddenly checked, and hopes which had led so many devout and earnest men to renounce the conveniences of home for the perils and discomforts of a wilderness were rudely crushed at the very moment when they seemed nearest their fulfillment. The same blow which fell upon Rhode Island fell with equal fatality upon Massachusetts and Connecticut. The government by charter ceased. The two most active agents of James in this remoulding of the government of the colonies were Dudley, President of the Council, and Randolph, the Secretary, whose despotic conduct in Boston has already been mentioned. Here was a broader and more congenial field.

It was resolved as has been seen to address the King in behalf of the Colony, and John Greene, venerable by years and illustrious by public services, was appointed to carry the address to

England and advocate it as agent for the Colony. He had watched over the cradle of the Colony—who so fit to stand by its grave.

Unfortunately, party had lost none of its virulence even in this supreme hour, and a small minority of dissentients was found to the sober and judicious conduct of the Assembly. Among them were members of the Atherton company, and among their methods of attack were bitter aspersions upon the personal character of the colonial agent. The provisional government found enough to do in preparing the colonies for their new life, and one of their earliest measures was a final organization of King's Province. Among the changes that they made was the changing of the names of its three towns. Kingston, the largest, was called Rochester, Westerly, the next in size, became Haversham, and East Greenwich, the smallest, took the name of Dedford. The western boundary of Haversham was Pawcatuck River. Dedford was extended on the north to Warwick, and enlarged by the peninsula of Potowomut. Part of the actual settlers were living on land to which they had no legal claim. Preëmption rights were granted them and time given them to "arrange with the owners by rent or purchase."

At last, on the 20th of December, 1686, the Royal Governor, Sir Edmond Andros, arrived in Boston. He came in a ship of the royal navy and brought with him two companies of the royal army, the first regular troops that had ever been seen in Massachusetts. He had already been in the colonies and knew the spirits with whom he would have to deal. Rhode Island, like her sisters, had everything to fear from his abitrary will. But she had treated him with respectful consideration on his former visit, and was now treated by him with less than his usual harshness.

He entered at once upon his welcome task, the transformation of a constitutional government into a despotism. Massachusetts came first in order, and the very first blow was a deadly one, an outrage upon her convictions and a deep humiliation to her pride. Her Puritan theocracy, which had penetrated every part of her civil polity, was overthrown, and the service of the church of England was openly celebrated. In this Rhode Island had no change to fear, for freedom of conscience was, till other ends were accomplished, the doctrine of the King himself. In all other things all the colonies fared alike.

We have seen how watchful Rhode Island was of the taxing power, and how nearly she had reached the great fundamental principle that taxation and representation go together. Andros sent out his tax-gatherers without consulting the tax-payers. His object was to raise money, no matter how. Farming the revenue, always a favorite device of despotism, offered facilities which he promptly turned to account. The augmentation of fees was an abundant source. Those of probate were increased twenty-fold. Writs of intrusion opened another channel for organized robbery. No one could tell how soon he might be compelled to buy his farm over again. Even marriage afforded a field for the display of arbitrary power.' Necessity at first compelled the government to recognize the validity of civil marriages. But as the transformation of laws and usages progressed, no marriages were recognized as valid which were not celebrated according to the rights of the Church of England. To feel the odious tyranny of this law it should be remembered that there was but one Episcopal clergyman in the Colony. Another oppressive act was the introduction of passports, whether for the fees they brought in.or in order to throw obstacles in the way of a free communication among the colonies, it would be difficult to tell.

Andros's commission gave him the power to appoint and remove his counselors at will. The council consisted of nineteen members, five of whom were from Rhode Island. One of them, John Greene, was absent on his agency in England. Their first meeting was held at Boston. In this the usual oaths of allegiance and office were taken, the two Quaker members from Rhode Island being allowed to make their affirmation. All officers in commission were continued in office during the Governor's pleasure, and all laws that did not clash with the laws of England, were retained. The first was the only full meeting of this impotent board, which only met to confirm the resolves of an arbitrary Governor.

In substance Andros had his own way, though not without occasional opposition and now and then humiliation. In Rhode Island the charter was adroitly put out of his reach by Governor Clarke and not reproduced till he had left Newport. In Connecticut it was hidden in the hollow of an oak. The seal of Rhode Island was broken. The members of the council were constantly changing, and few of them, according to Randolph, cared for the King. "His Excellency has to do with a perverse people."

We meet some of the questions of our own day. Licenses for the sale of liquor were granted in Newport, but no liquor could be sold in King's Province. How well the prohibition was obeyed it is impossible to say. Poor laws also appear in the guise of taxes for the support of that perplexing part of the population. It would be tedious and useless to follow the despotic Governor through all the changes of his administration of two years and four months. Suffice it to say that he had fully imbibed the spirit of his master, and did all that he could to reduce the colonies to servitude. A few provisions, however, may be mentioned as illustrating the condition of the country. With the growth of the towns fires became sources of danger. To enforce watchfulness the person in whose house a fire broke out was fined two and sixpence, and for still greater security every householder was required to set "a ladder reaching to the ridge pole, to every house that he owned." Attention was called to the fishing in Pettaquamscot pond and an order passed for encouraging it. A tax was laid for the extermination of wolves, which seem still to have been very numerous.

In April, 1688, Andros's commission was enlarged so as to comprise New York and the Jerseys, all under the general appellation of New England. Enlarged powers and minute instructions accompanied the new commission, and among the former was the subjection of the press to the will of the Governor.

But another change was drawing nigh. There was nothing in common between James the Second and the New England colonist, and Andros represented his master too faithfully not to be bitterly hated. Even Thanksgiving, that thoroughly New England festival, was neglected when announced by his proclamation. Some spoke out their detestation openly to his face. "I suppose," he said one morning to Dr. Hooker, the great clerical wit of Hartford, "all the good people of Connecticut are fasting and praying on my account." "Yes," replied the Doctor, "we read, 'This kind goeth not out but by fasting and prayer.'"

Rhode Island suffered less at his hands than any other colony. The enforced toleration which excited such strong feelings in Massachusetts met with no opposition in a territory where Baptists and Quakers and Puritans and Separatists worshipped according to their own convictions. John Greene soon became aware that there was no prospect of a return to the free life of the charter so long as James held the throne. Therefore, without renouncing the hope of a better future, he confined his negotiations for the present to questions of minor, though important bearing. Chief among them was the putting an end to the intrusions of the outside claimants to Narragansett. This brought up all the unsettled claims which had been so pertinaciously enforced and so firmly resisted. The Atherton claim was thrown out by the Commissioners as extorted from the Indians by fear. The Connecticut claim was repudiated upon grounds set forth in the Rhode Island charter. Several individual titles, both Indian and English, were considered, and after careful examination, the right of Rhode Island to King's Province was confirmed for the third time—"against Connecticut in point of jurisdiction, and against the so-called proprietors in point of ownership." This report was met in England by a petition of Lord Culpepper in behalf of the Atherton company for grants of land not already occupied and the bass ponds, upon such quit rents as might seem good to the King. The petition was granted in part and Andros was intrusted to "assign them such lands as had not already been occupied—at a quit rent of two and sixpence for every hundred acres."

Thus far Rhode Island has come off with honor

in her contests with her neighbors. There was one, however, in which she won no honor. A party of unfortunate Huguenots had established themselves in King's Province, forming a little settlement of their own and paying honestly for their lands. But the French name was not loved in the colonies and their Protestant neighbors persecuted them away. Traces of them may still be found in the neighborhood where they settled, which bears to this day the name of Frenchtown.

Meanwhile great changes were taking place in England, where James was rapidly running his career of bigotry and oppression. Slow as the communications between the mother country and her colonies were there was still communication enough to enable the latter to form some conception of the state of public feeling in the former. The new government had never acquired any stability in New England. The Council was constantly changing, and after the first meeting never all met together again. The public mind was ripe for revolution, and when the first tidings of the fall of James reached New England she was prepared to accept them with all their consequences. Unfortunately for Andros he was in Boston at this critical moment, and Boston was ready to act with her wonted vigor. The Governor was summoned to surrender his authority, and refusing, was thrown into prison. Massachusetts made haste to reörganize her government, but her charter was gone.

CHAPTER XV.

CHARTER GOVERNMENT AGAIN RESUMED.—FRENCH WAR.—INTERNAL IMPROVEMENTS.—CHARGES AGAINST THE COLONIES.

RHODE ISLAND had never hated Andros as bitterly as the other colonies had hated him, for the freedom of conscience which he endeavored to force upon them was in her a fundamental principle. But she loved her charter and rightly believed that it was the only sure pledge of her liberties. Therefore, when Dudley, the Chief-Justice, undertook to open his court, he was seized and put in jail. This was a bold casting off of the new government. The next step was a cautious return to the old. A letter from Newport came out calling upon the freemen of Rhode Island to meet there "before the day of usual election by charter," to take counsel together concerning public affairs. When the day came the freemen met, and doubtless with all their usual freedom of debate, prepared a statement of their reasons for resuming their charter government. Party lines were already sharply drawn. On one side were the Royalists, led by the rich merchant, Francis Brinley, who opposed the resumption of the charter, and called for a general government by immediate appointment of the King. On the other were the Republicans, stronger both by number and by fervor of opinion. Their boldness secured the freedom of the Colony. In an address to "the present supreme power of England," they gave their reasons for returning to their charter, and asked to have their action approved. Deputy-Governor Coggeshall, with several assistants, resumed their functions, but Governor Clarke, whose characteristic trait was caution, declined and the Colony was ten months without a governor.

Still, in May, all the old officers were reinstated and "all the laws superseded in 1686" resumed their place on the schedule. "The charter was produced in open Assembly" and then restored to Governor Clarke for safe keeping. When the question of the legality of the resumption of charter government came before the King, he approved it upon the written opinion of the law officers of the crown that "the charter, never having been revoked, but only suspended, still remained in full force and effect." Heartily must Rhode Island and Connecticut have rejoiced that theirs had been so successfully guarded. In May came the welcome tidings that William and Mary had been acknowledged in England. They were promptly and joyfully acknowledged in the colonies. Dr. Increase Mather, a great name in Massachusetts, was in London on behalf of the colonies when the revolution broke out. He obtained an early audience of William and pleaded for the recall of Andros. The recall was granted, and after ten months of confinement the crestfallen Governor was sent to England for trial. But his conduct was viewed in a different light in the mother country from what it had been in the colonies. "The charges against him were dismissed by the royal order, on the ground of insufficiency — and that he had done nothing which was not fully justified by his instructions." As a compensation for his long imprisonment, he was presently made Governor of Virginia.

In February, 1689-90, the Assembly met for the first time in four years and entered upon the work of organization. Seventeen deputies, together with the officers chosen in May, were present. Absentees were summoned. Clarke refused to serve as Governor. Christopher Almy also declined. The bold but aged Henry Bull was chosen in his stead. After some hesitation Clarke gave up the charter and other official papers. Funds which had been appropriated to the building of a Colony House were held by Roger Goulding, who promptly paid them over. Andros had broken the original colonial seal. A new seal, Hope with her anchor, was procured. Rhode Island's exposed situation laid her open to attacks by sea, and thus imposed the necessity of new expenses. War had broken out between England and France, and the colonies were to come in for their share of war's sufferings. Some

, fear was felt of the colony in Frenchtown, and the few survivors of the unfortunate settlement were required to repair to the office of John Greene, in Warwick, and take the oath of allegiance to the King.

Thus the government was regularly organized and public business began to move on in its accustomed track. At the May session of 1690 Governor Bull declined a reëlection, and John Easton was chosen in his place. John Greene was chosen Deputy-Governor. One more was added to the list of assistants, who thus became ten. Here ends the probation of Rhode Island.

Poor and weak, through toil and sacrifice, in spite of internal dissensions and external enmities, calumniated for the great truth on which she was founded, coveted for the beautiful territory which she had redeemed from the wilderness, she had solved the problem of self-government and proved that the religious virtues may flourish without the aid of civil authority. The struggle for existence is over. She now enters through industry upon the path to wealth and culture.

The sessions of the Assembly had been held hitherto in taverns or private houses. But now a proper edifice, the town house, is built for public use and the public meetings are held in it. Thus far, also, the governor, the deputy-governor and the assistants have received no compensation for their services. They are henceforth exempted from the Colony tax. War with the

French and Indians was raging all along the northern frontier. New York was the colony most exposed. Leister, her Governor, called on the other colonies for aid. Rhode Island, whose extensive water fronts left her open to attacks by sea, could not send men, and therefore taxed herself three hundred pounds to send money. The wisdom of this course was soon apparent. Seven French privateers made a descent upon the islands on the coast, committing horrible excesses. Bonfires were kindled at Pawcatuck to alarm the country, and a sloop well manned sent out from Newport to reconnoitre. A night attempt was made upon the town but failed. One upon New London was repulsed. Two sloops carrying ninety men were sent out under Thomas Paine and John Godfrey to fight the enemy. A bloody battle which lasted two hours and a half followed, and the French were driven off with the loss of half their crews and a valuable prize. Block Island was particularly exposed during this war. Four attacks were made upon it, the inhabitants ill treated and their cattle driven off. In the last invasion the privateersmen were defeated in "an open pitched battle."

The war pressed so "heavily on the commercial interests of the community that it was found necessary to lay a tonnage duty of a shilling a ton upon the vessels over ten tons burthen of other colonies that broke bulk in Newport harbor. The payment might be made in money or in powder, at the rate of a shilling a pound, and the products of the duty were employed in keeping up a powder magazine on the island. Rhode Islanders had not yet learnt to pay their taxes promptly, and more than once the Assembly was called together to devise the means of collecting sums already voted. The tonnage duty was a welcome, though a small contribution, to the scanty resources of the little Colony. A few years later a new source was opened by the levy of a duty upon foreign wines, liquors and molasses—that upon molasses being a half-penny a gallon. In the August session of 1698 an elaborate tax law in twelve sections was enacted, and a tax of eight hundred pounds currency was voted. By this act a poll tax of a shilling a head was imposed upon all males between sixteen and sixty. But this, also, was not easily collected, and years passed before an adequate method of taxation was devised and applied.

Shortly after the return to the charter the small-pox broke out. "Rhode Island is almost destroyed by the small-pox," says a cotemporary letter." When the Assembly met they were unable to open the session with the prescribed formalities, for the only copy of the charter was in the keeping of the recorder, who was sick with the dreaded disease, and the reading of the charter was the first step towards organization. When the pestilence was passed, the attention of legislation was directed to the militia laws, which were revised and brought more into harmony with the material wants of the Colony. In this connection it may not be out of place to remember that the town house was enlarged and a belfry added to it. Government 'was gradually putting on the external forms of authority.

In 1691 a change occurred on the eastern border which threatened her inter-colonial. relations. Plymouth was merged in Massachusetts, which was thus brought into larger contact with Rhode Island. Sir William Phipps, a native of Massachusetts, was appointed Governor, with a commission which gave him command over all the forces of New England, by land and by sea—a flagrant violation of the charters of Rhode Island and Connecticut, and which was vigorously repelled. Older grievances were not entirely healed. Some Pawcatuck men asked to be placed under the laws of Connecticut. The leaven of the Atherton company dispute had not yet spent its force. But the change of tone in the language of the correspondence shows that the bitterness which had distinguished its early stages was gradually passing away.

This (1692) was the time of the witchcraft trials in Massachusetts, a delusion in which Rhode Island did not share, for though she gave witchcraft a place on her statute books as a tribute to a superstition of the age, she never brought it into her courts. She was busied with more important questions.

Phipps was urging his claim to command the New England forces. John Greene, now Deputy-

Governor, went to Boston with one of the assistants to discuss the matter. They got no satisfaction from the aspiring governor, either upon the question of command or upon the equally important question of the boundary line. The whole matter was referred to the Board of Trade and by them to the Attorney-General, who decided in favor of Rhode Island. A distinction, however, was made between peace and war. In time of war the commander-in-chief might, in conjunction with the governor, call out the quota prescribed by the Board of Trade. Rhode Island's quota for service under the Governor of New York was forty-eight men. The eastern boundary question was referred to the New York Council as being disinterested and near the spot. The Narragansett dispute though so often decided in favor of Rhode Island, still reappeared from time to time. Several years were yet to pass before the boundaries both on the east and the west were definitively settled and the stout little Colony secured in the possession of her own territory. I shall no longer attempt to follow the story through its obscure ramifications. It has served thus far to illustrate colonial life, and show with what tenacity of purpose and devotion to a great principle Rhode Island followed up her labor of organization. It was the border war of our colonial history.

The necessity of regular communication between the colonies began to be seriously felt, and part of John Greene's mission to Boston in 1692 was to negotiate the establishment of a post office. Early in the following year Thomas Neale, acting under patent from the King, established a weekly mail from Boston to Virginia. Rhode Island came in for her share of the advantage. The rate of postage upon a single inland letter from Boston to Rhode Island was sixpence. And thus was woven one of the first links in the chain which, before another century was passed, had bound all the colonies in an indissoluble union.

We have seen a gradual approach towards a just comprehension of the relations of the state to its officers. The decisive step was taken in 1695, when a salary of ten pounds was voted to the governor, six pounds to the deputy-governor, four pounds to the assistants and three shillings a day to the deputies while in session. Absentees forfeited twice their pay.

In the following year an important change was made in the organization of the Assembly, the deputies becoming a separate house coördinate with the assistants, each house occupying a separate room and having a veto upon the action of the other. It will help to form a correct idea of daily life in the country if I add that a bounty of ten shillings was paid for killing old wolves, and of the seaports and sea coast that privateers were fitted out from them with very irregular commissions. Blackbirds fared hard in Portsmouth, where every householder was required to kill twelve before the tenth of May, under penalty of two shillings, and with a premium of a shilling a head for all over twelve. This was to serve as a protection for fields. But the serious danger was from the Indians, for the treaty of Ryswick gave for sometime but an imperfect peace to the colonies. Inroads of Indians were frequent and sudden. Never had the councils of war been more active or more constantly in session, and never had the men who were fit for service been more constantly under arms. Scouting parties of ten men were sent out every two days to serve beyond the limits of the plantations. Such were the trials of the second generation of colonizers.

The violation of the acts of trade and lax dealing with privateers became so flagrant that the home government after many vain complaints resolved to establish courts of admirality in all the colonies. The attorney-general was consulted and said there was nothing in their charters to prevent it. The colonial agents exerted themselves earnestly to ward off the blow, but without success, and when the Rhode Island agent, Jahleel Brenton, returned in December, 1697-8, he brought a commission to Peleg Sandford as Judge, and to Nathaniel Coddington as Register. Governor Clarke opposed it and tried to induce the Assembly to join in the opposition. Brenton advised that he should be impeached, whereupon Clarke resigned in favor of his nephew, Samuel Cranston.

The Colony was entering upon a new period of trial and danger. The enemies of her chartered rights were numerous and powerful, and unhappily for her were supported in their charges by a dangerous array of specious evidence. The rival interests were represented by men admirably fitted for their respective tasks. The Royal Governor of Massachusetts, Lord Bellemont, a man of singular ability and strength of character, represented the party that would have made New England a vice-royalty. Cranston, firm, resolute and self-possessed, held that Rhode Island under the protection of her charter had fully proved her capacity for self-government.

The great interest at stake was the interest of trade. Domestic trade was fostered and protected. Peddling was prohibited as injurious to regular traffic. Pains were taken to secure uniformity of weights and measures. In all this no power was assumed which the spirit if not the letter of the charter did not fully grant. But the act of navigation had raised up an enemy to foreign trade which in time of war encouraged privateering and in time of peace led to piracy. The treaty of Ryswick left many hardy spirits afloat, greedy for gold and unscrupulous in their pursuit of it.

The American coast offered great facilities for smuggling, and it was only as smugglers that pirates or privateersmen could convert their prizes into money. Much of this money it is said was buried in retired nooks of the inlets and bays along the coast. The royal revenues suffered greatly by this illicit trade, and the royal agents accused the colonists of openly favoring it. "The people of New York," wrote Lord Bellemont to the Board of Trade, "have such an appetite for piracy and unlawful trade that they are ready to rebel as often as the government puts the law in execution against them." Rhode Island was held to be a favorite resort of these bold adventurers. Both Cranston her Governor, and John Greene her Deputy-Governor were accused of favoring them. Greene, who had been elected ten years in succession, was dropped in 1700, but Cranston was reëlected from year to year, thirty years in succession.

Meanwhile Bellemont, whose hostility was embittered by the instigations of Randolph, went on collecting document upon document, till the formidable list amounted to twenty-five heads of accusation—chief of which was connivance with pirates—and, as he wrote to the Board of Trade, "making Rhode Island their sanctuary." Should the Board of Trade accept these accusations, what could preserve the Colony from a quo warranto? Nothing did save her but the death of the Royal Governor.

To this period belongs the story of Captain Kidd, long the subject of many a fearful tradition and all the more widely known from having exchanged an admiral's flag for the black flag of the corsair. After a wild and adventurous career in the Indian ocean he came to the American coast, and showing himself boldly in the streets of Boston was arrested, sent to England for trial and hanged.

CHAPTER XVI.

COLONIAL PROSPERITY.—DIFFICULTIES OCCASIONED BY THE WAR WITH THE FRENCH.—DOMESTIC AFFAIRS OF THE COLONY.

If we may judge the prosperity of the Colony by the increase of taxation—and taxes it must be remembered were self-imposed — we shall find that Rhode Island at the beginning of the new century had made real if not rapid progress in all the branches of national prosperity. Her population in 1702 was estimated at ten thousand, exclusive of Indians. She drew supplies from foreign ports in bottoms of her own, and raised the staples of life on her own farms. Her citizens were merchants, farmers, fishermen and sailors. There was a beginning, also, of manufactures—to the sore displeasure of the Board of Trade.

We perceive, also, by the same test that Providence had regained the relative position which she had lost during Philip's war, and was once more the second town of the Colony.

The soul liberty of which I have spoken so often had borne rich fruits. Baptists, Quakers, Congregationalists, Episcopalians, Puritans and Sabbatarians had their respective places of worship and their independent pastors. Among the

Baptist pastors we find John Clarke. Among the Congregationalists Samuel Niles, a native of Block Island, and the first Rhode Islander that graduated at Harvard. In 1704 the Society for the Propagation of the Gospel in Foreign Parts sent out James Honeyman to build up an Episcopal church in the southern part of the Colony. He found much to do as rector of Trinity, in Newport, and missionary to Freetown, Tiverton and Little Compton on the main. His memory is still preserved in Episcopal traditions and Honeyman's Hill, the highest land in the southern extremity of the island, is a familiar name to the inhabitants of Newport. In 1706 an Episcopal society was founded in Kingston, with Rev. Christopher Bridge for rector. So well was the work on the church done, that after remaining where it was built ninety-three years, it was removed to Wickford, where it is still used under the name of the Church of St. Paul. One of the most interesting of these denominations was that of the Sabbatarians, or Seventh-day Baptists, who had also a flourishing church in Westerly. To meet their peculiar views two weekly market days were set apart for them.

The meetings and acts of the Assembly still continue to form the principal record of our history. The Assembly itself claimed equal rights with those exercised by Parliament over its own members, and at a special session in 1701, suspended an assistant who had married a couple illegally and refused to acknowledge his error. The Board of Trade had more than once called for a printed copy of the laws of the Colony, and as a proof that they were regularly administered Governor Cranston sent a full statement of the mode of procedure in all the courts. I have already spoken of Lord Bellemont's plan for the formation of a great vice-royalty over all the colonies, including the Bahama Islands. After his death this wild scheme, fatal to the freedom and prosperity of British America, was revived by Dudley. The irregular administration of the navigation laws was the chief pretext, and it probably was held to be a sufficient concession to freedom that the local government was left in the hands of the colonial assemblies. A bill for this purpose was drawn up near the close of William's reign and brought forward early in that of Anne.

But the rights of the colonies were boldly and ably defended by Sir Henry Ashurst, the agent of Connecticut, and the fatal bill rejected after a full discussion. Dudley himself, however, was in high favor. He was appointed Governor and Vice-Admiral of Massachusetts and New Hampshire, and what was still more objectionable Vice-Admiral of Rhode Island and King's Province, a fruitful source of jealousies and bickerings.

Meanwhile the Assembly went on in its work of legislation, taking advantage of its experience to correct old errors, and gradually adapting the laws to the increasing wants of society. At the May session of 1701 we find justices of the peace first mentioned in connection with a general election. Thirteen were then appointed. In the same session a resolution for the reörganization of the militia law was again brought forward and the law of marriage revised and made more stringent. New powers were given the governor for enforcing the navigation act. Progress had been made towards a correct estimate of the obligations of society to its officers. The governor's salary was raised to forty pounds—a sum much increased during the year by special gratuities. The recorder was forbidden to practice at the bar except in cases which concerned himself or the town or Colony. Protection against vagrants was sought in a rigid vagrant act, extending to comers from other colonies, deserters from the King's service and "passengers brought in by sea and landed without consent of the authorities."

The short lived treaty of Ryswick was broken, and in the May session of 1702 preparations were made for the defence of Newport harbor by building a fort on Goat Island. In the town itself a battery was erected near the ground now occupied by the Union Bank. The funds for these defences were to be drawn from "forfeitures to the treasury and the gold plate and money taken from convicted pirates." The pay of the garrison at the fort was fixed at twelve pounds a year, with rations. Scouts, that essential element of every good army, but especially necessary where the enemy were part Indians, received three shillings a day while in active service. The spirit of adventure was awakened. Captain William Wanton, of Portsmouth, took out a commission as privateersman and brought in several valuable prizes.

In September Dudley undertook to take command of the Rhode Island troops—about two thousand men in all, and coming to Newport directed that they should be called out in his name. The calm but firm resistance of Governor Cranston and Major Martindale thwarted his usurpation, and he left the town in disgust.

In 1703 the long boundary line contest between Rhode Island and Connecticut was brought to a close, and Rhode Island confirmed in the jurisdiction over Narragansett which had been assigned to her in the arbitration of Clarke and Winthrop. Much of this was owing to the staunch loyalty of the men of Westerly, where its good effects were immediately felt. Yet so little were the true interests of the colonies understood by their transatlantic rulers, that it was not till twenty-three years later that the decision of the Commissioners was formally approved by the King.

This failure to comprehend the character and interest of the colonies showed itself in various ways, but in none more offensively than in the attempt of the Board of Trade to make Dudley Governor of Rhode Island by royal appointment.

But fortunately for Rhode Island, the powerful William Penn had been enlisted on her side, and the Queen's Council refused to accept the recommendation of the Board of Trade.

Another question which menaced serious danger to the Colony by placing it in a false position towards the mother country arose from the war. How far was she bound to send troops to the support of her sister colonies? Dudley claimed them for the defence of the Massachusetts frontier, Lord Cornberry for that of New York. Rhode Island pointed to her long water front, broken by bays and coves and constantly exposed to the fleets and privateers of the enemy, and claimed that she needed her men for her own protection. As a proof, however, of her willingness to do all that could justly be asked of her, she appealed to her past conduct and to the fact that during the last seven years she had spent nearly a thousand pounds a year for military purposes.

The war bore hardly upon the resources of the Colony. A French fleet was expected on the coast. Scouts were constantly on the look-out. Block Island was garrisoned. The fleet did not come, but one incident occurred which, though upon a small scale, brought out in strong colors the maritime spirit of the Colony. A French privateer in a cruise off Block Island took a sloop laden with provisions. The news reached the Governor the next day. In two hours two sloops, manned by one hundred and twenty volunteers, and commanded by Captain John Wanton, were on their way in pursuit of the enemy, and in less than three hours more took her, recaptured her prize and brought both safe into Newport.

The current of our history still continues to flow in a narrow channel. Each new session of the Assembly added to the body of the laws and met new wants. Newport had no charter. One was granted her by special statute. The other towns held theirs by grants of the Assembly. The subject of a court of chancery began to attract attention in 1705, but was held to be premature, and its duties were still left for the present with the Assembly.

Boundary questions still continued to occupy the Assembly and annoy the inhabitants of the border. The northern boundary brought Rhode Island into direct collision with Massachusetts, which was now the heiress of the claims of Plymouth. Commissioners were appointed who made no report, and it was only by slow steps that the Colony assumed its permanent form and dimensions.

Among the laws which were brought every day to every door was the law which made the price of wheat the standard of the price of bread. Every baker was required to have his trade mark and make every loaf of a specified weight. The bread that fell short was forfeited to the poor.

As an aid to commerce the Colony granted the control of the shores of all the waters comprised within a township to the town itself. This led to the building of wharves and store houses, and added to the wealth of the town.

In the midst of the progressing civilization we find occasional traces of barbarism. A slave had murdered his mistress with circumstances which aggravated the crime, and despairing of escape drowned himself. A fortnight after his body came ashore at Little Compton, and "the Assembly ordered that his head, legs and arms should be hung up in some public place near Newport, and his body be burnt to ashes."

We now meet the odious slave-trade, carefully watched over and protected by England as a source of wealth, but generally disliked by planters for "the turbulent and unruly tempers" of its miserable victims. Rhode Island drew most of her slaves from Barbadoes at the rate of twenty or thirty a year, and sold them at the average price of from thirty to forty pounds each. The moral question had not yet come up, but according to the old record the trade did not flourish because the people "in general" preferred white servants to black.

In 1708 the first census was taken by order of the Board of Trade, giving for result seven thousand one hundred and eighty-one inhabitants, of whom one thousand and fifteen were freemen. The militia amounted to one thousand three hundred and sixty-two. There were fifty-six white servants and four hundred and twenty-six black.

In the same year we meet for the first time, "vendue masters" and public auctions. The subject of "a uniform value for foreign coins in the colonies" was discussed in Parliament, and made the subject of a circular letter from the Board of Trade. The increase of the settlements made it necessary to provide for the Indians. A committee was appointed to confer with Ninigret about lands for his tribe, the Niantics, and choose the site of a new town in Narragansett.

I have already spoken of the judicial functions of the Assembly. They had increased so much that it was deemed necessary to impose a tax of two pounds upon every appellant before his case could be taken up.

The reports to the Board of Trade and the commutation table of taxation throw much light upon the commercial and agricultural progress of the Colony. In the commutation roll Indian coin was rated at "two shillings a bushel, barley at one and eightpence, rye at two and sixpence, oats at fourteen pence, wheat at three shillings, and wool at ninepence a pound." From the statistical reports to the Board of Trade, we learn that the annual "exports sent to England by way of Boston amounted to twenty thousand pounds; that the principal direct trade was by the West Indies; and that within the past twenty years the amount of shipping had increased six-fold." This increase it was said was owing to the superiority of the colonial shipwrights.

Eighty-four vessels of all sizes had been built in the Colony within eleven years. The population was divided. Aquidneck "was taken up in small farms," and the young men took to the sea.

In 1709 a printing press was set up in Newport and a public printer appointed. This pioneer printer was the son of a New York printer named Bradford, who offered to do the public printing of the Colony for fifty pounds a year. The offer was accepted for one year.

The war dragged heavily on, eating into the resources of the Colony and driving her to that most fatal of all expedients, the issue of paper money. A great expedition against Canada was planned, and failed. Rhode Island, which had been very active in raising men and supplies and had taxed herself liberally, shared the common disappointment.

The next attempt was more successful. A fleet of twelve ships of war and twenty-four transports sailed from Nantasket roads on the 18th of September, reached Port Royal in six days and took it after a short siege. The colonists were very happy. The name of Port Royal was changed to Annapolis, the city of Anna. The martial spirit of the colonies was roused and in the following year, 1711, they eagerly entered into the plans of the English ministry for the invasion of Canada. But although the greatest exertions were made the expedition failed.

Meanwhile the Assembly still continued its labor of legislation. The Court of Trials adopted the course which had been established two years before by the Court of Appeals, and began to charge a fee before entering a case upon the docket. Education was a subject of legislative interest. In Newport the public school was placed in charge of the town council, and provision made for opening a Latin school under Mr. Galloway. Various other minor incidents show the progress of the Colony. Public highways were a subject of general attention in Newport. Providence, which lay on the bank of a navigable river, was more directly interested in bridges. Names were given to the streets and alleys, and, as an element in the growth of the Colony, it may not be uninteresting to know that the first town crier was appointed in 1711. As an encouragement to commerce all "river craft trading as far as Connecticut" were exempted from custom dues, and no fees were exacted for free goods. The profits of the navigation act, as has already been stated, had been seriously affected by clandestine traders. To guard against this evil a law was passed requiring "all persons resident for three months in the Colony and intending to leave, to advertise their intention ten days before hand, so that their creditors might have due notice."

CHAPTER XVII.

PAPER MONEY TROUBLES.—ESTABLISHMENT OF BANKS.—PROTECTION OF HOME INDUSTRIES.—PROPERTY QUALIFICATIONS FOR SUFFRAGE.

The treaty of Utrecht gave peace to England and her dependencies, leaving them free to follow out the peaceful development of commerce and manufactures. War had brought on paper money, which was first issued to meet the expenses of the second expedition against Port Royal. This first issue was of five thousand pounds in bills of from five pounds to two shillings, equal in value as far as legislation could make them so, "to current silver of New England, eight shillings to the ounce. They were to be received in all payments due the treasury, to be redeemed in specie at the end of five years," and meanwhile were secured by an "annual tax of a thousand pounds." To counterfeit or deface them was felony. Further issues of eight thousand pounds were made by the end of the war, and secured by new taxes. Thus was opened the great gulf which was to swallow the fruits of much laborious industry.

The Assembly made another step towards its present form by electing a clerk outside the house. The pay of this first clerk was six shillings a day.

The military stores which had been collected during the war were divided into two classes. Those of a perishable nature were sold. The rest were carefully stored away to be ready for the chances of another war. "The cannon were tarred and laid on logs on the governor's wharf." The garrison of Fort Anne was dismissed. The labors of peace began. Increased attention was given to public highways. The old road which ran through the Colony from Pawtucket to Pawcatuck was repaired, and a new one opened to Plainfield through Warwick and West Greenwich. But in this the enterprise of the Colony outran its wants, and the new road was soon abandoned.

As we follow the sessions of the Assembly we find acts for the repression of litigation renewed three times in five years. The provision of the charter by which commissioned militia officers were to be elected by the Assembly had been neglected for more than a generation, and the elections made by the towns. While the population was small and most of the inhabitants freemen this mode of election proved good. But with the increase of population disputes and difficulties arose, and in 1713 a new law was passed in accordance with the provisions of the charter. But after a short trial and in spite of the protest of the governor and four assistants, the old law was revised.

One of the difficult questions of legislation

came before the Assembly of 1713. Merchants had exported grain too freely and the home market began to feel the drain. The Assembly interfered, and not only forbade further exportation but set a tariff of prices for the markets of the Colony. An account of the stock of provisions in Newport was taken. The price of wheat was ten shillings and sixpence a bushel, of rye five shillings, of corn and barley four shillings, and of flour and biscuit thirty shillings a hundred.

Among the laws of trade which were passed at this time was a stringent law against peddlers, prohibiting them from selling dry goods under heavy penalties. But the apple of discord which divided the whole community was paper money. All New England was disturbed by it. In Massachusetts there were three parties, each very bitter against the other. Smallest of the three was the hard money party, which insisted upon withdrawing the bills of credit and putting all business transactions upon a metallic basis. The other two were in favor of banks, but of banks founded upon very different principles. One advocating a private, the other a public bank system. By the former bills of credit secured upon real estate were to be issued by the company and received by its members as money, but without any fixed relation to gold and silver. The other advocated a public bank, with bills to be loaned by government on mortgage of real estate and paying an annual interest for the support of government. Each party represented a distinct class. The hard money party was composed of men for the most part free from debt and ready to pay their way in cash. The private bank party were owners of real estate who were unable to use it to advantage for meeting their engagements. The hard money party after a severe struggle coalesced with these, and a "bank or loan of fifty thousand pounds" was established for five years.

In Rhode Island there were but two parties— the hard money party and the paper money party. The struggle was long and bitter, and ended by the adoption of the public bank system of Massachusetts. The contest was felt in the elections, each party striving to secure an Assembly favorable to itself. In the May election of 1714 "the specie party triumphed." Twenty-two deputies out of twenty-eight lost their seats. An act had been passed requiring the treasurer to burn two thousand bills of credit. He disobeyed and lost his place. Bills to the amount of one thousand one hundred and two pounds eight shillings and sixpence were collected and burnt.

In the new election the paper money question still agitated the public mind. Only five out of the old members were returned to the Assembly. Of the assistants only one. Joseph Jenckes was chosen Deputy-Governor in the place of Henry Tew. So complete was the change that it was called "the great revolution." Yet amid all these changes Governor Cranston held his place.

The death of Queen Anne and accession of George I. excited little attention in the colonies. South Carolina was suffering from the Yemassee war, which brought new emigrants to Rhode Island, and among them some females of Huguenot origin who had their Indian slaves with them. Their coming seems to have been acceptable, for the Assembly upon petition remitted to them the importation tax. The population was not yet sufficient to protect farmers from wolves and foxes. The old bounty was increased, and rewards were offered by Portsmouth for blackbirds and crows, and by Providence for gray squirrels and rats. A few years later still higher bounties were offered for wild-cats and bears.

The great public question was still the question of the bank, and we have already seen that the form adopted was that of public banks. In the July session of 1715 a bank or loan of thirty thousand pounds was established, which in a later session was raised to forty thousand. "Bills from five pounds to one shilling were issued and proportioned among the towns." Whoever could give good mortgage security could claim a loan. But the interest instead of being secured by bond and mortgage was secured by bond alone, and thus the greater part of it was eventually lost, a very serious defect in the system, for it was from this interest that the bills were to be redeemed and the expenses of government paid. We shall meet this subject again, but never in a pleasant form.

It is interesting to see by what devices the increasing wants of the Colony was met. Newport had wants of her own as "the metropolitan town of the Colony." The street leading to the Colony House needed paving, and to meet the expenses a grant was made of funds drawn from the duty on imported slaves. Other streets were paved and a bridge built over Potowomut River by funds drawn from the same source.

The criminal code also, grows with the Colony. Fraudulent voting is punished with fine, whipping or imprisonment. To facilitate detection every voter was required to endorse his name in full on his ballot. A large proportion of the crimes in the Colony were committed by Indian slaves. The fear of punishment was an insufficient protection against this class of criminals, and a law was passed prohibiting their introduction into the Colony.

We have seen that Newport and Providence made early provision for schools. Portsmouth followed their example, and "having considered how excellent an ornament learning is to mankind," made in 1716 an appropriation for building a school-house. The experiment was successful, and six years later two others were built—one of them sixteen feet square, the other thirty by twenty-five.

It is deserving of remark that in this young society slander was not suffered to go unpunished. A Gabriel Bernon had brought a false accusation against one of the assistants. He was compelled to make "a written acknowledgment to the injured party," and ask pardon in writing of the Assembly which he had treated with disrespect on his examination.

The condition of the Indians called for legislative interference. On the petition of Ninigret their lands were taken under the protection of the Colony, and overseers appointed to lease them for the benefit of the tribe and remove trespassers. The following year an attempt was made to enforce temperance among them by increasing the difficulty of their obtaining liquor on credit.

The militia law was revised from time to time and various changes introduced. In that of 1718 the governor was styled "Captain-General and Commander-in-Chief," and the deputy-governor "Lieutenant-General."

It will be remembered that colonial laws were required to conform as far as possible to English laws. The colonial legislatures put a large interpretation upon this provision, and in providing for the estates of intestates modified materially the law of primogeniture. The eldest son, instead of the whole estate, received only a double share—one-third being given to the widow and the remainder divided among the children.

The Board of Trade had repeatedly called for

a complete copy of the laws, and the Assembly had appointed more than one committee to revise and print them. It was not, however, till 1719 that the work was taken seriously in hand. That it should have been printed in Boston shows how old prejudices were passing away. This first edition was distributed among the towns and the Assembly.

Boundary questions revive from time to time. The northern boundary gave rise to bitter discussions, and though often on the point of being decided, was not really brought to a decision for several years. The western boundary, also, had been practically decided in favor of Rhode Island. But this question, too, was reöpened, and the uncertainties and inconveniences which such disputes engender idly prolonged to the sore annoyance of the inhabitants of the border. How imperfectly the serious nature of the question was understood in England may be seen by the proposition of the Privy Council that both Rhode Island and Connecticut should surrender their charters and be annexed to New Hampshire. It was not till 1727 that Westerly knew whether she belonged to Connecticut or to Rhode Island.

Protection begins about this time to manifest itself as essential to the success of domestic industry. Acts also were passed for the protection of river fisheries. The manufacture of nails and hemp duck were encouraged—nails by a loan and duck by a bounty. With the increase of population new guarantees were required to secure purity of suffrage. In the winter of 1724 the freehold act was passed "requiring a freehold qualification of the value of one hundred pounds, or an annual income of two pounds derived from real estate to enable any man to become a freeman." With modification of detail but none of principle, this law held its place on the statute book for a hundred and twenty years. "Freemen of the towns who were not freemen of the Colony were allowed to vote for deputies."

In 1721 a new bank or loan for forty thousand pounds was established upon the same principle as the first. Hemp and flax were received in payment of interest. Specie had become so scarce that an English half-penny passed for three half-pence, and it was soon manifest that the introduction of paper money had raised prices and encouraged speculation in land.

But nothing occurred to break the monotony of colonial life so important as the capture in 1723 of a pirate schooner and the trial of her crew by a court of admiralty. Twenty-six of the prisoners were condemned to death, hanged at Gravelly or Bull's Point, and buried on Goat Island between high and low water mark.

One of the important events of 1722-3, and which must be considered as a favorable indication of the increase of population was the division of Kingston into two towns. In 1724 the failure of the crops led again to the prohibition of the exportation of grain. Two thousand bushels of Indian corn were bought on public account and sold to the people at low prices. In Newport no one was allowed to have more than four bushels at a time—in the other towns not more than eight. The temperance question, also, began to attract attention at an early day, and various efforts were made to check drunkenness. Among them was an act prohibiting the selling of liquor to common drunkards, and to ensure the carrying out of the act town councils were required to post in their own and the neighboring towns those who came under it. In nothing, however, was the progress of the Colony more evident than in the growth of the religious sentiments. The soul liberty of its founder had been mistaken for license. Towards the close of the seventeenth century Cotton Mather had written: "Rhode Island is a colluvies of Antinomians, Familists, Anabaptists, Anti-Sabbatarians, Arminians, Socinians, Quakers, Ranters, everything in the world but Roman Catholics and true Christians." A quarter of a century later he wrote: "Calvinists with Lutherans, Presbyterians with Episcopalians, Pedobaptists with Anabaptists, beholding one another to fear God and work righteousness, do with delight sit down together at the same table of the Lord." In strict accordance with the fundamental principle of the Colony the pay of the clergy was made by voluntary contribution of their parishioners.

We have recorded the deaths of Williams and Clarke. In April, 1727, Governor Samuel Cranston followed them to the grave, leaving no public man so universally loved behind.

It is a proof of the progress of the Colony that vagrants and "mad persons" began to be provided for by law. Among the laws adopted from England at this period was the act of limitations for personal actions.

CHAPTER XVIII.

CHANGE OF THE EXECUTIVE.—ACTS OF THE ASSEMBLY.—JOHN BERKELY'S RESIDENCE IN NEWPORT.—FRIENDLY FEELING BETWEEN THE COLONISTS AND THE MOTHER COUNTRY.

NEARLY a generation had passed since a new governor had been chosen, but the place made vacant by death was now to be filled. The choice fell upon Joseph Jenckes, (May, 1727.) He was a resident of Pawtucket, and in those days of irregular communication Pawtucket was too far from the seat of government for the prompt transaction of public business. It was voted, therefore, that it was "highly necessary for the Governor of this Colony to live at Newport, the metropolis of the government," and a hundred pounds was appropriated for the expense of his removal. While the Colony was passing into the hands of a new executive a similar change was taking place in the mother country. George I. died suddenly, and George II. succeeded to the throne.

But the change of sovereign brought no change with it in the policy of the mother country. The act of navigation was still the rule by which she measured her relations to the colonies. They were still to supply the raw material and she the profitable manufacture.

The first eight years of George II.'s reign were years of peace. Party spirit in England ran high under the names of court and country, the first as supporters of the ministry, the second of parliamentary opposition. But Sir Robert Walpole did not love war, and in the cabinet his voice was supreme.

In the Colony we find the same indications of growth and development. The records of the Assembly are still our principal guide. The criminal code, the surest indication of the moral condition of the community, was revised. Intemperance, in spite of repeated attempts to suppress it by legislation still seems to prevail, and in 1728 a new license law was passed. Unforeseen crimes, also, sometimes call for special action. An Indian lad attempted to kill his master, a crime unforeseen in the code, and was branded on the forehead with the letter R., whipped at the cart tail at every street corner in Newport, and ordered to be sold out of the Colony for his unexpired term. A slanderous pamphlet was publicly burned by the town sergeant in front of the Colony House and the author compelled to make a written confession of his fault.

The unsettled boundary lines though still causes of uneasiness and vexatious delays, are gradually approaching final decision. The controversy concerning the western boundary had lasted sixty-five years. More effectual means are employed to enforce the registry of births, marriages and deaths. Peddlers, the field of whose industry had already been reduced by previous statutes, were forbidden to sell any kind of goods under pain of forfeiture. Early attention is paid to the preservation of deer and the protection of fish. The planting of hemp and flax, and the manufacture of duck are again the subject of legislation, and receive increased bounties. James Franklin sets up a printing press in Newport after having failed to establish a newspaper in Boston. Not discouraged by his failure, he made a similar attempt at Newport with a similar result. He was in advance of his time. Important laws were enacted for the encouragement and regulation of trade. Special officers were appointed for special departments. Lumber of every kind was placed under the protection of surveyors. Packed meats and fish were examined by viewers. Casks were measured by official surveyors. The whale and cod fisheries were encouraged by bounties. And to incite the efforts of honest but unfortunate men, bankrupt laws equally useful to creditor and debtor were established.

Roads and bridges continue to call for legislation. The Pawtuxet bridge had fallen to decay, and Rhode Island and Massachusetts united, first in pulling it down and soon after in building it up again. A new ferry was established between Portsmouth and Bristol. Lands in Westerly were set apart for an Indian house of worship.

The fortifications of the Colony were not neglected. "A regular and beautiful fortification of stone" was built at Newport and the new King petitioned to give forty cannon for its armament.

The records of the time tell of an earthquake which in October, 1727, was felt through New England, exciting much alarm but doing little damage—far less indeed than the attempt to build up commerce upon public loans and paper money. To this period also belongs the first appearance of the Palatine Light, a curious electric phenomenon according to some, produced according to others by hydrogeneous gas, but believed by local superstition to be the phantom of a wrecked emigrant ship whose passengers had fallen prey to the avarice of her captain and crew.

The Legislature continues its labor of law-making, and among its provisions is one prohibiting the manumission of slaves without bonds from the owner to prevent them from coming upon the town. Another act sets bounds to the authority of moderators in town meetings, and requires that any motion supported by seven freeholders shall be put to vote. Another requires that all money questions shall be announced in the call for the meeting.

Among public annoyances we find Indian dances especially mentioned and the regulation of them referred to the town councils, and the selling or giving of intoxicating drinks upon the dancing ground strictly forbidden.

To meet the growth of the Colony a new division of it into three counties was made, and the judicial system altered to meet the change. "Each county was to have its court house and jail." The responsibility of public officers increases with the increase of the Colony in wealth. The public treasurer was required to give bonds to the amount of twenty thousand pounds and his salary raised first to one, and two years later to two hundred pounds. A distrust of lawyers found expression in the October session of 1729 in an act forbidding them to serve as deputies. At the next session it was repealed and though never reënacted was more than once brought up for discussion.

Among the eminent Englishmen of the first half of this century was George Berkeley, Dean of Derry, better known by his later title of Bishop of Cloyne, and still better by Pope's line :

"To Berkeley every virtue under Heaven."

He had taken high rank among the philosophers of his age by his new theory of vision and other writings in which he denied the existence of matter. Advancement in the church made him master of a large income, which he resolved to employ in the service of religion by founding a college in the Bermudas for the training of pastors for the colonial churches and missionaries to the Indians. The benevolent object failed through the failure of Lord Carteret to give him the aid of government. Instead, therefore, of establishing himself in Bermuda, he purchased a farm near Newport and built a house on it, which is still known by the name of Whitehall. He brought with him a choice library, a collection of pictures and a corps of literary men and artists, among them the painter Smibert, who thus became the teacher of Copley and West.

The influence of such a man is quickly felt in a young community, and Berkeley soon gathered around him a body of cultivated men, who joined with him in the discussion of questions of philosophy and the collection of books. These books became the basis of the Redwood Library. Not far from his house among what the modern tourist knows as the hanging rocks is a natural alcove, which opening to the south and roofed with stone commands an extensive view of the ocean. Here, tradition says, Berkeley wrote his Alciphron or Minute Philosopher, which was printed in Newport by James Franklin. But Berkeley had lived too long among men of letters and in large cities to be contented with the limited resources of a colonial town, and after a residence in Newport of two years and a half, he returned to Europe and a broader field of usefulness and honor. His library of eight hundred and eighty volumes he left to Yale. Brown University was not yet established.

Legislation begins to take notice of charitable institutions. Attention had already been called to the condition of the insane, and now a fund was formed for the relief of disabled sailors and their families by deducting sixpence a month from the wages of every seaman in active service. This money was paid over to the town in which he lived and which was bound to support him.

The respect for the rights of conscience which forms the fundamental principle of the colonial polity, still meets us from time to time in some new application. In 1730 the militia law was modified for the protection of the Quakers. Provision was also made for the protection of the Indians by an act requiring the assent of two justices of the peace to give validity to any bond of apprenticeship in which they were concerned.

In 1730 the Board of Trade called for a census. The population was found to have increased six thousand in ten years—numbering fifteen thousand three hundred whites, sixteen hundred and fifty blacks, and nine hundred and eighty Indians—nearly eighteen thousand in all, almost equally divided between the three counties. Of these eighteen thousand nearly nine hundred were enrolled in the militia. Providence was divided into four towns.

The question of paper money still excited the Colony. Governor Jenckes was against it, but it was upheld by a majority of the Assembly. By September, 1731, one hundred and ninety-five thousand three hundred pounds had been issued in bills of credit, of which one hundred and twenty thousand pounds were still outstanding. Silver had risen from eight to twenty shillings an ounce. Yet such was the general infatuation that in this very year a new bank was voted of sixty thousand pounds.

Yet trade increased and the Colony prospered. The shipping had risen in ten years from thirty-five hundred tons to five thousand, manned by four hundred men. Boston was the principal mart for supplies, but two ships came annually from England, two from Holland and the Mediterranean, and ten or twelve from the West Indies. The exports which comprised live stock, logwood, lumber, fish and the products of the field and dairy, amounted to ten thousand pounds a year. The ordinary expenses of the government amounted to two thousand, the extraordinary to twenty-five hundred pounds a year, colonial currency.

The paper money controversy had raised a question as to the governor's power of veto. The law officers of the crown were consulted by the Board of Trade and declared that he had none. They decided also that the King himself had none.

The publication of the laws had met a public want. The first edition was soon exhausted and a new one called for. For many years small pains were taken to secure accuracy in the text, the preparation of it being left to the clerk. A wide door was thus left open for interpolation, and it was through this door that the clause against Roman Catholics, so contrary to the spirit and policy of the Colony crept into the statute—to be silently dropped as soon as attention was called to it.

We have already seen that provision had been made for the defence of the Colony by building a fort in Newport harbor. Additional provisions were made at the October session of 1732, by imposing a duty of sixpence a ton upon all vessels that entered the harbor except fishermen. We have already seen that several attempts had been made for the suppression of intemperance, and apparently with little success. In 1732 another moral principle was made the subject of legislation, and "these unlawful games called lotteries" suppressed by statute. We shall soon find them legalized and in some instances doing the office of insurance companies. A more legitimate source of gain was found in the whale fishery, which was successfully encouraged by a premium. Whales were often taken in Narragansett Bay. But the first regular whaler that entered Newport harbor was owned by Benjamin Thurston, and brought a hundred and fourteen barrels of oil and two hundred pounds of bone.

It was not till many trials had been made that a satisfactory regulation of the tenure of office was reached. On revising the statutes good behavior was made the term of tenure for the judges and clerks of common pleas. But the democratic element was too strong to allow this prolongation to gain a footing of authority, and a semi-annual election was soon substituted to the more conservative system. The deputies had been chosen semi-annually. In 1733 this also was changed to the whole year, but after a short trial changed back again to the half year. The first printed schedules were distributed in the summer of 1733. The October sessions were to be held alternately at Providence and South Kingstown. The certificates of election were carefully scrutinized and irregular proxies rejected. In 1734 the House consisted of thirty-six deputies, ten assistants and three general officers, a secretary, attorney and treasurer.

We have seen that vessels engaged in fishing were exempted from the harbor duty. As a further encouragement the first year's interest on the new loan was set apart for building a pier or harbor on Block Island. Westerly harbor was repaired. The river fisheries also came in for their share of protection, and dams or weirs were prohibited and no fishing except by hook and line permitted during three days in the week. The first session of the Assembly at East Greenwich was distinguished by an act for the preservation of oysters, which the thoughtless inhabitants were burning in large quantities for lime. Important acts were passed for the regulation of mills. An attempt to cut through the beach on Block Island failed, and the old pier was enlarged.

The close of Governor Jenckes's term of office was embarrassed by disputes arising from the paper money controversy. He declined a reëlection, and William Wanton, brother of the Deputy, was chosen in his stead. This was the only instance of brothers holding the two principal offices of the Colony at the same time. The dispute between Massachusetts and Rhode Island was referred to Commissioners from New York and Connecticut. No decision was reached, but the Assembly in acknowledgment of their services voted them three silver tankards of the value of fifty pounds each, with "the arms of Rhode Island handsomely engraved on them."

We have seen that Massachusetts like Rhode Island had sought a temporary relief in the issue of paper money. The King interfered and the Massachusetts bills were withdrawn. This was a severe blow to Rhode Island, and hardly a less one to the tradesmen of Boston, whose relations with Rhode Island were very intimate. Various devices were recurred to for their protection, among them a combination to refuse to take Rhode Island bills in payment for goods. But the necessities of trade were too great. The combination gave way. Silver rose to twenty-seven shillings an ounce. Debts were paid at a loss to the creditor of thirty-three per cent. The future looked very dark.

Attention was called to the security of marriage. Till 1733 none but Quakers or clergymen of the Church of England could perform the ceremony. In 1733 authority to perform it was extended by the Assembly to clergymen of every denomination.

The death of Governor William Wanton, which occurred in 1733, produced a deep sensation throughout the Colony, where he was greatly respected for his civil and military services. Few colonists stood higher with the King. On a visit to England with his brother John, he was presented by the Queen with a silver punch-bowl and salver and permitted to add a game-cock lighting on a hawk to his arms. On his death his brother, John Wanton, the Deputy-Governor, was chosen to fill his place.

Education still forced its claims, and we find George Taylor successfully petitioning for leave to open a school in a chamber of the county house of Providence. Fifty years before the first school in Providence had been taught by William Turpin—of whom, unfortunately, we know only the name.

From time to time come questions from the Board of Trade showing how carefully England watched over her revenues. In one the Colony was asked what revenue duties were laid upon British commerce. The impost on slaves brought from the West Indies had been removed by the King's orders, and Governor Wanton could answer that there were no duties affecting the direct commerce with England. Yet a consciousness of rights appears in more than one act of the Assembly. The Court of Vice-Admiralty sometimes exceeded its legitimate authority and tried causes over which it had no jurisdiction. This was a delicate matter for the colonial legislature to interfere in, for the court was appointed by the King. But without heeding this the Assembly conferred upon the Supreme Court the power of injunction.

The small-pox was a frequent cause of alarm. In 1735-6 another fearful disease desolated New England. It was called the throat distemper, and is described as "a swelled throat, with white or ash-colored specks, an efflorescence on the skin, great debility of the whole system and a strong tendency to putrefaction." No age was exempt from it, but it was most fatal among children.

Roads and bridges as we have already seen had received early attention. Communication between the different parts of the Colony increased with the increase of population. In 1736 a line of stages with special privileges for seven years was established between Newport and Boston. The natural development of trade was preparing the way for a closer union among the colonies. Increased attention was given to the duties and privileges of citizenship. It is sad to find that laws against bribery at elections were called for at an early day. By those of 1736 both briber and bribed were fined double the sum offered or received and deprived for three years of the right to vote. Illegal voting was forbidden under the penalty of a fine of two pounds and disfranchisement for three years.

The kindly feeling which the colonists cherished for the mother country sometimes received a practical illustration. In the spring of 1737 His Majesty's ship Tartar lay in Newport harbor, and that she was a welcome visitor the Assembly proved by ordering that "a score of the best sheep that may be got be presented to her commander, Mathew Norris, for the use of the crew." None foresaw that the day would come when a British press gang would seize free citizens in this same harbor.

The expenses of local government increased. To provide for this increase authority was given the towns to assess traders from abroad for a fair proportion of the outlays of the town. Changes were also made in the mode of paying jurors. Hitherto they had been paid out of the treasury—a mode liable to abuses and attended with great inconvenience. It was voted that they should receive a fixed pay of six shillings a day and pay their own expenses. Public attention had been called early to protection from fires. As the population of the larger towns grew, better protection was required. In Newport two companies of firemen were organized, and to compensate them for their services they were exempted from serving on juries or in the militia.

CHAPTER XIX.

WAR WITH SPAIN.—NEW TAXES LEVIED BY ENGLAND.—RELIGIOUS AWAKENING AMONG THE BAPTISTS.

EVENTS were preparing a closer union of the colonies. England declared war against Spain—a war of commercial rivalry, for Spain was a maritime power of the first class, and claimed the right of search. England sent out her ships of war and privateers, and carried on a lucrative contraband trade among the Spanish islands and on the Spanish main. The colonies were called upon to furnish their part of men and munitions of war. Rhode Island sent out privateers and prepared to defend her harbors and coast. Fort George was put in fighting order and a garrison of fifty two men stationed there under Colonel John Cranston. New Shoreham was garrisoned and Block Island provided with six heavy guns. For the protection of the coast and shores of the bay seven watch-towers were erected and constant guard kept in them by night and by day. Five beacons were stationed between Block Island and Portsmouth to give warning of the first approach of danger, and the Colony's war sloop, the Tartar, of a hundred and fifteen tons burthen held in readiness for instant service. Newport merchants also entered actively into the game and sent out in the second year of the war five privateers manned by five hundred men.

A great expedition was preparing against the Spanish West Indies. Rhode Island's contingent was two companies of a hundred men each. The Newport company was commanded by Captain Joseph Sheffield, the Providence company by Captain William Hopkins. The Colony was proud of its work and feasted both officers and men before they set sail to join the British squadron at New York and bear their part in the disastrous attempt upon Carthagena. Meanwhile it had proved its mettle by taking a French contraband schooner and carrying her into Newport for adjudication.

Rhode Island was loyal, loving the king and accepting the supremacy of Parliament. But she was quick to discriminate between usurpation and legal authority. The northern colonies carried on a lucrative commerce with the West Indies and particularly with the French Islands. Upon this trade England had imposed a heavy tax under the title of molasses act, and was preparing to increase it. The colonies protested. Newport dealt largely in the distilling of rum and was thus a great consumer of molasses. All looked alike to the trade with the islands for the means of paying for their importations from the mother country. But the objection did not stop here. Colonial development had reached the underlying principle of the revolution. Parliament taxed Englishmen as their representative. But by what right could an English Parliament tax Americans?

Richard Partridge, the colonial agent, and a Quaker in faith, acting in the name of Rhode Island and other northern colonies, "strenuously opposed" the new restrictions, and the Assembly requested the Governor "to write to the neighboring governments, inviting them" to join in the opposition. Thus concerted action and the right of self-taxation begin to claim their legitimate place in colonial polity, and prepare the way for independence. In the midst of these agitations Governor John Wanton died. I have already spoken of him as of one of the great names of colonial history and happy as few public men are in the recognition of his deserts. He was elected Deputy-Governor five times in succession and Governor seven. Deputy-Governor Richard Ward was chosen to fill his place, and William Greene was promoted to the place of Deputy-Governor made vacant by the promotion of Richard Ward. Henceforth these two names become prominent in Rhode Island history.

Disease came with war. The small-pox broke out again. Portsmouth and Jamestown were compelled to call on the Assembly for aid and Dutch Island was used as quarantine ground. While the minds of the colonists were thus prepared for thoughts of suffering and death, George Whitefield came among them calling them to repentance and prayer. Crowds gathered round him to listen to his burning words, and all New England was filled with the fame of his eloquence. His disciples joined the Baptists who increased greatly in numbers and influence. Samuel Fothergill, also, the calm and persuasive Quaker, passed at this time a half year in Newport in the house of his brother-in-law, John Proud, and Quakerism throve under his gentle teaching as the Baptists throve under the fervid exhortations of Whitefield.

The war continued. Spain against whom it had been first directed formed an alliance with France, and the colonies were called upon for new exertions. Ten more cannon were mounted in Fort George which was enlarged to receive them. Ten new field-pieces were ordered. A brick magazine was built for the safe keeping of powder and the supply of military stores was increased in every county. To secure promptness of action the Governor and Council together with the field officers and captains were formed into a permanent council of war. By a former act of the Assembly the men were allowed to choose their own officers. This act was repealed and the right of choice vested in the Legislature where the charter placed it. The drill system was incomplete. A more thorough one was established and two more companies were raised in Newport. In the midst of these warlike preparations the rights of conscience were respected and those who were scrupulous about the shedding of blood were employed as scouts and guards, or required to furnish horses in case of sudden alarm, or do any other duty consistent with their religious scruples.

The House of Commons ever watchful over the interests of British commerce, began to look with suspicion on the frequent "emissions of paper currency in His Majesty's colonies in America, in which Rhode Island has too large a share." An address to the King was followed by instructions to the colonial governors from the Board of Trade to transmit to the home government "an account of the tenor and amount of the bills of credit" issued by each colony, the times when they fell due, the number actually outstanding and their value in "money of Great Britain, both at the time such bills were issued and at the time of preparing the account." The Governor's opinion was also required upon the still more difficult subject of "sinking and discharging all such bills of credit."

Governor Ward replied on the part of Rhode Island by an elaborate history of the colonial currency and an able exposition of the causes and necessities from which it arose. Unfortunately these necessities still existed, and without heeding the warning implied by the action of the House of Commons the Assembly "created a new bank of twenty thousand pounds for ten years at four per cent." The paper issued under this act was called the new tenor, because unlike the earlier issues the bills bore on their faces the exact amount of gold and silver they were supposed to represent. Silver on the new tenor notes was rated at six shillings and ninepence sterling, gold at five pounds an ounce, and thus the value of a new tenor bill was four times that of an old tenor bill. The seeds of bankruptcy were thickly sown in both.

The question of the eastern boundary line, one of the bitterest of the many disputes with Massachusetts, had after several vain attempts to come to an amicable agreement, been referred, in 1741, to a royal commission. With the decision of this commission neither party was altogether satisfied, Massachusetts claiming a great deal and Rhode Island something more than it awarded them. Both parties appealed. But the commission adhered to its decision, and the line fixed by it continued to be the boundary between the two colonies till after the adoption of the Federal constitution.

CHAPTER XX.

PROGRESS OF THE WAR WITH THE FRENCH.—CHANGE IN THE JURISDICTION OF THE COURTS.—SENSE OF COMMON INTEREST DEVELOPING AMONG THE COLONISTS.—LOUISBURG CAPTURED.

War still continued to give its stern coloring to legislation. The Tartar was held ready for instant service. The Governor and his council were vested with the power of laying an embargo upon outward bound vessels. Speculation turned seaward, and the money which in peace would have been employed in building up commerce and manufactures was spent upon privateers.

Still the interests of peace were not altogether neglected. The productive enterprise which was to raise Rhode Island so high in the list of manufacturing states, was already awakened, and as early as 1741 James Greene and his associates petitioned the Assembly for permission to build a dam across the south branch of Pawtuxet river and lay the foundation of those iron works which in the sequel became so celebrated throughout the colonies. Population was increasing. The large townships became too large for the demands of local government and were divided. Thus

Greenwich, carrying out the suggestions of its position, was divided into East and West. About the same time Warwick was divided and a new township set out under the name of Coventry. In the next year North Kingstown was divided and the Town of Exeter incorporated, and a year later the country district of Newport, which was separated from the town by thick woods, was incorporated as Middletown. The territorial struggle was nearly over and Rhode Island was settling down into its permanent proportions. The schedules still continue to record the progress of organization as experience called for new changes. The office of attorney-general was abolished and a King's attorney for every county appointed instead. A Court of Equity composed of five judges, annually elected by the Assembly, was formed to try all causes of appeal in personal actions from the Superior Court to the General Assembly—a course which "by long experience had been found prejudicial." To draw closer the ties of loyalty a form of prayer for the royal family was sent from England to be read in every religious assembly throughout the colonies as a part of public worship.

The dissensions with Connecticut concerning the western boundary had taken a new form. The line, as the reader will remember, had been drawn and marked by competent authority. A committee appointed by Connecticut displaced the bound at the southwest corner of Warwick.

The Rhode Island Assembly sent surveyors to examine the ground and restore the line. This outrage was repeated twice.

The history of the war does not belong to the history of Rhode Island, although the spirit engendered by it led to the formation of some military institutions. Among these was the Newport Artillery, which was chartered in 1741, and is still one of the best disciplined corps in the State.

I have spoken of the substitution of King's attorneys to attorneys-general. It was made in the hope of enforcing the payment of interest bonds. But after a short trial the original form was resumed. The root of the evil was too deep. Another of the chronic evils of paper money vexed the Colony sorely. Counterfeit bills followed close upon the issue of genuine bills, and the Colony was flooded with bad money.

The Court of Equity was not continued long, and many other changes of brief duration were made in various branches of government. But what deserves especial mention is the instinctive perception with which Rhode Island detected the slightest invasion of her chartered rights and the courage with which she defended them. The clerkship of the naval office in Newport was claimed by one Leonard Lockman in virtue of a royal commission. The claim was referred to a committee which reported "that His Majesty was mistaken in said grant" which belonged to the Governor, who alone was responsible for the conduct of that officer. The question of custom fees and vice-admiralty fees was brought forward about the same time, and "the undoubted right of the General Assembly to state the fees of all officers and courts within the Colony" boldly asserted.

The expenses of the war still increased, straining the resources of the Colony to the utmost. Questions of organization were still rising, but the question of finance was the most difficult of all. New bills were issued with reckless profusion, and various devices adopted for the relief of the exchequer. Several bounties, and among them the bounties on hemp and oil, were withdrawn. The tonnage duty upon all vessels entering the Colony was revived. The lottery so wisely condemned in 1733 was legalized in 1744. Weybosset bridge was built by lottery.

The great military event of the campaign of 1745 was the capture of Louisburg by colonial troops. In this gallant feat of arms which fills so bright a page of colonial annals Rhode Island bore her part—especially through the Tartar, which, supported by two other war sloops, defeated at Famme Goose Bay a flotilla which was advancing with large reinforcements to the relief of the enemy. Captain Fones, who commanded the Tartar in this memorable campaign, has not received the honorable mention to which he was entitled for his gallantry and skill.

New exertions were required for securing Louisburg, and the colonies were again called upon to furnish men and supplies. In this also Rhode Island bore her part, propping as best she might her tottering treasury and using impressment for raising men. When the war was over England acknowledged her services by special grants.

In this year Rhode Island lost one of her faithful sons, Colonel John Cranston, son of the popular Governor, and commander of her forces at the capture of Port Royal. Towards the close of the year another great loss, though of another kind, fell upon the Colony. Two new privateers, mounting twenty-two guns each, with crews of over two hundred men went to sea the day before Christmas in a gale of wind and were never heard of again. Privateers held a place in war then which they do not hold now, and there was bitter sorrowing in more than two hundred households when the months passed away and no tidings of husband or father or brother came.

The success of the expedition against Louisburg increased the desire to carry the war into Canada. Commissioners from the colonies were invited to meet and take council together concerning the common interest. Here we meet for the first time the names of Stephen Hopkins and William Ellery, whose names stand side by side on the Declaration of Independence, which is already drawing nigh. The sense of common interest and mutual dependence gradually gains ground. Every exertion was made to call out the strength of the Colony. Popular feeling went with government and strengthened its hand for the great contest. Canada and Indian warfare were inseparably connected in the minds of the people, who, to rid themselves of the dreaded enemy submitted cheerfully to what they would otherwise have resisted as tyranny. Impressment was authorized by the Assembly.

In the midst of these efforts depreciation was undermining the strength and corrupting the moral sense of the community. The property tax of freemen had doubled. Bribery and fraudulent voting gained ground, and an attempt was again made to meet them by increasing the severity of the law. Every voter and every officer was required to declare under oath that he had neither taken nor offered a bribe ; and a single fraudulent vote was sufficient to invalidate an election. The evidence of the briber held good against the bribed ; and that the law might not be forgotten it was ordered to be "read in town meeting at every semi-annual election for five years and the name of every transgressor stricken from the roll of freemen."

Again, the vacillation of the ministry defeated the expedition against Canada. Then came tidings of a great French armada which was coming to the conquest of New Engand. Great was the alarm of the colonies. But help came from another quarter. Disease and tempest scattered and infected the hostile fleet. One commander died. His successor committed suicide, and the shattered remnants of the unfortunate armada had hard work to make their way back to the French coast.

Before the tidings of this disaster could reach New England it had been resolved to send reinforcements to the succor of Annapolis Royal, the supposed point of attack. The Rhode Island troops sailed early in November. The Massachusetts troops soon followed. Both were overtaken by heavy gales which cast some of them ashore at Mt. Desert. Some, like their adversaries, the French, were crippled by disease and a few made their way to the nearest port. Winter set in and the campaign of 1746 closed in gloom.

This was the year in which the royal decree concerning the eastern boundary was enforced. Rhode Island gained by it a large accession of territory—the towns of Bristol, Tiverton, Little Compton, Warren and Cumberland, which were incorporated and brought under the control of Rhode Island laws. Thus ten new deputies were added to the colonial representation. Thus, also, a revision of the judicial and military system of the Colony became necessary, and a new court was established under the title of Superior Court of Judicature, Court of Assize and General Jail Delivery, and consisting of a chief-justice and four associate justices annually chosen by the Assembly. The judicial powers of the assistants or upper house of Assembly ceased, though they still continued to act as a court of probate. Two militia companies were formed in Tiverton and one in each of the other new towns.

The previous history of the new towns belongs to Massachusetts and Plymouth. Their annexation to Rhode Island brought her an increase of about four thousand inhabitants, well trained most of them in the tenets of religious freedom.

CHAPTER XXI.

ATTEMPT TO RETURN TO SPECIE PAYMENTS.—CHANGES IN THE REQUIREMENTS OF CITIZENSHIP. — NEW COUNTIES AND TOWNS FORMED.—FRENCH AND INDIAN WAR.—WARD AND HOPKINS CONTEST.—ESTABLISHMENT OF NEWSPAPERS.

THE war was almost over, although privateers still endangered maritime commerce. First an armistice was agreed upon for four months and then peace was signed at Aix la Chapelle, on the 30th of April, 1748. It was a welcome peace although the war had brought lessons with it which were never forgotten. The men who had fought at Louisburg were looked upon as veterans, and when the final struggle came brought experience to the service of the revolting colonies. Parliament, well aware of the readiness with which the colonies had contributed to the support of the war both by men and by money, made them a grant of eight hundred thousand pounds as an indemnity. Rhode Island's share for the expedition against Cape Breton was six thousand three hundred and twenty-two pounds twelve shillings and tenpence; for the expedition against Canada, ten thousand one hundred and forty-four pounds nine shillings and sixpence. But deductions were afterwards made in a caviling spirit which excited bitter feelings. Still more irritating to colonial pride was the article restoring to France her conquered territories, for among them was Louisburg. Of the right of search, the original cause of the war, no mention was made, a precedent not forgotten in the war of 1812. Now was the time to heal the wound which paper money had inflicted upon the commerce of the country. Hutchinson, an aspiring young statesman of Massachusetts, formed a plan for sinking the paper money and restoring specie payment by means of this grant. Massachusetts after a long discussion, wisely adopted Hutchinson's plan. Rhode Island and Connecticut rejected it. Rhode Island presently felt the consequences of her error by the loss of her West India trade.

The records of the labors of peace again fill the schedules. Charlestown was divided into two towns and the name of Richmond given to the portion north of Pawcatuck river. The communications between the different parts of the Colony were carefully watched over. There were already nineteen ferries when peace returned, and of these thirteen served to keep up the connection with the seat of government.

The year before the peace the first public library in the Colony, the Redwood Library, was founded. It was fruit of the good tree planted by Berkeley. In 1754 Providence followed the noble example and founded the Providence Library Association. In the following year we find another attempt to enforce a moral law by legislative enactment. The act against swearing was revised, and a fine of five shillings or three hours in the stocks imposed as a penalty for every offence.

The increase of population called for a revision of the statute of legal residence. "New comers were required to give a month's notice of intention to become residents, after which if they remained one year without being warned to leave they were admitted as lawful inhabitants of the town." A freehold estate of thirty pounds sterling also gave a legal residence. "Apprentices having served their time in any town, might elect their residence there, or return to the place of their birth. Paupers not having acquired a legal settlement might be removed by the councils on complaint of the overseer of the poor, to the place of their last legal residence or to that of their birth." So careful was the watch kept over the conditions and privileges of citizenship. The Board of Trade called for a new census. "The population was found to consist of thirty-four thousand one hundred and twenty-eight souls, of whom twenty-nine thousand seven hundred and fifty were whites, the remainder blacks and Indians. Newport contained forty-six hundred and forty souls, Providence thirty-four hundred and fifty-two."

The lottery had taken a strong hold upon the

innate love of chance. The two first lotteries had been applied to public improvements. The third was formed for the relief of an insolvent debtor. Henceforth we meet it as a common relief in business misfortunes and a natural assistant in new enterprises.

The winter of 1748–49 was made memorable in Rhode Island annals by the death of John Callender, her first historian and pastor of the First Baptist Church in Newport. Among the public works of the year which the growing commerce of the Colony called for, was a light-house at the south end of Conanicut, still known as Beaver Tail Light.

Depreciation began to make itself deeply felt as the interests of English commerce became more and more interwoven with those of colonial commerce. Their raw products were the only articles that the colonies could give in exchange for English manufactures. Their West India trade was their only source of coin. Colonial bills out of the colonies were worthless. The subject was brought before the House of Commons, which called for a full and accurate statement of the condition of the currency. A committee was appointed by the Assembly to prepare the statement, and Partridge the colonial agent directed to present and support it. By this report it was shown that three hundred and twelve thousand three hundred pounds in bills of credit, emitted to supply the treasury since May, 1710, of which one hundred and seventy-seven thousand had been burned at various times and one hundred and thirty-five thousand pounds were still outstanding, amounting in all in sterling money to about thirty-six thousand pounds.

An interesting incident of this year was the organization of a Moravian mission.

The statute book records several new criminal statutes. It is an illustration of domestic relations that the first divorce was granted by the Assembly in 1754—more than a hundred years after the foundation of the Colony. And it may be taken as proof of the feelings of the Colony towards England, that a large number of English statutes were transferred to the colonial statute book. New precautions against fire were taken in Newport by the formation of firewards, and a fire engine was sent for from England. Providence soon followed the example. Another step was taken towards a satisfactory distribution of the territory by forming East and West Greenwich, Coventry and Warwick into a new county under the name of Kent County, with East Greenwich for its county town. The new county was required to build a court house at its own expense, which was partly done by lottery. Four years later another town was formed from Providence County and incorporated under the name of Cranston. In spite of the increased depreciation of the currency the Colony continued to grow in numbers and strength. Seventeen hundred and fifty-two was made memorable both in England and her colonies by the adoption of the Gregorian calendar. Henceforth the new year begins on the first of January instead of the twenty-fifth of March.

But the great event of the year was the decision of the lawsuit for the possession of the glebe lands in Narragansett, a suit of nearly thirty years standing, and which after passing through many phases was decided in favor of the Congregationalists against the Episcopalians, upon the ground that "by the Rhode Island charter all denominations were orthodox, and that a majority of the grantors when the deed took effect were Presbyterians or Congregationalists."

Meanwhile paper money was doing its bad work. The calendar of private petitions bears sad witness to the evil. Bankruptcy became frequent, and among the bankrupts of those days of gloom was Joseph Whipple, the Deputy-Governor, who, surrendering all his property to his creditors was relieved by a special act of insolvency. The spirit of enterprise though dulled, was not crushed.

The first recorded patent was granted in 1753. Parliament had passed an act to encourage the making of potash in the colonies, and Moses Lopez took out a patent for making it for ten years by a process known only to himself. The next year a similar patent was granted to James Rogers for the manufacture of pearl-ash. The industrial instinct which was to receive in the sequel so great a development, was already girding itself up for the trial. The spirit of association, also, was awakening. A society of sea-captains was incorporated for mutual assistance under the name of the Fellowship Club. From this grew the Newport Marine Society.

A new war was at hand, a war known to our childhood as the old French war, and the last waged by France and England for the dominion of North America. The treaty of Aix-la-Chapelle had left the door wide open for new claims, and these soon led to a new war. Here again Rhode Island displayed great energy, sending Stephen Hopkins and Martin Howard, Jr., to represent her as Commissioners at the Albany Congress of 1754, in which Franklin brought forward his plan for developing by union the resources of the colonies, she took promptly the steps necessary for her own defence and complied cheerfully with the requisitions of the English commanders. In this as in former wars she sent out her privateers to harrass the enemy's commerce. But her part in the contest was a limited one. Her troops went as contingents not as armies. She had no generals to give their names to great victories, and when peace returned her soldiers and sailors returned cheerfully to the duties and avocations of common life.

The annexation of the eastern towns in 1757 marks an important period in the history of

Rhode Island. With two unfriendly neighbors on each side she had been compelled to contend inch by inch for her territory. All the obstacles which impede development had accumulated in her path. All the dangers which menace the existence of feeble colonies had beset her. She had faced them all, she had overcome them all. A great principle lay at the root of her civilization, and humanity itself was inseparably connected with her success.

From the annexation of the eastern towns in 1757 to the peace of Paris in 1763, all the leading events were more or less connected with the war. Privateering took the place of commerce. Taxes were levied to build and arm forts and raise and equip soldiers, not to erect churches and court houses and libraries and schools.

The war was lingering but decisive. It gave England one brilliant victory and one illustrious name—the Heights of Abraham, and Wolf—to the colonies the lesson so valuable a few years later that English troops might be driven where colonists held their ground, and the name of Washington. Recorded in European history as the seven years war, for the colonies it was a war of nine years, hostilities having begun two years before war was declared. Nowhere is man's place in history more distinctly marked than in this war, which till the right man came was a succession of blunders and defeats. With William Pitt came victory.

While the war was still confined to the colonies a large number of French residents had been thrown into jail as prisoners of war. What was their legal position? The question was brought before the Assembly by a petition for release, which was so far granted as to authorize their transportation to some neutral port, and so far rejected as to still subject them to the laws of war.

We have seen how watchful the home government was to enforce the laws of trade. But with all its watchfulness smuggling still prevailed in every colony. New orders came from the King directing the Assembly to "pass effectual laws for prohibiting all trade and commerce with the French, and for preventing the exportation of provisions of all kinds to any of their islands or colonies." The Assembly passed the necessary acts. But too many and too powerful interests were involved to admit of their rigorous execution.

To this period belongs the bitterest party contest in the annals of Rhode Island, generally known as the Ward and Hopkins contest. Samuel Ward and Stephen Hopkins were the foremost Rhode Islanders of their time; both men of self-acquired culture and both illustrious by public services. Hopkins was the elder of the two, being born at Scituate on the 7th of March, 1717. Ward was his junior by eighteen years. Both were farmers and merchants, and both sincerely devoted to the interests of their native Colony. But as to what those interests were they differed widely, and their difference soon took the form of town and country parties. Newport was the leading town of the Colony, not only in commercial enterprise but in intellectual culture. Berkeley had not left his foot-prints there in vain. This seat of Rhode Island culture was best represented by Samuel Ward. The name of Hopkins stood for the country. The distribution of taxes was one of the questions at issue. Paper money was another. By degrees all questions of public policy were classed under the one or the other of these two leading names. There were sharp contests at the polls, painful severings of social ties and all the bitterness which partisanship gives to political discussion. At last the aid of the law was invoked and Hopkins sued Ward for slander. It is a singular illustration of the altered relations between Rhode Island and Massachusetts that in order to obtain an impartial jury the trial should have taken place at Worcester. Ward was acquitted and Hopkins condemned to pay the costs. In a few years the party contest gave way to the graver contest of the Revolution wherein the two leaders took their seats side by side in Congress Hall.

Among the events of domestic interest which belong to this period was the burning of the Providence Court House—not so much for the loss of the building as for that of the Providence Library which was kept in one of its rooms. The want of a public library was keenly felt, and when a lottery was granted for rebuilding the court house, half of its proceeds were set apart for the library. Rhode Island already felt the importance of libraries and schools. She will persevere in this course till it secures her a comprehensive school system and an admirable university.

The theatre found less favor, although its founder, David Douglass, brought with him the recommendation of the Governor and Council of Virginia. His first application for a licence in Newport failed; a second was more successful; and this pioneer of the American stage drew for a while good houses. He moved to Providence and built a permanent theatre. Many came from Boston to seek an enjoyment which they could not find at home. But the current soon turned. The Bostonians met with a cold reception, and the short-lived pleasure was condemned as a nuisance.

A newspaper was a want more generally acknowledged. Hitherto there had been none in the Colony. But in the summer of 1758 the *Newport Mercury* was established, and has held its ground with varying fortunes to our own day. Four years later William Goddard established in Providence the *Providence Gazette and Country Journal*. Among its first contributors was Governor Hopkins, who began for it his "Account of Providence," but called to other subjects by the excitement of the times he never went beyond the first chapter. Enough, however, was published to call out several insulting letters from Massachusetts.

Times were daily becoming more and more critical. The Board of Trade insisted upon the rigorous enforcement of the navigation act. The colonial governments passed the necessary laws but could not enforce them. It was then that writs of assistance were first called for, and from this call arose that trial so celebrated in colonial annals, the first mutterings of the tempest which was at hand. James Otis became a familiar name throughout the colonies.

For thirty-four years the Quaker diplomatist, Richard Partridge, had faithfully and skillfully served Rhode Island as her agent in London. In 1759 mindful to the last of the interests of the Colony, he wrote on his death bed to recommend a brother Quaker, Joseph Sherwood, for his successor.

In this same year freemasonry was introduced, a charter was granted by the Assembly with permission to raise twenty-four hundred dollars by lottery for building a hall in Newport.

We have seen how early attention was called to the subject of fires. In 1759 the immediate action at fires was placed under the direction of five presidents of firewards, three of whom were elected at annual town meetings with authority to blow up buildings if necessary in order "to stop the progress of the flames." These details though minute, serve to show how far our fathers carried their ideas of the powers and duties of government.

The increase of population called for a new division of territory. In 1757 Westerly was divided and its northern portion incorporated under the name of Hopkinton, a choice of name which shows that in that legislature the Hopkins party was in the majority. Two years later the new town of Johnston was formed out of Providence and named after the attorney-general.

CHAPTER XXII.

RETROSPECT.—ENCROACHMENTS OF ENGLAND.—RESISTANCE TO THE REVENUE LAWS.—STAMP ACT.—SECOND CONGRESS OF COLONIES MET IN NEW YORK.—EDUCATIONAL INTEREST.

Thus far we have traced the progress of Rhode Island, step by step from the first small settlement on the banks of the Mooshausick to the flourishing Colony, which, by its firmness and perseverance had made it mistress of the shores and islands of Narragansett Bay. We have seen it taking for its corner stone a vital principle of human society, unrecognized as yet by the most advanced civilization. We have seen this principle and society with it constantly endangered by misinterpretations, and the little Colony brought more than once to the brink of the precipice by the malignity of implacable enemies. We have seen it gradually growing in strength and enlightenment, drawing abundant harvests from a niggard soil, spreading its ships of commerce over distant seas and protecting its coasts by its own ships of war. We have seen it working out its civil organization by patient experiment, making laws and unmaking them as they met or failed to meet the want for which they were made. And now we shall see her strong by virtue, resolute by conviction and rich by intelligent industry, gird herself up for the contest which was to decide forever the relations of the British colonies of North America to their mother country. But before we enter upon this part of our subject let us pause a moment and consider somewhat more closely our new starting point.

The society which Roger Williams brought with him to the banks of the Mooshausick was a morally constituted society, in which all the questions of moral law had been studied and discussed as revealed in the Scriptures. It was not till their numbers increased and their wants with them that the idea of law took root amongst them and they became a legally constituted society. Their laws arose from their necessities and followed the development of their legal sense. They felt the want and strove by experiment to discover the remedy. Successful experiment became law and the statute book the record of the progress of civilization.

To this statute book, therefore, we must go for our knowledge of colonial life in all its relations. It defines the condition of the individual and the qualifications, the rights and the duties of the citizen. It defines the powers and prerogatives of government, and assigns to each department its limits and its sphere. Its enumeration of crime is the key to the moral sense of the community, and its provisions for the moral and intellectual training of the citizen show how far it has comprehended the reciprocal obligations and true nature of the ties which bind the citizen to his commonwealth.

Following this guide we find that Rhode Island has worked out her problem of self-government and soul liberty, framing for herself a pure democracy and surrounding it with all the provisions required for protection against foreign violence and internal dissension. After many trials she has organized a judiciary system adequate to the protection of person and property and the prompt administration of justice. She has cultivated the sense of right and wrong and made careful provision for the enforcement of contracts and the punishment of crimes. She has opened highways, established ferries and built bridges. She has favored navigation by the institution of judicious harbor laws. She has provided for the extermination of wolves and foxes by the offer of liberal bounties, and for the protection of fish and deer by stringent laws. She has broached the difficult subject of public charities and made a beginning of provision for the poor and the insane. She has initiated a system of public schools and founded a college which in the course of half a century becomes a university. She has opened her doors wide for different creeds, and required only that they all should be equally free.

Her relations with the mother country had taken their coloring from the attitude of self-defence which she was compelled to maintain towards the adjacent colonies of Massachusetts and Connecticut, which were eager to divide her territory between them. Against their long persecutions her last appeal was to the King, and she made it without humbling herself, for her enemy was at her own door and of her own household.

From the beginning of her civil life she had been contemptuously refused admission to the league from which Massachusetts and Connecticut derived the strength that made them bold both for aggression and for defence. More than once she seemed to be upon the point of being crushed, but of yielding—never. Hence in her relations with the mother country she never assumed the defiant attitude which her stronger sisters assumed and which at an early day awakened suspicions of their loyalty. Rhode Island was loyal as it behooved her to be; but she never carried her loyalty so far as to imperil the rights guaranteed to her by her charter.

We enter upon a new period of colonial history. The contest with France was over. The contest with England was beginning. For England, not satisfied with the advantage which she had derived from her colonies by constitutional means, resolved to deprive them of the protection which the constitution accorded to the humblest subject of the crown. They would gladly have contributed their portion to the expenses of the war and taxed themselves to pay it. But English constitutional law had prescribed the forms and conditions with which taxes could be raised, and colonial constitutional law taught that representation was an essential condition of taxation. This led to the stamp act and that train of disasters so fatal to English supremacy.

Equally fatal was the ill-timed jealousy with which she sought to fetter the commerce and check the manufacturing spirit of the colonists. It was from their commerce with the French islands that they drew not only many articles which habit had made essential to their comfort, but the greater part of their hard money. To England they sent their raw material, and receiving it back in the shape of manufactured goods paid liberally for the English labor and skill. England's best customers were her colonies.

War had been a severe school in which much needed lessons had been learned. Farmers and mechanics had learned to be soldiers and bear the hardships of a soldier's life. Taxes had increased and legislation had been compelled to busy itself largely with questions of military organization, with the building of forts, the raising of recruits, the providing of supplies. Maritime enterprise had lost none of its ardor, but had encountered sore rebuffs. From the port of Providence alone forty nine vessels richly laden had fallen into the hands of the enemy. On the land, also, many valuable lives had been lost and many industrious hands taken from the tilling of the soil to waste their strength in the barren offices of war. The time when these lessons would be turned to account was drawing nigh.

Meanwhile internal improvements continued to receive the attention of the legislature. Church's Harbor was made safer for fishermen by the erection of a breakwater. Providence Cove was the seat of a prosperous trade, and especially of shipbuilding. To facilitate the communication with the water below a draw was opened in Weybosset bridge.

The cancer of paper money was still eating into the vitals of the community, in spite of the legislative palliatives which were from time to time fruitlessly applied to it. Party spirit also had reached its fullest development, and the two rival factions of Ward and Hopkins continued to hate each other bitterly and fight each other obstinately at the polls. These were minor evils. But in the great northwest new war clouds were gathering under the influence of the mighty Pontiac, its king and lord. Parliament prepared for the outbreak, and voted an appropriation of a hundred and thirty-three thousand pounds and an army of ten thousand men for the defence of the American colonies. The regulars were sent against the Indians and parts of the provincials were distributed through the frontier garrisons. The Rhode Islanders were stationed at Fort Stanwix. We are spared the story of the war of Pontiac. It belongs to the frontier and is in no way connected with Rhode Island history. Another contest on which hung the fate of all the colonies is already begun.

I have often spoken of the Board of Trade and the jealous scrutiny with which it watched the growth of the colonies. Too short-sighted to see that their prosperity was intimately connected with the prosperity of the mother country, the ministry by advice of the Board of Trade drew tight the bands of commerce and encumbered the communications of the two countries with dangerous restraints. Trade had increased, but the revenue had not increased in its natural proportion. The form of the evil was smuggling, but its root was the imposition of oppressive duties. Walpole alone had seen forty years before that the surest way to enlarge the revenue was to make the importation of the raw material and the exportation of the manufactured goods as easy as possible. But Walpole stood alone in his wisdom. An attempt was made to enforce the acts of trade. New officers were appointed, a ship of war was stationed in Newport harbor during the winter of 1763 and the noisome tribe of revenue officers stimulated to zealous exertion.

In 1739 a heavy blow had been dealt the commercial and manufacturing industry of the colonies by the molasses and sugar act, imposing a duty on those articles which looked very much like taxation. The colonists looked anxiously to 1764 when the odious act would expire by limitation. But when the time came it was promptly renewed and extended to other articles of domestic consumption. And now was first heard the ominous words stamp act and committees of correspondence. By the stamp act no legal or commercial act was valid unless it was written on stamped paper. The price of this paper was fixed by government and a body of agents appointed to carry on the sale. Thus every transaction in which there was a legal form became tributary to government. In what does this differ from taxation without representation? asked the colonists. But so little did government comprehend the real nature of what it was doing that instead of foreseeing the collision of the two constitutions Parliament assumed by a formal vote the right to tax the colonies. All that remonstrance could gain was a postponement of the stamp act till some more acceptable form of impost could be devised. Even the colonial agents in London failed to see that a radical change in the relations of the two countries was at hand. "The sun of liberty is set," wrote Franklin from London to Charles Thompson at Philadelphia. "The Americans must light the candles of industry and economy."

"They will light a very different kind of candle," was the reply.

The spirit of resistance gained strength daily. Massachusetts took the lead in recommending the call of a Congress of Delegates to meet at New York and take counsel concerning the condition of the country. Rhode Island followed close in her footsteps. In Virginia Patrick Henry brought forward a series of resolutions which going directly to the fundamental principles of constitutional taxation found adherents everywhere. In Providence the *Gazette* reappeared in an extra number with "*vox populi vox Dei*" for superscription, and "where the Spirit of the Lord is there is Liberty," for motto. Augustus Johnston, the attorney-general, was appointed stamp distributor, but refused to "execute his office against the will of our sovereign Lord the People."

In Newport riots took place and popular feeling manifested itself with extreme violence. The effigies of three obnoxious citizens were kept hanging on a gallows in front of the court house through the day, and in the evening cut down and burned in the presence of a great crowd. Next morning the violence of the mob increased, the obnoxious three and equally obnoxious revenue officers were compelled to take refuge on board the Cygnet sloop-of-war that was lying in the harbor.

Meanwhile a calm, firm voice came from the soberer and more thoughtful citizens assembled in town meeting, instructing their deputies to give their "utmost attention to those important objects, the court of admiralty and the act for levying stamp duties." . . . . . "It is for liberty, that liberty for which our fathers fought, that liberty which is dearer to a generous mind than life itself that we now contend."

The day for the enforcement of the stamp act came. But the Congress at New York and the town meetings and assemblies of the different colonies had done their work thoroughly. In a session of the Assembly held at East Greenwich, Rhode Island declared her intention to assert her "rights and privileges with becoming freedom and spirit, ... and to express these sentiments in the strongest manner." Six energetic resolutions were passed pointing unequivocally at independence if grievances were not redressed. The grave duty of representing her in the New York Congress was entrusted to Henry Ward, colonial secretary, and Metcalf Bowler. Governor Ward, Governor Fitch, of Connecticut, and the Royal Governors were called upon to make oath that they would support the obnoxious act. Samuel Ward alone refused.

The fatal day came, and with its inauspicious dawn legal life ceased. Ships lay idle at the wharves for want of clearance. Merchants could not fill an invoice, the officers of the law could not enforce its decrees. Men and women could not marry or be given in marriage. Civil life was paralyzed in all its functions. Whither will this lead us? was the question that rose to every lip. It was soon evident that the colonies were terribly in earnest. They would rely upon personal honesty and do without stamps. Mobs and riots showed to what lengths the heated popular mind was prepared to go. Engagements to suspend all commercial intercourse with England and employ their means in fostering their own manufactures and productions manifested an intelligent union of purpose which could not be mistaken. Of the stamp distributors some resigned, some refused to act. Throughout the whole country, in town and village not a stamp was to be found, not an agent dared to receive or sell the hateful ware. England bowed to the blast and repealed the act, but as if to leave the way open for future taxation coupled the appeal with an act declaring that Parliament had a right "to bind the colonies in all cases whatsoever." The wound was salved over, not healed.

There were other subjects of collision. We have seen that British ships of war visiting Newport harbor were sometimes welcomed. Sometimes, however, they were held to strict account for their conduct. Lieutenant Hill, of the schooner St. John, was fired into from Fort George for some unrecorded offence. In the following year the Maidstone roused the indignation of the inhabitants by impressing seamen openly in the harbor. Even market boats were stopped and their men taken violently from them. A ship from the coast was boarded as she entered the harbor and her crew impressed. Popular forbearance could go no further. In the evening a mob of sailors five hundred strong seized one of the Maidstone's boats and burned it on the common. The way was opening for the burning of the Gaspee.

Meanwhile there were great rejoicings over the repeal of the stamp act. Very soon men will begin to look closely to the act that was tacked to it—the declaratory act.

The great step towards securing the concurrent action of the colonies in their resistance was taken. On the 7th of October, 1765, the second colonial Congress met in New York, and after a three weeks earnest discussion sent forth an address to the King, an address to the people, and a memorial to both houses of Parliament, claiming that as Englishmen they could not be taxed without their own consent or deprived of the right of trial by jury. It was soon made evident that the country would stand by them. Associations were formed under the name of "Sons of Liberty." Rhode Island went a step further, and formed associations of the "Daughters of Liberty." Hitherto the correspondence with the colonies had been conducted by the Board of Trade. But as the dispute assumed a more definite shape, the infatuated King, who was resolutely persisting in his unconstitutional scheme of personal government, gave orders that the colonial dispatches should be addressed to him.

It has been seen that Parliament had resolved to indemnify the colonies for their expenses during the late war. Several payments for this purpose had already been made. But after the stamp act riots the balance though voted was withheld under the pretext that the sufferers by those riots should first be indemnified for their losses. As the Colony had exerted itself beyond its strength to bear its part in the war, this withholding of its just compensation was felt to be a great wrong. When the day for summing up her share in the common grievances came, Rhode Island did not forget this wrong.

Taxes continued to excite bitter complaints, and though called for to meet the daily wants of government, were not collected without great difficulty. In 1767 this dissatisfaction reached its height, unseating Governor Ward and working a complete political revolution. A new valuation of ratable property was made to serve as the basis of a just taxation, but was opposed as favoring trade at the expense of the landholders.

Among the laws demanded by the growing trade was an act fixing interest at six per cent., and making contracts for higher rates usury to be punished by the forfeiture of principal and interest. The true nature of money loans was not yet understood. Among the important civil acts of this period was the completion of an elaborate digest of the laws, two hundred copies of which were printed and distributed among the people.

We have seen that early attention was given to education, and schools opened in Newport, Portsmouth and Providence. In 1766 a grammar school was founded in Exeter upon a gift of five hundred acres of land made seventy years before by Samuel Sewall, of Boston, one of the original purchasers of Pettaquamscot. But more important still was the effort that was made about the same time for the establishment of free schools in Providence to be supported by taxation. Like all such movements it met with most opposition where such schools were most needed, among the poor. In part, however, it was successful, a brick school-house was built and the supervision of all the schools given to a committee of nine, composed in part of the town council.

The foundation of a university, chiefly in order to secure for Baptists the same educational advantages that were enjoyed by other denominations, also belongs to this period. Foremost among its founders was the Rev. Morgan Edwards, and among its benefactors John Brown, of Providence, in record of whose liberality it was removed from Warren, its first seat, to Providence, and its name changed from Rhode Island College to Brown University. Four denominations were represented in its corporation, but a large majority reserved to its founders, the Baptists. Religious tests were forbidden by charter, but the president was required to be a Baptist. Its property and all those connected officially with it were exempted from taxation.

To the ecclesiastical history of this period belongs the Warren Association of Baptist Churches.

The pen also claims its part in the discussion of rights, and among the causes of the rupture we must count the "Farmer's Letters," among its instruments committees of correspondence.

Among the things effecting the material interests of the Colony was the discovery of a new bed of iron ore on the Pawtuxet River, in Cranston. In the preparations which were immediately made for working it, the rights of the fish, which had so often been the subject of legislation, were not forgotten.

CHAPTER XXIII.

TRANSIT OF VENUS.—A STRONG DISLIKE TO ENGLAND MORE OPENLY EXPRESSED.—NON-IMPORTATION AGREEMENT.—INTRODUCTION OF SLAVES PROHIBITED.—CAPTURE OF THE GASPEE.

THE feud of the two parties which had so long divided the Colony ceased at the approach of danger from abroad. A new Governor was elected, Josias Lyndon, and a new Deputy-Governor, Nicholas Cooke, whose name meets us so honorably during the first years of the war, now close at hand. For Ward and Hopkins a broader field of honorable rivalry was opening, and we shall soon see them working earnestly together in the Congress of the Declaration.

England had grown very angry over the attempts of the colonies to organize a system of concerted action. But the times were full of lessons, and the chiefest and most heeded among them was the lesson of union. The Parliament of 1761 was as blind as its predecessors had been, and came together firmly resolved to chastise the Americans into obedience. Where both sides were equally suspicious and equally embittered positive collision could not long be avoided. The first occurred in Newport harbor between three midshipmen of the Senegal man-of-war which was lying in the harbor, and some of the citizens. A citizen, Henry Sparker, was run through the body by an officer named Thomas Careless. Careless was indicted for murder, but acquitted on trial by the Superior Court on the plea of self-defence. Collisions occurred at Boston, all of which served to fan the flame of discontent. To hasten the crisis a regiment supported by a naval force was sent to overawe the rebellious town.

At the June session of the General Assembly (1758) an address was voted to John Dickinson for his "Letters of a Farmer." In closing it they "hope that the conduct of the colonies on this occasion will be peaceable, prudent, firm and joint." Resistance was becoming a familiar idea, and one of the most significant ways of expressing it was by liberty trees. A large elm in front of Olney's tavern, in Providence, was dedicated in the presence of an enthusiastic crowd, and an oration embodying the popular sentiment pronounced by Silas Downer.

In the September session several important State papers were prepared, and the withholding of the war money complained of as a great injustice. Still in the midst of this growing disloyalty the King was always spoken of with affection and respect.

While attention was thus anxiously directed to England, purely domestic interests were not forgotten. The deputy-governor's salary was fixed at fifteen pounds, half that of the governor. An educational society was incorporated at Providence under the name of Whipple Hall. Laws relative to real estate were passed, making it liable for debt after the death of the holder. School and church lands were exempted from taxation, and Trinity Church, in Newport, was incorporated, the first incorporation of a church in Rhode Island. An act was passed, also, wherein the old policy of protecting the river fish was changed, and the Scituate Furnace Company allowed to keep up the dam in the spring. In a previous year a general estimate of ratable estates had been ordered. In 1769 it was reported and found to amount to two million one hundred and eleven thousand two hundred and ninety-five pounds ten shillings and sevenpence, or seven million thirty-seven thousand six hundred and fifty-two dollars, at the current value of lawful money, six shillings to a dollar, which was made by statute the basis of taxation

This was the year of the transit of Venus, to which astronomers were looking forward with deep interest. In this band of observers Rhode Island was represented by Governor Hopkins and other unprofessional scientists in Providence, and by Ezra Stiles of Newport—and here we again meet the name of Abraham Redwood, who was never either governor or deputy-governor, but still lives in fresh remembrance as founder of the Redwood Library. He furnished the instruments for the Newport observation. The local memory of this event is still preserved in Providence by the name of the street in which the observatory stood. The latitude of Providence was found to be 41°, 50′, 41″; its longitude 71°, 16′ west from Greenwich.

Meanwhile the current was daily sitting more decidedly towards armed resistance. Opinions which four years before had been cautiously whispered in corners, now formed the chief topic of declamation in every private and public gathering. Virginia passed unanimously another series of resolutions more decided than the first, and sent copies of them to every colonial assembly. Rhode Island thanked her through the Governor. The Wilkes riots in London strengthened the hands of the opposition, and Lord Hillsborough gave assurance at a meeting of several colonial agents that the idea of drawing a revenue from America had been given up, and the offensive revenue act would in all but the tax on tea be repealed. Ministers failed to see that it was an inherent right, not a sum of money for which the colonists were contending. And in this contention they were prepared to go all lengths.

There was smuggling it was true, and thereby a constant loss to the revenue, but the method of enforcing the revenue laws was vexatious and intolerable to a free people. The officers employed in collecting the revenue belonged to a class immemoriably odious, and even where the collection was entrusted to officers of the Royal Navy it was conducted with an insolence and disregard of the rights and feelings of the colonists which made it doubly odious. Things had already reached the pass at which compromises become impossible. Either the King or the people must yield. Fortunately for mankind victory was where the young fresh life lay, with the colonists.

Among those who had made themselves most offensive in their endeavors to suppress the contraband trade was Captain William Reid, of the armed sloop Liberty, which was cruising in quest of smugglers in Long Island Sound and Narragansett Bay. Under the pretext of putting down illicit trade he had sorely annoyed legitimate commerce. After bearing with his annoyances till they could be borne no longer, the people of Newport seized his vessel, scuttled and sank her, cut down her mast and burnt her boat. This was the first overt act of the War of Independence. Proclamations were issued and rewards offered, but the offenders were never detected. Another wrong inflicted by the revenue officers was in claiming higher fees than were allowed by law. After bearing this also till their patience gave out, the merchants of Newport banded together to resist the imposition.

The question of renewing the non-importation agreement came up for decision. New York, which on this occasion had taken the lead, was for extending them "indefinitely until every portion of the revenue act shall be repealed." Boston followed the example. In Providence and throughout the country opinion was divided, but after much discussion nearly all concurred in admitting everything but tea, and Newport brought down the indignation of the other colonies upon her by admitting prohibited articles.

In these same days the chronicle records a murrain among the cattle and hydrophobia among the dogs. From the first, relief was sought by forbidding the exportation of cattle from the island, from the last by giving general leave to kill all dogs running at large. These acts were to hold good for four months.

This was the period of Newport's greatest prosperity. Her population was over eleven thousand. She had seventeen manufactories of sperm oil and candles, five rope-walks, three sugar refineries, one brewery and twenty-two distilleries of rum, an article which in those days was deemed essential to the health of the sailor and the soldier, and all hard working men. Her foreign commerce found employment for nearly two hundred ships, her domestic trade for between three and four hundred coasting craft. A regular line of packets kept open her communications with London for passengers and mails. Her society had never lost the intellectual impulse given it by Berkeley. Ezra Stiles, the most learned American of his day, filled one of her pulpits, Samuel Hopkins, the founder of a new school of theology, another. A public library, which still bears the name of its founder, furnished the means of literary recreation and research. She would gladly have drawn Rhode Island College to herself also, but though great efforts were made to bring this about Providence made the better offer and obtained the preference.

While this question was still under discussion the first Commencement came round. Seven young men, clad like their officers in the products of American looms, presented themselves for graduation. It was a holiday in which all citizens could heartily unite, for it was the only one which brought them together in the gratification of a common pride. Commencement Day and Election Day continued to be the gathering days of the Colony long after the Colony had become a State.

The greater part of the slaves of the Colony were in Newport, and special laws were enacted concerning their general treatment and their manumission. In the autumn session of 1770 these laws were revised, and a bill introduced prohibiting their further importation. Unfortunately this movement went no farther. The evil had struck too deep.

There was a lull in the storm. Even men not used to indulge vain hopes began to think that the cloud which had so long darkened the horizon might pass away. The revenue acts were still the chief obstacles to harmony. Smugglers were as bold and as successful as ever. But nothing occurred in 1771 to show that the final rupture was so near. Rhode Island's peculiar grievance was the old war debt. To make one more effort, Henry Marchant, the new attorney-general, was directed to join Sherwood in enforcing the claim. Another old question was also revived, that of the northern boundary. Among the acts of the Assembly was a new bankrupt law. The evils of a paper currency still continued to bear their fruit.

But one of the most dangerous movements of this year was a claim advanced by Governor Hutchinson to the command of the Rhode Island forts and militia. This claim Rhode Island had contested when advanced by former governors, nor was she disposed to yield to it now. Still less was she disposed to accept a proposal which at this time came from Bristol under the signature, "A Friend to Property," to divide Rhode Island between Massachusetts and Connecticut, or ask that she should be made a royal government upon the ground that "an elective legislature must always be a source of disorder and corruption" in a small state.

That Rhode Island was not disorderly nor corrupt was proved by the conduct of her courts. A merchant of Wrentham named David Hill was detected by the New York Committee of Inspection "in selling goods included in the non-importation agreements." By the persuasion of the committee he was prevailed upon "to deposit his goods with a merchant till the revenue acts should be repealed." But the suspicions of the people were excited, and they seized the goods and destroyed them. Hill finding in Rhode Island "property belonging to some of the committee," sued them in the Rhode Island courts, asserting that in giving up his goods he had acted upon compulsion. The sympathies of the courts and the people were against him. But, guided by the law and the evidence the Court of Common Pleas awarded him heavy damages and the Superior Court confirmed the award. In the next year when a new election came round and the voice of the people was heard, they also confirmed it by reëlecting the same men for judges. These righteous judges were Stephen Hopkins, James Helme, Benoni Hall, Metcalf Bowler and Stephen Potter.

While these things were a doing the insolence of the officials employed in enforcing the revenue laws reached its highest point. The suppression of smuggling in Narragansett Bay was entrusted to Lieutenant Duddingston, of the Royal Navy, with two armed vessels—the Gaspee, a schooner of eight guns, and the Beaver. Not contented with performing the duties of his office, still vexatious even when considerately executed, he multiplied its annoyances by a thousand acts of petty tyranny. He stopped vessels of every kind without discrimination—ships just from sea, and market boats on their way to Providence and Newport with their perishable freights, and to increase the indignity refused to show his commission or the authority by which he acted. Admiral Montague, who commanded on the station, justified him in his oppression. Complaints were sent to England, but the day of complaint was past.

On the 8th of June the sloop Hannah, Benjamin Lindsey, master, arrived at Newport from New York, and having reported at the custom house set sail the next day for Providence. No sooner was she seen from the deck of the Gaspee than the watchful servant of the King gave chase, and venturing too near a point which ran out from the right bank of the river took ground. Captain Lindsey kept on his course with the welcome tidings that the common enemy was at bay. At the beat of the drum the exasperated citizens came crowding to the gathering place, James Sabin's house in South Main Street. Eight long boats with five oars each were manned. Powder was prepared and bullets run, and when night set in with its friendly shades the resolute band set forth on its mission of vengeance.

It was long after midnight when they came within sight of the doomed vessel hard set in the sand, and heard the first hoarse challenge of the guard. Without heeding it they dashed forward and as a second challenge came were at her side. Duddingston sprang upon the gunwale—he had no time to dress, no time to arm himself or call his men to quarters—but as he stood full in view his figure caught the eye of Joseph Bucklin who was standing on one of the main thwarts. "Eph.," said Bucklin to Ephraim Bowen, who was sitting on the thwart on which Bucklin was standing and who lived to tell the story in his eighty-sixth year, "reach me your gun, I can kill that fellow." As Eph. was reaching him the gun, Whipple, one of the leaders was beginning to answer Duddingston's hail :—"I am the sheriff of the County of Kent, God damn you,"—but while he was yet speaking Bucklin fired and Duddingston fell, wounded in the stomach. The surprise was complete. The crew with their wounded commander were sent ashore and the vessel burned to the water's edge.

Who were these bold men? Everybody in Providence knew; but although large rewards were offered for their detection and a special tribunal formed to try them, nobody was ever found to bear witness against them. So deep were the feelings that prepared the way for the separation from England.

CHAPTER XXIV.

PROPOSITION FOR THE UNION OF THE COLONIES. — ACTIVE MEASURES TAKEN LOOKING TOWARDS INDEPENDENCE.— DELEGATES ELECTED TO CONGRESS.—DESTRUCTION OF TEA AT PROVIDENCE.—TROOPS RAISED.—POSTAL SYSTEM ESTABLISHED.—DEPREDATIONS OF THE BRITISH.—"GOD SAVE THE UNITED COLONIES."

THE 22d of June, 1772, was memorable in the history of humanity, for it was on that day that Mansfield solemnly declared as Lord Chief-Justice of England that slavery could not exist on English soil. This declaration met with a hearty response in Rhode Island. On the 17th of May, 1774, the citizens of Providence met in town meeting to take counsel together upon the questions of the day. Two resolves of this meeting stand fitly side by side. An intestate estate comprising six slaves had fallen to the town. In the meeting it was voted that it was "unbecoming the character of freemen to enslave the said negroes, that personal liberty was an essential part of the natural rights of mankind, and that the Assembly should be petitioned to prohibit the further importation of slaves, and to declare that all negroes born in the Colony should be free after a certain age."

In the June session of 1774 the question was brought before the Assembly. "Those" says the preamble, "who are desirous of enjoying all the advantages of liberty themselves, should be willing to extend personal liberty to others." . . . Therefore, says the bill, "for the future no negro or mulatto slave shall be brought into this Colony." To perfect the act clauses were added defining the condition of slaves in transit with their masters, and protecting the Colony against pauper freedmen.

Having taken this high ground concerning the individual, they took ground equally noble concerning the Colony, "resolving that the deputies of this town be requested to use their influence at the approaching session of the General Assembly of this Colony for promoting a Congress, as soon as may be, of the representatives of the general assemblies of the several colonies and provinces of North America for establishing the firmest union, and adopting such measures as to them shall appear the most effectual to answer that important purpose, and to agree upon proper methods for executing the same." Thus in Rhode Island the condemnation of slavery and the call for union went hand in hand.

The time for hesitation was past. Event came crowding upon event. Virginia, also, called for a Congress. But it was on Boston chiefly that all eyes were fixed. Her example had strengthened the hands of the discontented, and both the

King and his Parliament had resolved to make her a warning example of royal indignation. For this the bill closing her port and cutting off her commerce and known in history as the Boston Port Bill was passed. It was to go into operation the 1st of June, 1774. Never did a great wrong awaken a more universal resentment. Old jealousies and rivalries were forgotten in the sense of a common danger. On the 1st of June the voice of mourning and commiseration was heard throughout the land. Virginia set it apart as a day of fasting and prayers. From every Colony came contributions in sheep and oxen and money. Rhode Island sent eight hundred and sixty sheep, thirteen oxen, four hundred and seventeen pounds in money. Boston in this day of suffering was for her no longer the Boston of the Atherton Company and disputed boundary lines.

But intelligent as Rhode Island had proved herself in her political measures, she could not altogether raise herself above the ignorance of her age in sanitary measures. The small-pox was in Newport, and inoculation was still an undecided question. Should the legislature be asked to declare for it or against it? After four days of discussion it was decided in the negative by a close vote.

We have already seen that a special tribunal had been organized to follow up the question of the Gaspee. In its instructions directions were given to send their prisoners to England for trial.

Hutchinson, the renegade Governor of Massachusetts, proposed to annul the charter of Rhode Island. The committee applied to Samuel Adams for counsel. "An attack upon the liberties of one colony," was his answer, "is an attack upon the liberties of all."

The new year, the eventful 1773, began amid anxious doubts and firm resolves. The Assembly was sitting at East Greenwich, the Gaspee court at Newport. "What shall I do?" asked Chief-Justice Hopkins. The Assembly bade him follow his own judgment. "Then for the purpose of transportation for trial," said the brave old man, "I will neither apprehend any person by my own order nor suffer any executive officers in the Colony to do it." The question fortunately never rose, but questions equally important were at hand.

The burning of the Gaspee was a sudden outbreak of popular indignation. To thoughtful minds it was a still more alarming indication of popular feeling that the senior officer on the station, Captain Keeler, of the Mercury, should have been seized and verdicts of trespass and trover found against him in the colonial courts. But England did not heed the warning.

But the great work was done by the Committee of Correspondence, already formed in Massachusetts and Rhode Island in 1764, but more effectively organized in Virginia in 1775—the railroads and telegraphs of those days. They bound the colonies in a union which doubled their strength and fanned their zeal into a flame. Through them the earliest and "most authentic intelligence of all such acts and resolutions of the British Parliament, and measures of the ministry as may relate to or affect the British colonies in America" was obtained, and a correspondence concerning them kept up with the other colonies. In all these preparations for the struggle, now so near at hand, Rhode Island bore her part. And while they were going on, and as if his part had been done, her faithful agent, proved by fourteen years of assiduous service, Joseph Sherwood, died.

In October, 1773, the tea act went into operation, leading the discontent still more directly to action. But as no tea was sent to Rhode Island, and the story is well known I shall not repeat it here, only saying that public meetings were held in all of which it was resolved to confirm the Philadelphia resolutions. Rhode Island had another grievance to complain of.

The story of the Hutchinson letters is well known to every reader of American history. Some unknown friend of the colonies had put them in the hands of Franklin, and Franklin had sent them to America. "Among them was a letter of George Rome, written six years before, denouncing the governments and courts of Rhode Island." It was immediately published in newspapers and on broadsides, and in every form which could give it circulation. Everywhere it was read with the strongest expressions of condemnation. The author was brought to the bar of the house of deputies, and refusing to plead, sent to jail for the remainder of the session.

Among the acts of revenge which disgrace the English legislation of this period, was the removal of Franklin from the responsible office of superintendent of the American post-office. In his hands the post-office had become a trustworthy institution, paying its way and meeting the wants and commanding the confidence of the country. As a means of communication it had become a bond of union. To suppress it would be a serious blow to the social and commercial relations of all the colonies. The blow fell, but not according to its aim. We have already recorded the name of William Goddard as founder and editor of the *Providence Gazette*. When Franklin was removed Goddard conceived the idea of a colonial post-office adapted to the new relations between England and the colonies. To secure the concurrence of all the colonies he visited them all, explaining his plans and awakening everywhere that confidence without which all his efforts would have been vain. It was another step towards union.

On the eve of such a contest it was wise to count heads. A census was ordered and gave as its result fifty-nine thousand six hundred and seventy-eight, of whom fifty-four thousand four hundred and thirty-five were whites, three thousand seven hundred and sixty-one blacks, and one thousand four hundred and eighty-two Indians.

Two events of grave significance mark the month of May, 1774. General Gage entered Boston as Governor, and a town meeting was held at Providence wherein it was resolved, "that the deputies of this town be requested to use their influence at the approaching session of the General Assembly of this Colony, for promoting a Congress as soon as may be, of the Representatives of the General Assemblies of the several colonies and provinces of North America for establishing the firmest Union, and adopting such measures as to them shall appear the most effectual to answer that important purpose; and to agree upon proper methods for executing the same."

In the same meeting it was recommended to break off all trade with Great Britain, Ireland, Africa and the West Indies till the Boston Port Bill should be repealed. Everywhere the warmest sympathy with Boston was expressed and effective measures taken to assist her by contributions of provisions and money. East Greenwich was the first to open a subscription for her. The example was promptly followed by Newport, Westerly and other towns in which her name had never awakened kindly feelings before. Some of the poor sought refuge in neighboring colonies, and found work and sympathy. Some Tories, alarmed at the prospect of a siege, removed to Providence, but found it a dangerous residence for men of their political creed. One of these, a hardware dealer named Joseph Simpson, seems to have been particularly obnoxious to the Whigs, who of a Saturday night covered his doors and windows with tar and feathers. A public meeting was called to protest against allowing the town to be made a receptacle of the enemies of the country and request the council to have such persons legally removed. Some indications of disorder appearing, another meeting was called to "insist upon the supremacy of the laws."

Measures of defence, also, began now to attract the attention of the Assembly. The stores at Fort George were examined. Some thirty years before an independent company had been chartered under the name of the Providence County Artillery. This name was now changed to Cadet Company and the corps formed upon a regimental basis, taking its position field days on the right. The Light Infantry Company, of Providence, was chartered at the same session. It was to consist of a hundred men and be stationed "in front of the left wing of the regiment." A day of fasting and prayer was appointed and religiously observed. But the most important step of all was the election of Stephen Hopkins and Samuel Ward for delegates to that Congress towards which all eyes were anxiously directed. Thus

Rhode Island had been the first to propose a Congress and the first to take action upon the proposal. In the same session six resolutions were passed "counseling Union and an immediate meeting of Congress to petition for redress, and to devise measures to secure their rights." And as if they foresaw how entirely government was passing away from the King and Parliament, they recommended also that Congress should meet annually. Copies of these resolves were sent to all the colonies.

On the 5th of September, 1774, Congress met in Philadelphia, and after careful deliberation adopted a Declaration of Rights, and recommended the formation of an "American Association," the chief articles of which were "non-intercourse with Great Britain till their grievances should be redressed, abolition of the slave trade, encouragement of home industry, and the appointment of committees of inspection in every town and district to see that its terms were kept inviolate." To these were added "a petition to the King, letters to the other British colonies, addresses to the Canadians and to the people of Great Britain, and votes of thanks to the friends of America in Parliament." The tone through all was decent, earnest and resolute. As they circulated through the country the people felt that their convictions had been faithfully represented.

In this agitated state of the popular mind a

riot was stirred up in Providence by the license question, and in East Greenwich by the Tory question. The first was put down by the citizens, but the second called for the intervention of the military.

The attention of the General Assembly was largely given to measures of defence. The colonial fire-arms at Newport were distributed by counties in proportion to their tax rate. Simeon Potter, of Bristol, was chosen major-general, a new office created for the occasion and subject to annual election. The militia law was carefully revised, and provision made for the "manner in which the forces within this Colony shall march to the assistance of any of our sister colonies if invaded or attacked." The cannon and powder at Fort George were removed to Providence for greater security and more convenient use. Independent companies were formed and carefully trained. Among the Kentish Guards were Nathanael Greene, the future liberator of the South; Christopher Greene, the future hero of Red Bank; James M. Varnum, a future brigadier, and others whose names reappear in higher grades as the progress of the war brought superior merit to view. In Providence County the militia was divided into three regiments under the command of a brigadier.

Among the recommendations addressed by Congress to the people, was a recommendation to stop the exportation of sheep to the West Indies, for domestic manufactures were growing daily in importance and wool was wanted for colonial looms. The recommendation was promptly acted upon, and a temporary committee of inspection appointed to see it carried out. The manufacture of fire-arms was successfully begun.

In February, 1773, the day for suspending the use of tea came. In Providence three hundred pounds of it were publicly burned, the fire being lighted with ministerial documents and other obnoxious papers. While this was a doing by the "sons of liberty" in Market Square, some other sons of liberty went round from store to store, effacing with lamp-black the word tea on the signs.

In April there was a general muster of the militia, when it was found that Providence County had two thousand infantry and a troop of horse under arms, and Kent County nearly fifteen hundred. The returns of the other counties have not been preserved.

The day of decision came. The battle of Lexington was fought. The tidings reached Providence in the night. By the next day a thousand armed men were on the road to Boston. But before they could reach it expresses met them announcing the retreat of the British.

The Assembly met. They voted to raise an Army of Observation of fifteen hundred men, in spite of the protests of the Governor, the Deputy-Governor and two assistants. Nathanael Greene and William Bradford were appointed a committee to confer with the Assembly of Connecticut about this raising of arms. The public ammunition was distributed—to each town its proportion. For greater security it was voted to hold the election session of the Assembly at Providence. A day was set apart for fasting and prayer.

The May session for the election of officers came. The dividing line between Whig and Tory was more sharply drawn. Several changes were made in the board of assistants. Deputy-Governor Sessions gave place to Nicholas Cooke. Governor Wanton himself was suspended for having in various ways "manifested his intentions to defeat the good people of these colonies in their present glorious struggle to transmit inviolate to posterity those sacred rights they have received from their ancestors." A Committee of Safety was appointed, which, with the two highest military officers, was to superintend the paying and furnishing the troops and direct their movements when called out of the Colony. The public offices were removed to Providence.

"The army was formed into one brigade of three regiments, each regiment consisting of eight companies, with a train of artillery." Of this little army, called Army of Observation, Nathanael Greene, who had never held military rank before, was placed in command with the rank of brigadier-general. To anticipate jealousies of rank and position it was provided that "each regiment should occupy the flanks in rotation."

Paper money with all its evils now became a necessity, and bills of credit were issued to the amount of twenty thousand pounds. To give them the character of an investment they were to bear an interest of two and a half per cent., and be "redeemable by taxation at the end of two and five years." An embargo was laid on provisions.

Another battle, the battle of Bunker Hill, was at hand. Collisions between the King's troops and the people were frequent. By the 1st of June nearly a thousand men of the Rhode Island Army of Observation with their artillery were encamped on Jamaica Plains. The committees of inspection for enforcing the American Association were very active. Articles of war were framed. Tories were jealously watched. The suspension of Governor Wanton was a bold step resolutely persevered in. He attempted to explain and defend his conduct, but his explanations were not accepted.

The persecutions of the Gaspee were renewed by Sir James Wallace, Captain of the Rose frigate, and brought on an action between a tender of the frigate and a colonial sloop commanded by Captain Abraham Whipple. After some sharp firing on both sides, the tender was driven ashore under Conanicut and captured.

Wallace already owed Whipple a grudge for his part in the burning of the Gaspee, and wrote him: "You, Abraham Whipple, on the 10th of June, 1772, burned His Majesty's vessel, the Gaspee, and I will hang you at the yard-arm. James Wallace." To which Whipple replied: "To Sir James Wallace, Sir: Always catch a man before you hang him. Abraham Whipple."

This was no longer a sudden uprising of popular indignation against insufferable wrong, but a conflict between two regular armed vessels—the first naval battle of the War of Independence. It led directly to the equipping of two vessels, the Washington and the Katy, for the defence of the Colony—the largest carrying ten four-pounders and fourteen swivels, with a crew of eighty men—the smallest with thirty men.

In this June session in which the foundations of the navy were laid, William Goddard's postal system went into operation six weeks before its adoption for all the colonies by Congress.

During this same eventful month of June the waters of Narragansett Bay were the scene of another bold enterprise. The Rose frigate, Swan sloop-of-war, and a tender were lying with five prizes in Newport harbor. Other vessels came in sight and the royal squadron set out in pursuit of them, following them up the bay and leaving the five prizes unprotected. No sooner did the people of Newport see the opportunity than they seized it, boarded the prizes and carried them off in triumph.

The next event of general interest was the battle of Bunker Hill. An extra session of the Assembly was called. Committees were appointed to take account of the arms and ammunition in the Colony and report it to Congress. Saltpetre and brimstone were sent to the powder mills of New York. Fort George was dismantled. A signal post was established on Tower Hill, and a beacon at Providence, on Prospect Hill. The Colony was put upon a war footing, every man able to bear arms being required to hold himself in readiness for active service. A fourth of the militia were held for minute men and drilled half a day every fortnight. The independent companies were drilled with them. The Army of Observation, which now numbered about seventeen hundred men, was placed under the command of Washington. Everywhere were sights and sounds of war.

The national fast day came, July 20th. From every pulpit, from every family altar, rose fervent prayers for Almighty guidance and protection. For Newport it was a day of terror, for Wallace, enraged at the desertion of some of his men, threatened to bombard the town. Two days he lay in position before it. On the third he sailed away.

Providence harbor was now fortified between Field and Sassafras Points, and a battery of six eighteen-pounders erected on Fox Point. The Beacon was proved and found to shed its light over an area extending from Cambridge to New London and Norwich, and from Newport to Pomfret. All through August the preparations for war continued. The live stock was removed from Block Island and the islands of the bay. The incipient navy was enlarged and the Rhode Island delegates in Congress instructed "to use their whole influence for building at the Continental expense, a fleet of sufficient force for the protection of these colonies, and for employing them in such manner and places as will most effectually annoy our enemies, and contribute to the common defence of these colonies." This recommendation led to the appointment of a committee of which Governor Hopkins and John Adams were members, and which presently laid the foundation of the Continental Navy.

From time to time there were sudden alarms. Once it was given out that Providence was to be attacked, and the works in the harbor were manned and the troops called out. But Wallace, contenting himself with taking a brig from the West Indies and plundering the shores, retired down the bay. In October he was reinforced, and after holding Newport in suspense bombarded Bristol. Domestic enemies also were to be guarded against. George Rome reappears and is sent to Providence "to be dealt with according to his demerits." Furnishing supplies to the enemy or holding correspondence with them was made punishable with death and forfeiture. Exception was made in favor of Newport on account of her exposed situation. The sufferings of the poor both in Newport and on the islands were so great that the Assembly found it necessary to come to their assistance, helping some to move away and supplying others with provisions. How business suffered may be seen by the repeal of the statute of limitations. In November Governor Wanton was formally removed from office and Nicholas Cooke elected in his stead. With the burning of the Gaspee the sword was drawn, with the deposition of Governor Wanton the scabbard was thrown away.

Meanwhile new emissions of bills of credit were made and the overwhelming debt overwhelmingly increased. But it was no longer the debt of a single colony but a part of the war debt of all the colonies, and therefore Congress assumed forty-five thousand pounds of it as such. Of this forty-five thousand pounds a hundred and twenty thousand dollars were presently paid. One more battle was fought in Narragansett Bay, and one more day set apart for fasting and prayer.

We have seen that Rhode Island had called for a navy. In November Congress took the subject up, appointed a marine committee and voted to arm and equip four vessels. Esek, brother of the Governor, was put in command of them with the title of commodore. Two hundred and fifty Rhode Islanders followed Arnold through the wilderness, and none of all the invading army bore with greater fortitude the privations of the weary march or fought more gallantly under the walls of Quebec than Christopher Greene, Samuel Ward and Simeon Thayer, all of whom we shall meet again on the ramparts of Red Bank. Over a hundred were sent to Philadelphia under Captain Whipple, to serve in the new navy.

Meanwhile at Newport and on the islands the presence of the British squadron held men in constant alarm. A considerable force was encamped at Middletown, and a constant watch kept up to guard against the secret machinations of the disaffected. Row gallies patrolled the bay and a night guard was established. But in spite of every precaution the trees were cut down on Hope Island, twelve dwelling houses were burned and their occupants plundered on Conanicut, and the live stock carried off wherever a secure landing could be effected. General Lee, who had been sent from Cambridge to direct the fortifying of the island, made his entrance into Newport at the head of eight hundred men, and after imposing upon the suspected a comprehensive oath and giving instructions for the erection of fortifications, returned to the army. To express their sense of his services the Recess Committee voted "that one of the best beds, with the furniture taken from Charles Dudley, be presented to General Lee."

In the last days of December there was a riot in West Greenwich to prevent the enlistment of minute men. In the middle of January there was some sharp fighting on Prudence Island. In the course of the first day the British, who had come up in twelve vessels, landed two hundred and fifty men, drove off a body of a hundred minute men, burned seven houses and carried away a hundred sheep. Next day reinforcements arrived from Bristol and Warren and the fighting was renewed. This time the victory was with the Americans, and after a battle of three hours the enemy were driven to their ships with a loss of fourteen killed and many wounded. War in one of its worst forms raged at all the most vulnerable points of Narragansett Bay.

And thus the gloomy days went by, slowly but surely bringing nearer and nearer the now inevitable problem of independence. Rhode Island, with her hundred and thirty miles of coast line, her two navigable rivers, and triple passage from the ocean, was in constant exposure. We have seen how she was harrassed by Wallace in January, 1776. In February more houses and a windmill were burned and more stock plundered on Prudence, and a descent for plunder made on Point Judith. With this last the names of several persons suspected of being Tories were mixed up, giving the Committee of Safety much to do. Difficulties between the citizens of Newport and the soldiers under General West, encamped on the island, arose in a measure from the same cause. West resigned because men whom he had arrested as Tories had been set at liberty by the Assembly. Among them was Governor Wanton.

The first act of the eventful drama closes with the evacuation of Boston, on the 17th of March. For a day it was believed that the British fleet was entering the bay, but the alarm proved false. The American army went to New York, passing through Rhode Island on its march.

While these events, so grievous in the present, so full of a glorious future, were passing, Samuel Ward, who had so nobly represented the highest conscience and culture of Rhode Island in the Continental Congress, was dying of small-pox in Philadelphia—the advanced post of civil heroism. An upright and conscientious man, who had drawn from books and men those lessons which make men wise in judgment and firm in principle and bold in action. Had he lived a few weeks longer his name would have been foremost among the signers. A marble monument was voted him by Congress, "in testimony of the respect due to his memory, and in grateful remembrance of his public services."

The last Colonial Assembly of Rhode Island met on the 1st of May. On the 4th, two months before the Congressional Declaration of Independence, it solemnly renounced its allegiance to the British crown, no longer closing its session with "God save the King," but taking in its stead as expressive of their new relations, "God save the United Colonies."

CHAPTER XXV.

RHODE ISLAND BLOCKADED.—DECLARATION OF INDEPENDENCE INDORSED BY THE ASSEMBLY.—NEW TROOPS RAISED.—FRENCH ALLIANCE.—UNSUCCESSFUL ATTEMPT TO DRIVE THE BRITISH FROM RHODE ISLAND.

FROM the 4th of May, 1776, the Declaration of Independence of Rhode Island, to the battle of Tiverton Heights, on the 29th of August, 1778, she lived with the enemy at her door, constantly subject to invasion by land and by water, and seldom giving her watch-worn inhabitants the luxury of a quiet pillow. For months, as we already have seen, British ships of war had infested her shores, driving off the stock, plundering the inhabitants and burning their houses and barns. In November a still greater calamity befell her, a British fleet took possession of her waters, a British army of her principal island. The seat of government was removed to Providence. The points most exposed had already been fortified as well as the means and military science of the Colony permitted. These were strengthened and other points fortified. A battery was erected on the southern projection of Warwick Neck, commanding the entrance of Coweset Bay. The women and children of the seaboard towns were advised to take refuge in the interior. The militia were called out. The troops on the island, about seven hundred in number, were removed to the main land, part under Colonel Cook taking post at Tiverton, part under General West at Bristol. Massachusetts and Connecticut sent immediate aid to their imperilled sister. And thus Rhode Island entered upon the humiliating life of a district held by its enemy.

The story of these three years should either be told in detail, or told very briefly. In detail it presents some striking pictures and some important lessons. The pictures are for the chief part marine views, most of the fighting having taken place on the water. The lessons are to be found in the skill or want of skill with which legislation adapted itself to new wants and new means. Our limits do not admit of detail. We shall glean sparingly from the statute book.

The first duty of the Assembly was to draw out the resources of the State and give them efficiency. The census of Providence in February gave a return of four thousand three hundred and fifty-five souls, with about five hundred stand of arms. Of this population one-sixth were effective men. The other towns furnished their proportion, and the distribution and equipment of them received the constant attention of the Assembly and fills a large space in the schedules. In the new arrangement of the Continental Army the three Rhode Island regiments were formed into two battalions. We shall not attempt to follow the schedule through the various changes which were made in the quota furnished by Rhode Island to the main army. The fuller page of history gives it a noble record, and the names of Christopher Greene, of Angell, of Thayer, of the two Olneys, of Samuel Ward and their companions, stand very high in the regimental history of the war.

Another subject which occupied from time to time the anxious attention of the Assembly was the treatment of the small-pox. How could its ravages be staid? How could the prejudice against inoculation, which still prevailed so widely even among the intelligent and well informed, be overcome? The question was brought before the Assembly in June, when it was resolved, though not without opposition, to establish an hospital for inoculation in each county. It was resolved also to ask Congress to establish a uniform system of inoculation in the army and navy.

There could no longer be any doubt as to the treatment of Tories. Rhode Island was an independent state, and justifiable in employing, to protect herself against treason, the same means which other independent states employed. A test oath was framed, which all who were suspected of Toryism were required to subscribe. Yet, even in this dark day of trial she did not forget her fundamental principle, and the conscientious scruples of the Quakers were respected. Commerce was permitted with all parts of the world except England and her dependencies.

The Declaration of Independence by Congress was received with general satisfaction, and proclaimed with a national salute and military display. At Providence the King's arms were burned, and the Legislature assumed its legal title, "The State of Rhode Island and Providence Plantations," and voted that "we do approve the said resolution, and do most solemnly engage that we will support the said General Congress with our lives and fortunes."

Congress, as we have seen, had voted to build a navy at the original suggestion of Rhode Island, and directed that two of the thirteen frigates that were to compose it should be built there. Ship building was one of the arts to which the Colony had directed its attention on its first planting, and Rhode Island workmen had grown skillful therein. The direction first taken by her maritime enterprise was privateering, which not only made the fortunes of individuals, but met many wants which the regular commerce of the country was unable to meet. To this great fleet Rhode Island contributed sixteen vessels, manned by men in the prime of life, and animated by love of adventure, love of country, and love of gain. Sometimes their numbers were kept full at the expense of the army, and it was found necessary to lay a general embargo till the Continental quotas were filled.

In December the Assembly met at Greenwich, but finding that place too exposed, adjourned to Providence. The chief subject of discussion was how to raise an army, and the New England States were invited to send committees to Providence to concert some general plan of action. The Recess Committee gave place to a Council of War, composed of ten members. The dangerous system of short enlistments still prevailed and a brigade of three regiments, two of infantry, each composed of seven hundred and fifty men in eight companies, and one of artillery composed of three hundred men in five companies, were voted for fifteen months. The command was given to General Varnum, and Malmedy, a French officer, recommended by General Lee, was appointed "Chief Engineer and Director of the works of defence in this State, with the rank of Brigadier" When brought to the test of enlistment its roll filled up very slowly.

The Convention of the Eastern States met in Providence. Each state was represented by three delegates. Stephen Hopkins was chosen President. After long and frequent consultations with the Assembly, it was recommended that an army of six thousand men should be concentrated in Rhode Island, of which Massachusetts was to furnish nineteen hundred men, Connecticut eleven hundred, New Hampshire three hundred, and Rhode Island eighteen hundred and a thousand Continental troops.

Other questions called for equal attention. Men no longer dared to look to paper and a printing-press for their money, but to taxing and borrowing. A loan of forty thousand pounds at five per cent. was voted. But the borrowers were many, the lenders few, and taxes hard to collect. With less wisdom it was voted to prevent monopolies and regulate prices. All of these questions recur from time to time till men grow weary of contending with the natural laws of trade. Meanwhile the army was almost naked, and more than once on the brink of starvation and mutiny. The plans of the convention for concentrating a large force were never wholly carried out, and the army of the State, like the army of Congress, was too often an army on paper.

Yet one great step was taken at the suggestion of General Varnum. Colonel Christopher Greene, Lieutenant-Colonel Olney and Major Ward were sent home to enlist a battalion of negroes for the Continental service. When the question came before the Assembly in the form of a resolution to enroll slaves, compensate their masters and give them their freedom, it met with some opposition upon the ground that it would be disapproved of in other states, that the masters would not be satisfied with the compensation, and that there were not slaves enough to make a regiment. But the wiser opinion prevailed, the regiment was raised, and when the day of trial came the freedman proved himself an excellent soldier.

In February, 1778, the Articles of Confederation were adopted, not as perfectly satisfactory, but as the best that could be had. Certain modifications were proposed. "Obtain them if you can," were the instructions to the Rhode Island delegates, "but in all events sign the articles."

In April came the happy tidings of the French alliance, joyfully received everywhere with ringing of bells and firing of salutes and military display. The 22d of April had been appointed for a fast day. It was changed to a thanksgiving. The hopes of the country were raised very high. "Surely," men said to one another, "now that France has declared for us, the end must be near."

In May Governor Cooke, who had served diligently since the beginning of the war, withdrew from his laborious office, and William Greene, son of the late Governor Greene, was elected in his stead, and with such general acceptance that he continued to be reëlected eight years in succession. Four delegates instead of two were sent to Congress.

We have seen how the islands of the bay had suffered. In the same month of May an expedition was sent by the British commander at Newport against Warren and Bristol on the main. Three churches and several private houses were burnt, and seventy flat-boats, together with the galley Washington and a grist-mill, were destroyed. There was loss of life and destruction of property, but not a step made towards the decision of the contest. Soon after an attempt was made on Fall River, but repulsed by the judicious choice of position and gallantry of Colonel Joseph Durfee.

The presence of the enemy in Narragansett Bay was a constant menace to the Eastern States, and to drive them out was the constant aim of the commander of that department. Under General Spencer great preparations had been made and great hopes entertained of success. But one of the brigades failed to be up with their boats in time, and a second attempt was prevented by the weather.

At last the favorable moment came. Sullivan, an active and intelligent officer, was in command of the Continental forces, and the coöperation of D'Estaing with the French fleet was secured. On the 29th of July twelve French ships of the line and four frigates arrived off Newport. The English were effectually blockaded, driven from their outposts, and compelled to destroy their vessels.

Preparations were made for an immediate advance. At no period of the war had greater enthusiasm prevailed. Volunteers came pouring in from Boston, Salem, Newburyport, Portsmouth—not merely those whom pay or bounty could call out, but men of wealth and position. John Hancock led the militia of Massachusetts. Greene and Lafayette came on from the main army. By the

8th of August Sullivan found himself at the head of ten thousand men. The right wing took post at Tiverton. The French fleet under D'Estaing held the outer harbor. The morning of the 10th was fixed upon for the attack. On the 8th the fleet ran up the middle passage in face of a heavy fire from the enemy's batteries, and secured the command of the bay. Sir Robert Pigot drew in his forces and stationed them in strong positions near the town. They numbered about six thousand in all.

Sullivan seeing that the British commander had abandoned his strong works at the head of the island, thought that no time was to be lost in securing them, and without waiting for the day agreed upon with the French admiral, set his right wing under Greene, in motion on the morning of the 9th and began to cross over to the island. D'Estaing felt the breach of etiquette, but had little time to dwell upon it. For about two in the afternoon a fleet of nearly twenty-five sail came in sight, standing in for Newport. It was the fleet of Lord Howe. He lay to off Point Judith for the night, and next morning began a trial of seamanship with D'Estaing for the weather-gage. The Englishman stood out to sea; a sudden change of wind enabled the Frenchman to follow him, and the whole of the first day and part of the second were passed in manœuvring. Meanwhile the wind kept rising, and in a few hours it blew a gale. Soon it was no longer a question of victory, but of life. The work of destruction by mortal hands ceased. The big ships were tossed helplessly about by the yawning billows. The invisible winds snapped the strong masts — once the pride of centennial forests — asunder. The Languedoc, with her ninety guns, the French admiral's own ship, lost masts and rudder. The shattered fleets made their way to port as best they might, the English to New York, the French to Newport, with occasional encounters on their way.

The tempest had raged with as much violence on shore as at sea. Nothing could withstand its rage. Trees were torn up by the roots. Tent poles were snapped asunder like reeds. Marquees were torn and dashed to the ground. The rain fell in torrents, swelling the brooks till they overflowed their banks and spread over the fields in ponds and pools. Men crouched under the stone walls. When the tempest ceased, horses and men were found dead together. Then was the time for Pigot to draw out his men from their snug quarters in the town and lead them against the exhausted Americans. The American general feared this, and anxiously watched the dangerous hours go by. But the Englishman let slip the golden occasion and it never returned.

It was not without many misgivings that Sullivan had seen the French fleet make sail and stand out to sea. But D'Estaing had pledged himself to return, and when on the 20th a swift frigate, and soon the Languedoc herself, hove in sight, he dispatched Greene and Lafayette to confer with the French admiral and his officers and secure their coöperation. But whatever D'Estaing's own wishes may have been, his officers, who were jealous of him as a landsman, pointed to his instructions and called upon him to repair to Boston. The Americans felt themselves deserted, for it was only by the aid of the fleet that the town could be taken. "There never," they said, "was a prospect so favorable blasted by such a shameful desertion."

Still Sullivan resolved to persevere in his attempt, and giving partial vent to his indignation in the order of the day, took up a position within three miles of the town and began to erect batteries. It was soon evident that it would be hazardous to attempt to hold it. On the 28th it was resolved to fall back and establish a fortified camp at the north end of the island. But already the army was melting away. Three thousand militiamen and volunteers went off in twenty-four hours, and presently the assailants scarcely outnumbered the assailed. The British fleet also would soon be back, while the French fleet could no longer be counted upon. D'Estaing indeed gallantly offered to bring up his land forces to the support of his allies. But now the only question was how to retreat without loss. A sharp battle was fought on the 29th, in which both sides contended obstinately for the victory.

Then in the night, men, baggage, artillery and stores, were transported across the ferry without the loss of a man or beast, or a single munition of war.

CHAPTER XXVI.

ACTS OF THE BRITISH TROOPS.—DISTRESS IN RHODE ISLAND.—EVACUATION OF NEWPORT.—REPUDIATION.—END OF THE WAR.

THE Americans were sorely disappointed. They had taken up their arms with such confidence of success that they could not bear to lay them down with so little done. Their murmurs were loud and deep. Some were ready to lay all the blame upon their allies. Nothing but the good sense of Greene and the good feeling and generous nature of Lafayette could have prevented an outbreak. The old leaven of English animosity toward France still lay deeply rooted in the colonial heart. It was an unfortunate beginning of the alliance that was to give them victory.

For still another year the principal island of Narragansett Bay was to remain in the hands of British soldiers, and its other islands and the shores of its mainland lie exposed to the ravages of British cruisers. It was a year of suffering. There was no more fighting in regular battles, no more laying siege by regular advances, but many plundering excursions for the wanton waste of property and the wicked waste of life. ' Houses were burnt from mere wantonness; woods and orchards cut down to serve for fire-wood, and for this the cold winter furnished a good excuse; but when at last the enemy withdrew, little was left of the sylvan beauty of Narragansett Bay.

The adventurous fighting was chiefly done on the water, and the hero of it was Silas Talbot, of Providence. Talbot had already distinguished himself early in the war, both on land and on the water. Nothing suited his adventurous spirit so well as the leadership in enterprises which to other men seemed hopeless, and his judgment and skill equaled his daring. Of these bold exploits one of the boldest was the capture of the Pigot galley, a vessel of three hundred tons, mounting eight twelve-pounders, protected by strong boarding nettings and manned by forty-five men. The force with which Talbot took her was a small sloop carrying two three-pounders and manned for the occasion by sixty men. As a recognition of his gallantry Congress sent him a commission of lieutenant-colonel, and not long after that of captain in the navy.

Among the miseries of these years was a scarcity of food, almost amounting to a famine. Speculation was active and remorseless, getting control of the market and growing rich on human suffering. An appeal was made to Connecticut for a suspension of her embargo on provisions in favor of Rhode Island. The question how to counteract "engrossers and forestallers," was one of the most difficult questions which Congress and state legislatures and special conventions were called upon to meet. Two thousand helpless poor were scattered through the State, dependent upon public and private charity for bread. Five hundred pounds were voted for the relief of the poor of Newport. The appeal to Connecticut for a relaxation of her embargo was met by permission to export seven thousand bushels of grain, and a recommendation of a general contribution by her citizens. The recommendation called forth gifts of four thousand three hundred pounds in money, and five hundred bushels of grain. The recommendation was extended through Congress to other states, and South Carolina assumed through her delegates fifty thousand dollars of Rhode Island's Continental quota.

It was in this year also that the storm, long known as the Hessian storm, from the number of those wretched mercenaries who perished in it, occurred. Sentinels froze at their posts—some were suffocated by the whirling snow. The roads were blocked up by it. Never had such a storm been known.

New taxes were regularly called for and voted, both for Continental and State expenses. But the currency was deranged and the sources from whence taxes were drawn well nigh exhausted. The treasury was empty. To enlist a new brigade, —the term of the old one having run out,—it was found necessary to borrow twelve thousand pounds from Connecticut for a month. There was not time yet for constitutional reforms, although attention was frequently called to the inequality of representation. But the more important reforms were the reforms of the army, and the great event of 1779 was the introduction of Steuben's Tactics.

The derangement of the currency made itself felt everywhere. Colonel Crary, of the First State Infantry, an excellent officer, was compelled to throw up his commission because he could not support his family on his pay. With many others it was merely a question of time—whether they should resign at once or wait a little longer till they were ruined utterly. As paper depreciated taxes were increased. Confidence, the basis of national prosperity, was gone. In June, 1778, two heavy taxes were levied, one of two hundred and twenty-five thousand pounds for Congress, and one of sixty thousand pounds for the State. Almost the only channel through which goods and money still continued to come was through privateers.

The vital question was the question of finance. Congress appealed to the states and the states to the towns. A convention met at East Greenwich and attempted to fix upon a maximum scale of prices for articles of consumption. The establishment of rates for labor and board and manufactures, was left with the towns. The fatal effects of a false system of political economy fell heavily upon both town and country. Trading in gold and silver was discouraged and desperate efforts made to relieve the country from the pressure of present debt; but the root of the evil lay too deep, and bankruptcy was already at the door.

One act, however, of these days of trial, we can still dwell upon with satisfaction. In spite of the manumission act an attempt was made to sell some slaves to the South. The Assembly interfered for their protection and forbade the sale.

The Greenwich Convention had left its work unfinished. A new convention was called in September to finish it, and every effort was made to raise the loan recommended by Congress. At the suggestion of Massachusetts a convention of the five Eastern States was called to meet at Hartford and take these difficult questions into consideration. And thus the days and months passed away, monotonously sad, with little of present enjoyment and still less of promise for the future. Men lived like those who carry their lives in their hands and have no hold on the morrow. At last the long looked for day came. Fifty-two transports entered Newport harbor and immediately the work of embarkation began. Six thousand men with their baggage and military stores and a melancholy train of Tories were to bid goodbye to their pleasant quarters. When all was ready the inhabitants were forbidden to venture into the streets on pain of death, and the march to the place of embarkation at Brenton's Point began. Then was heard for the last time in the streets of Newport the British drum and the measured tread of an enemy's march. All day long the boats were plying to and fro, and at sunset the fleet set sail. Forty-six Tories, with such property as they could carry, and a large band of liberated slaves went with it. The last act of the troops was to burn the barracks at Brenton's Point and the light-house at Beaver Tail. When the inhabitants began to look about them and count their losses, they found that over five hundred houses had been destroyed and property to the value of nearly one hundred and twenty-five thousand pounds ruined in the Town of Newport alone. The population had been reduced by more than half, and among the emigrants were the Lopez, and Hays, and Riveiras, and Touros, rich and enterprising Jews. One outrage it is difficult to explain, the robbery of the town records, which were put on board one of the transports and sent to New York. This alone would have been a great injury, for they contained the history of the Colony from its foundation, and as parts of that history the record of sales and grants of land. But to complete the loss the vessel on board which they had been put sunk in the passage of Hell Gate, and it was not till they had lain three years in the water that they were recovered. Parts only were legible.

The Assembly which met on the very day of the evacuation, found much to do. Many expenses which the presence of the enemy had made necessary, ceased. The coast-guard was dismissed. The ferries from Newport to South Kingstown were reopened. The four island towns resumed their charter administration. The non-intercourse act was repealed, and New Shoreham restored to the exercise of her corporate rights. To meet the embargos laid by the neighboring states, an embargo was laid upon all articles of exportation. The militia was reörganized. In August acts had been brought in confiscating the property of Tories, and forbidding the sale of slaves out of the State against their will. They were passed in October.

We come now, and reluctantly, to a disgraceful page of our annals, the Revolutionary debt of Rhode Island. In the December session of 1779, the State acknowledging "the proved fidelity, firmness and intrepidity in service, of its soldiers," pledged itself through its constitutionally elected representatives, to make good at the close of the war, "to them or their legal representatives, the wages of the establishment of Congress, wherever they engaged." Upon the strength of this solemn engagement many of the men and officers of the three Rhode Island regiments of the line, whose terms of service were about to expire, reënlisted for the war.

This pledge was broken, leaving an ineffaceable stain upon the shield of Rhode Island. Nor does it lighten the disgrace to say that other states also were untrue to their pledges. Other states persecuted for opinion, but in this Rhode Island did not follow their example.

A bitter winter followed the evacuation. The bay was blocked up with ice. Seaward the ice extended as far as eye could reach. Government had to come to the relief of the starving and freezing poor. Corn cost four dollars a bushel, potatoes two—famine prices, as prices ordinarily ruled.

We have marked the first appearance of the *Newport Mercury*. During the three years of British occupation it was published at Rehoboth, but at the evacuation was brought back to Newport, and resumed its original influence under the editorship of Henry Barber.

As time wore on things gradually assumed a more hopeful aspect. In April, 1779, Lafayette returned from France with the cheering assurance that a French fleet would soon follow him. Preparations for effective coöperation immediately began. The militia was called out for three months. Rhode Island's quota of men was one regiment of six hundred and thirty men; of supplies, seventy-one thousand six hundred and seventy-five pounds of beef, thirty hogsheads of rum, and twenty-two hundred and eighty-five bushels of forage grain; of transportation, two hundred draft horses.

The promptness with which the little State met the heavy calls upon her limited resources was warmly acknowledged by Washington in a letter to Governor Greene. And at the same time one of her regiments was winning high honor at

Springfield, under the guidance of one of her best officers, Israel Angell.

The arrival of the French fleet and army under Ternay and Rochambeau was the signal for universal rejoicing. The hopes and confidence of the first year of the alliance were revived. But this time the efforts of the combined forces were to be directed against the enemy's strongest post — New York itself. Some apprehensions were still felt from the secret machinations of the Tories, and an act was passed banishing them.

Meanwhile preparations were made for quartering and feeding the troops. In Providence, University Hall was set apart for a hospital. The barracks at Tiverton and a farm near Bristol were assigned to them for the same purpose, and Pappoosquash Point was given to them for a burial place.

To meet the expenses imposed by these preparations new taxes were assessed, founded upon a new estimate of taxable property, and designed to sink the remaining portion of the State's quota of old Continental bills and meet present and future expenses. Taken altogether the taxes voted in the July session of 1780, reduced to a specie standard, amounted to one hundred and twenty-six thousand three hundred and sixty-nine dollars and fifty cents. It was a heavy burden, and the good spirit with which the people bore it showed how thoroughly their hearts were enlisted in the cause of their country.

But suddenly there was a new alarm. An English fleet of sixteen ships of war appeared in the offing, staid just long enough to spread a general apprehension of invasion, and after a second alarm took up its station in Long Island Sound and blockaded the French from the sure position of Gardiner's Island. Thus for a time French coöperation once more failed.

In September the Assembly met in Newport, the first time in four years. The State House had been used by the British for a hospital, and all the churches except Trinity for barracks. The Assembly held its sessions in the Redwood Library.

Money was still the primary object of attention. Congress called on the states for three millions of dollars. For the first time Rhode Island was unable to meet her portion. She had also a large proportion of the French troops to provide for, whose headquarters were at Newport, where Rochambeau established himself in the Vernon House, which still bears his name. But the French brought hard money with them, and spent it freely.

In December Ternay, the French admiral, died, without having had an opportunity of doing any thing important for his allies. His tomb is still seen in Trinity church-yard.

We enter upon 1781, the decisive year of the war—and decisive also by its political significance. Connecticut and Virginia ceded their western lands to the Union, and Greene's successes in the South, and Washington's capture of Yorktown, virtually put an end to the war. In the same year the confederation was completed by the accession of Maryland. Rhode Island could not perform all her federate duties as heretofore, but the presence of the French fleet made her for a while an object of especial interest. Her daily quota of supplies was two thousand rations of fresh beef, besides rum and other stores.

In the same year she lost by surprise two of her best soldiers, Colonel Christopher Greene and Major Ebenezer Flagg, both distinguished by their part in the defence of Red Bank, in 1777. Peace was at hand, and with peace a new experiment in political life. The confederation had been tried in war and found wanting. How would it meet the requirements of peace?

CHAPTER XXVII.

ARTS OF PEACE RESUMED.—DOCTRINE OF STATE RIGHTS.

GREAT were the rejoicings over the surrender of Cornwallis—public balls, firing of cannon and display of fire-works—for close upon that surrender came the longed for peace. As a more enduring expression of gratitude to the man who had led in this great work, the Assembly decreed that "in order to obliterate, as may be, every trace and idea of that government which threatened our destruction . . . . . the same county, (King's), shall forever hereafter be known and distinguished by the name and style of Washington."

And soon the war-worn troops who had so gallantly borne their part in the burthen and heat of the day, came home rejoicing in their victory, but trembling for their future. Then came pressing the urgent questions of the hour, and first of all the question of finance. The Bank of North America had been established to strengthen the hands of the superintendent of finance, though not enough to make him listen to the appeal of Rhode Island to be allowed to pay part of her quota in army supplies. To ascertain on what ground the State stood for taxation a new census was ordered, which gave fifty-one thousand eight hundred and sixty-nine for the whole number of inhabitants, Newport returning five thousand five hundred and thirty-one, and Providence four thousand three hundred and ten. A new estimate of taxable property also was made, which was found to amount to nearly three millions of pounds in lawful money. Taxation had borne heavily upon this capital, but with peace war expenditures ceased, and productive industry began to return to its natural channels.

And very soon a Federal question arose. Congress resolved to levy an import duty of five per cent., but could not do it without the consent of the states. Here dawns upon us the question of state rights, soon to assume a more menacing aspect and delay for years Rhode Island's entrance into the Union. Nearly all the states but Rhode Island had given their consent to it, but she foresaw in it future danger to her liberties and persisted in her refusal. Two of her delegates, Howell and Ellery, held out vigorously against it. " Howell undertook to prove that the State, by adopting the impost, would lose four-fifths of its revenue collected upon it. Mr. Ellery went upon the common danger of altering the constitution, and frightened the people with the loss of liberty."

Varnum and Marchant used many arguments "to remove these prejudices, but to little purpose. The general spoke two hours and a half; his arguments were learned, sensible and conclusive; but they were unavailing." Such were the reasonings in the Rhode Island Assembly. "The truth of the matter is," wrote General Greene, "a large majority of the members are incompetent judges of so complicated a question. . . . . . . What is to become of us and our national honor God only knows. No people ever had brighter prospects shaded so unexpectedly."

In the midst of these exciting discussions it is pleasant to see what early attention was given to education. The college returned to the use for which it was built, and in September, 1782, seven students received their degrees.

In that same year and month died Nicholas Cooke, who had filled the Governor's chair so worthily at the begining of the war. More than once before peace was declared an armed enemy was seen in Narragansett Bay. Two vessels were cut out of Newport harbor in the night by Tory privateers, and at another time an armed party took possession of Hope Island and held it for several days. One of the most menacing signs of these troubled times, was the armed resistance to the collection of taxes which had threatened Massachusetts with civil war, but was sternly put down. Yet even when the strong arm of the law was raised to enforce, they who wielded it most firmly could not but feel that there was much ground for complaint.

I shall not attempt to follow step by step the progress of Rhode Island in her return to the life and arts of peace. New laws were called for and made. New fields of enterprise were opened and entered upon. The errors of the past were to be bitterly atoned for. But her resources were great, her will strong, and her courage unabated. From the mass of detail I select a few characteristic points.

The financial embarrassment made itself felt everywhere, endangering contracts, paralyzing industry and checking enterprise, and undermining both public and private credit. Eight millions were required for the Federal quotas of 1782. Less than half a million had been collected. Four states had paid nothing, nine next to nothing. The impost act failed, and Howell, who by his opposition to it had made himself numerous enemies in Congress, had greatly added to his influence at home. Rhode Island was looked up to as the champion of state rights. With time she will grow wiser.

We have seen that slavery became the subject of legislation at an early period of our annals. It reappeared at the return of peace, when gradual emancipation was minutely provided for, and the introduction of "slaves for sale under any pretext whatever, forbidden."

Among the purely local acts was the incorporation of Newport, and the regulation of the Pawcatuck fishery, and an attempt to annex Potowomut to East Greenwich. Among those which belong to the history of thought was that by which Sabbatarians were "allowed to pursue their usual avocations on Sunday." Among those that bore directly upon business was the revival of the statute of limitations, and an act for encouraging the manufacture of certain articles of general demand. Patents and copyright laws followed soon after the adoption of the Constitution, though not with a full recognition of an author's right to the product of his brain. For the support of government a tariff act was passed.

But the most historically interesting act of the February session of 1783 was the enabling act, by which the original harmony between the digests and the charter was restored. Into these digests, but when or how nobody could tell, the phrases: "Roman Catholics excepted," and "professing Christianity," had been interpolated in direct violation of the royal charter. Neither under Charles nor under James could this have been done. But in 1696 a plot against William had been discovered, which led to the formation of "associations of loyalty" in all the colonies but Rhode Island. Practically, the exception had no effect, and Catholics and Jews were admitted to the full rights of citizenship as they had always been. But as an historical question it is pleasant to know that the principle of universal toleration was never practically violated in the home of Roger Williams.

CHAPTER XXVIII.

DEPRECIATION OF THE CURRENCY.—INTRODUCTION OF THE SPINNING-JENNY. — BITTER OPPOSITION TO THE FEDERAL UNION. — RHODE ISLAND FINALLY ACCEPTS THE CONSTITUTION.

THE question of finance meets us at every turn, and in every phase bears fatal witness to the demoralizing effects of paper money unsustained by hard money capital. At the Spring election of 1786, the triumph of the paper money party was complete. A new bank was established of a hundred thousand pounds. And soon a Forcing Act became necessary to give the bills currency under heavy penalties. A complete stagnation of business presently followed. The old hostility between town and country revived. Commerce was suspended. Shops were closed. The farmers who had mortgaged their farms for the bills, found that they had got nothing but bits of paper in return for fruitful acres. To retaliate upon the tradesmen they refused to bring their produce to market. The necessaries of life fell short and much suffering ensued. In Providence a town meeting was held to devise a remedy, and it was resolved that the farmers should be left to make their own bargains, and that to relieve the immediate demand five hundred dollars should be borrowed and sent abroad to buy corn for the sufferers. At Newport an attempt was made to force the bills upon the grain dealers, which led to a riot. At a meeting in South Kingstown farmers were advised to break off their intercourse with the merchants.

A convention of the country towns of Providence County was held at Scituate and adjourned to meet the State convention at East Greenwich. Sixteen towns were represented and resolved " to support the acts of the General Assembly," and enforce the penal acts in favor of paper money. Providence was represented by five of its best and most popular men, but they were powerless against the torrent.

When the question came before the Assembly a new Forcing Act was passed, in which the right to trial by jury was withheld and all the common forms of justice violated. The protest of the indignant minority was refused a place on the records; and pushing their recklessness to the utmost, the triumphant majority enacted that the arrears of Continental taxes might be paid in the new bills, and proposed a system by which all trade was to be carried on by a committee in the name of the State. This, however, was a step too far even for these wild schemers, and when the Force Act was brought to trial, it was condemned by a full bench as unconstitutional.

But the Assembly persevered, summoned the judges to answer for their interference, and under the name of Test Act passed a new Forcing Act more outrageous than the last. It was something like a pause in this reckless career that the new act was referred to the towns for discussion. Only three towns accepted it. An attempt at conciliation failed.

The lowest deep of financial degredation was reached when the treasurer was ordered to pay one-fourth part of the State debt in the bills received for taxes. Never had party spirit assumed so dangerous a form. Among the bad doings of the Assembly was the resumption of the charter of Newport.

. It was at this critical moment, when rents were paid in corn and trade seemed about to return to its original form of barter, that the first spinning-jenny in the United States was constructed by Daniel Jackson, of Providence, and the foundations of Rhode Island's manufacturing prosperity securely laid. History is full of compensations.

We reach the beginning of a still greater struggle. The convention that was to transform the Confederation into a Union was to meet in May. Should Rhode Island be represented in it? Those who had faith in the Confederation, and there were many such, believed that with some amendments it might be made to answer all the purposes of a stable government. Those who were more impressed with its weakness called for a thorough and radical change. The first, who in the sequel were known as States Rights men, were also the advocates of paper money. The second, the Federalists of a later day, were in favor of hard money. The motion to send delegates was lost, and another step taken towards repudiation. "All holders of State securities were required to present them to the treasurer within six weeks and receive five shillings in the pound thereupon, or to forfeit that amount, and interest was to cease immediately upon the rising of the Assembly. The paper was now passing at the rate of six dollars in paper for one in silver." Never had the honor of the State been so imperilled. Fortunately, though, the Assembly was divided, the courts were firm, and it was only by removing four judges out of five that a decision in favor of paper payments was obtained. Meanwhile the bills continued to fall, and soon reached eight for one. But the moral sense of the community was not altogether stifled. Some churches refused to receive as communicants men who paid their debts in paper.

But soon all questions became absorbed in the question of the acceptance or rejection of the Convention. In the Senate it was voted to send delegates, but the bill was lost in the House, whose action was defended by a State Rights letter, setting forth the doctrine of popular sovereignty and "the entire subserviency of the legislature to the public will." None but the people could send delegates to a convention.

Meanwhile, the Convention, with Washington at its head, and Franklin, Hamilton and Madison among its working members, had reached the end of its arduous labors. The next step was to submit it to the people. The Assembly met and a bill was introduced for printing it for distribution, and appointing delegates as recommended by the Convention itself. The last was voted down by a large majority. The fruit was not yet ripe. But a resolve to print a thousand copies for distribution was agreed to, and thus the question was brought squarely before the people.

And now for three years it was the chief question in all public meetings, and was sure to come in either directly or indirectly wherever two or three met together for business or for pleasure. The merchants accepted it cheerfully, for they saw progress and development and protection in it. But it was opposed by the farmers, who saw in it a sacrifice of the rights of the State. Rhode Island had stood alone so long, had been so firm and self-reliant through the dark days of her long contest with Massachusetts and Connecticut, that she failed to see how completely the relations of the colonies to each other were changed, when from colonies they became states. There was no place for independent states in the domain occupied by a Federal Union.

The first to accept the Constitution was Delaware. Pennsylvania came next, and then New

Jersey. The opening of 1788 was marked by the accession of Georgia. Connecticut followed close. In Massachusetts the contest was long and bitter. In June New Hampshire gave in her adherence.

We have seen in what a dark hour Rhode Island first turned her attention to cotton spinning. In this hour of even deeper gloom she first opened a direct trade with India. About the same time a rolling and a slitting-mill was established near Providence. Women of all classes met together to spin flax, and men of all classes took pride in wearing homespun. Nor was the promise of navigation less. Providence already counted a hundred and ten sail in her waters, exclusive of river craft. In spite of all her errors her faith in the future was unimpaired.

Meanwhile the contest continued. Town was arrayed against country, the States Rights men still holding the majority in the Assembly, although in Providence the Federalists were strongest. The tidings of New Hampshire's acceptance was received with exultation. The Constitution was sure. In Providence it was resolved to unite the celebration of the Fourth of July with that of the completion of the National Union. The States Rights men took this for an intentional insult and marched upon the town. Nothing but the good sense of the leaders prevented a bloody collision. The rejoicings it was agreed, were for the Declaration of Independence, not for the Declaration of the Union. Then from five to six thousand people sat down in a tent a thousand feet long to feast upon a sumptuous banquet, the most attractive part of which was an ox roasted whole. On the very next day came tidings from Virginia. She also had accepted the Constitution. New York followed and then North Carolina, and the warmest enthusiam welcomed each new declaration of acceptance. But a bitter party spirit still held Rhode Island back.

Thus month followed month. New assemblies and new town meetings came together and fought over the same ground. In all the other states of the old thirteen the Constitution had been accepted, and was in successful operation. It was clear that Rhode Island could not long preserve her insulation. She was already compelled to ask vital favors of the Union, and petition Congress to exempt her commerce from paying duties in Union ports. For a while Congress bore with her and granted her prayer. Slowly but surely the decisive day drew nigh. All the artifices of parliamentary tactics were brought into play. In the midst of intense excitement and by the casting vote of Governor Collins, it was decided on the Sabbath morning of January 17th, 1790, to call a convention. But even in the convention the friends of the Constitution were in a minority. The familiar ground was to be fought over again with no less bitterness than in the beginning. Loud murmurs came from Congress. Shall this little strip of land prevent us from completing a union so full of promise? Louder still were the murmurs from the seats of commerce—Providence and Newport. We will break away from these impracticable men and go into the Union alone with our ships and our spinning-jennies. A coalition ticket was formed. So great was the eager crowd, in which each man had his opinion, that the State House was found too small to hold them, and the convention was compelled to adjourn to the Second Baptist Church. It still took three days more before a vote was reached; and then, at five o'clock of Saturday afternoon, on the 29th of May, 1790, Rhode Island declared her adhesion to the Union.

CHAPTER XXIX.

MODE OF LIFE IN OUR FOREFATHERS' DAYS.

WE have followed with as much detail as our limits would permit, the history of Rhode Island through the various phases of her colonial life. Before we enter upon the story of her development as a member of a great Union, we propose to bring together a few facts from the imperfect record of her social and domestic life, and endeavor to form for ourselves some idea of what manner of men and women our fathers and mothers were, and what kind of lives they led. Incomplete as our materials for such a picture are, there is still enough to be found in those sources from which history loves to draw to bring us very near to the life of those days.

And to begin with the soil; the inland in the beginning of English colonization was a vast forest, dotted with ponds of fresh water and watered by numerous rivers. In this forest the natives themselves had begun the work of clearing, and drawn between it and the sea a belt of arable land from eight to ten miles in depth, on which they planted their favorite food—the nutritious maize. The waters abounded with fish, the woods with game. The animals most to be feared were the wild-cat and the wolf—the most sought after by the hunter, the deer. In the earliest commercial intercourse of Indian and white man, the medium was maize.

There were no carriages nor carriage roads. All traveling was on foot or horseback, and when the first English settlement began, in almost every twenty miles you would find an Indian village.

As the soil came under more skillful cultivation and the colonist took the place of the Indian in field work, the harvests became more abundant, and the rich grasses which grew as high as the tops of the fences, became very valuable as butter and cheese. Thus farming was carried on on a large scale, and dairy farms gave employment to many hands. The Stanton farm was four miles long by two miles wide, and was cultivated by forty horses and forty slaves. The Champlin farm was a tract of a thousand acres, feeding thirty-five horses, fifty-five cows, from six to seven hundred sheep, and slaves enough to tend and utilize them all. Robert Hazard owned sixteen hundred acres on Boston Neck, and several thousand on the west side of the Pettaquamscot River. On one of these farms grazed a hundred and ten cows, two hundred loads of hay were cut, thirteen thousand pounds of cheese were made, and from seventy to eighty pounds of butter. The products on which all this labor was bestowed, were corn, tobacco, cheese and wool. The work was done by slaves and Indians. The cheese resembled in flavor and color the rich Cheshire cheese of England. Some attention was also given to fattening bullocks and raising horses, and cutting hay and grain for the West Indies.

On Isaac P. Hazard's farm twelve negro women were employed in making cheese, each woman having a girl under her and making from twelve to twenty-four cheeses a day. So rich and luxuriant was the grass that his hundred and fifty cows gave double the quantity of milk that cows give on the same farms now. Four thousand sheep furnished the materials for the woolen cloths of his numerous household, and extensive hemp fields the linen, both being woven in his own looms. This Hazard, when years came upon him, gave over the management of his estate into the hands of his children, and congratulated himself that he thenceforth had only seventy mouths to provide for between parlor and kitchen.

Traveling, as I have already stated, was on horseback, and a servant well mounted always went with the master to open the gates. The roads were mere driftways. A generous hospitality left the inns to justices' courts, town councils and tipplers. The guest chamber was seldom empty, and the fireside all the more cheerful for the face of a stranger.

Public provisions for education were insufficient. Their place was supplied for boys by private tutors, or by board in the family of a learned clergyman to prepare them for college. The girls were sometimes sent to Boston to study accomplishments. They loved reading, each generation having its favorite in verse and in prose. Of those nearest to us Pope was the poet. Private libraries were numerous and well selected, though not large.

Amusements took their character from country life. The young men loved races on the beach with their Narragansett pacers, and a silver tankard for the winner. They all loved quahaug roasts on the shores, where deep beds of shells still remain to bear witness to their festivities. They loved to hunt the fox and the deer with hound and horn, and exercise their skill in starting and following up the partridge and woodcock and quail. They would lie on the frozen ground in the cold winter dawn to get a shot at a duck or a wild goose and trap the timid rabbit in snow. No hardship was too great that brought them to their game. In May they went in merry parties to Hartford to eat bloated salmon.

In such a state of society weddings were great festivals, and more especially for the display of dress. The bride came robed in stiff brocade with towering head dress and high heeled shoes. The bridegroom, in scarlet coat, his limbs clad in small-cloths and silken hose, with laced ruffles on his wrists, and brilliant buckles on his shoes, and his hair curled and frizzled, or suspended behind in a queue. Friends and kindred came from far and near, sometimes as many as six hundred being gathered to witness the nuptial rites and join in the wedding dance.

But the great pastime for young and old, for matron and maid and for youth just blushing into manhood, was the autumn husking, when neighbors met at each other's corn-yards to husk each other's corn; sometimes husking a thousand bushels in a single meeting. Husking had its laws, and never were laws better obeyed. For every red ear the lucky swain could claim a kiss from every maid; with every smoot ear he smooched the faces of his mates amid laughter and joyous shoutings; but when the prize fell to a girl she would walk the round demurely, look each eager aspirant in the face, and hide or reveal the secret of her heart by a kiss. Then came the dance and supper, running deep into the night and often encroaching upon the early dawn.

I have spoken of slavery and the repeated attempts Rhode Island made to shake it off. The number of slaves was not large, and for the most part they were treated kindly. Still servitude implied degradation, and the habit of looking down upon human beings could not but react unfavorably upon the character and habits of the masters themselves. It was a softening of their lot that in the regular festivals the negroes had their share, their dances and their suppers, and even their elections, when they elected and installed their governor, and feasted luxuriously at the expense of their masters.

CHAPTER XXX.

COMMERCIAL GROWTH AND PROSPERITY OF RHODE ISLAND.

RHODE ISLAND came well prepared to her new duties. She had worked out in her own experience the most important problems of civil organization, rendering "unto Cæsar the things that are Cæsar's, and unto God the things that are God's." Her legislation was the reflection of her culture, and her statute book the record of her progress in the science of self-government. Her colonial life had been a constant struggle with jealous neighbors who coveted her beautiful bay and detested her "soul liberty." Out of this struggle she came stronger and more resolute for the discipline it gave her, yet not without some marks of the strife. She had learned to apprehend danger from afar off and cultivate jealousy as a safeguard, and hence she sometimes as in her refusal to grant the impost duty, was guided by a keen sense of her rights as a sovereign state, rather than a deep conviction of her obligations as member of a confederation. Hence also, she had hesitated three years on the borders of union, and seen her sister states enter it one by one before she could bring herself to make over to a central government even those portions of authority which a central government could administer so much more in her interest than she. But she was wiser for the struggle, and full of resolution and hope entered boldly upon her new career.

We have seen that Rhode Island began very early to seek her fortune on the water. Ship building was one of the earliest forms which her enterprise assumed. Already in March, 1790, the shipping of Providence alone consisted of nine ships, thirty-six brigs, forty-five sloops and twenty schooners, forming in all a tonnage of ten thousand five hundred and ninety. To man this commercial fleet the same town had a population of six thousand three hundred and eighty to draw from. Newport, though no longer holding the same position which she held before the war, was still an active seaport. The population of the whole State had risen to sixty-eight thousand eight hundred and twenty-five.

The most active commerce had been that of the West Indies. But with peace a wider field was opened, and ships sent directly to the East Indies. Raw material of various kinds was sent to Europe, and European manufactures brought back in return. It was soon evident that the new State would profit England more by equal commerce than by dependence. Yet it was not all at once that the financial errors of the Revolution could be repaired, or the bitterness engendered by civil war assuaged. A deep rooted hostility to England had taken hold of many minds, to bear its fruits when republican France claimed sympathy as a sister republic.

We have already registered the birth of manufactures. Circumstances favored their growth and prepared the way for a development which has made the smallest one of the richest states of the Union. A great river runs through it, widening at its mouth into a spacious bay. Deep ponds of pure water dot its surface, and limpid streamlets which swell with every rain send from every upland their tributes to the bay. How should these waters be subjected to the will of man? Samuel Slater, a native of Derbyshire, had served an apprenticeship to Jedediah Strutt, the partner of Arkwright, and learned the secret of the new method of spinning cotton. Heavy penalties were affixed to the exportation of the new machinery. But Slater had made himself master of the theory as well as the practice of the art, and seems to have been casting about him for a way of turning his knowledge to account, when he learned that the State of Pennsylvania had offered a bounty for the introduction of it. Thus American manufactures owe their birth to protection. The story was a simple one. Slater came to America bringing the secret with him. In Moses Brown, of Providence, he found a judicious counselor, in William Almy and Smith Brown enterprising capitalists. On the 21st of

December, 1790, and on the Pawtucket River, the first factory went into operation. On that day and by the hand of Samuel Slater, the destiny of Rhode Island was decided.

In these days of mingled hope and fear, on the 19th of July, 1785, closed the long and useful career of Stephen Hopkins, whose name is closely interwoven with all that is greatest and best in Rhode Island history; an astronomer of no mean pretensions, a statesman of broad views and deep penetration, a supreme executive, prompt, energetic and fearless, a genial companion when wise men relax from care, and a trusty counselor when the duties of life bear heaviest on the scrupulous conscience.

The tranquil growth of manufactures affords few materials for general history, in which it appears by its results rather than by its processes. Statistics take the place of narrative, and except in controlling and inventive minds the story of man himself is the story of a machine.

Meanwhile another seed was sown in this fruitful ground, and another name was associated with a great public benefaction, the name of John Howland, a native of Newport, but from his ninth year a resident of Providence and a barber by trade, became, in 1799, the father of the free school system of Rhode Island. Not all at once was this good work done, but slowly and in spite of much opposition, chiefly from the poor who were to profit most by it. Years were yet to pass before the pride as well as the consciences of the people became enlisted in its behalf.

In the commercial history of the State the foundation of the Providence Bank, in 1791, was an event of great importance, to be followed at intervals by others with various degrees of success. But among them all not one bore so directly upon the moral growth of the community as the Providence Institution for Savings, founded in 1819.

Great hopes were founded on a canal connecting the tide-water of Providence River with the north line of the State. A company for this purpose was formed in 1796, and so great was the confidence which the undertaking inspired, that John Brown, a leading merchant of Providence, subscribed forty thousand dollars to the stock. The project failed, and though enthusiastically renewed in 1823, failed again and forever.

The yellow fever belongs to our record, and Rhode Island came in for a full share of the destruction occasioned by the September gale of 1815. Most towns hand down from generation to generation the story of some great fire which swept over it in its young days, leaving ruin and desolation in its path. The "great fire" of Providence was the fire of 1801, the memory of which still lives in the traditions of our own generation.

Pleasant memories also belong to our record. When Washington made his first visit to the

East as President, Rhode Island had not yet entered the Union. When she did he made a second visit to the East in recognition of her accession, and was enthusiastically welcomed. He had already been there under very different circumstances during the war.

We have spoken of John Howland as a public benefactor. Another of these benefactors of their race was Ebenezer Knight Dexter, founder of the Dexter Asylum, who having amassed a large fortune in honorable commerce, gave sixty thousand dollars of it to the support of the poor. A still more important movement was made in the interest of the poor, when the first temperance meeting was held in Providence in 1827.

We saw how a charter had been granted to Newport and taken from her. In 1829 an attempt was made to obtain a charter for Providence and failed. Two years later a serious riot occurred in which some property was destroyed and some lives were lost. It became evident to the friends of good order that a more efficient government was required to hold in check a population of sixteen thousand eight hundred and thirty-two souls; for to that number had Providence risen in 1830. A charter was applied for and easily obtained, and on the 22d of November, 1832, the Town of Providence became a city. Samuel W. Bridgham was the first Mayor.

Though never the seat of war during the war of

1812, the name of Rhode Island is closely connected with it, through Oliver H. Perry, one of the greatest of naval commanders. She bore her part also in the sufferings occasioned by the embargo, and the other rash measures of a government which rushed headlong and wholly unprepared into a war with the most powerful nation on earth. Fully sharing also in the just discontent of the Eastern States, she sent four delegates to the much maligned Hartford Convention.

CHAPTER XXXI.

THE DORR REBELLION.

WE have seen that the relation of the citizen to the State became the subject of attention and experiment at an early period in the history of Rhode Island. Although an avowed democracy, she regarded suffrage not as an inherent right, but as a privilege dependent upon the fulfillment of certain specified conditions. Inequality of representation was a natural consequence of the unequally increased population; some towns growing faster than others, but having no more voice in legislation than they had had at the beginning of their civil existence. The right to vote was held to be an important right, and great pains were taken to secure purity at the polls. But it was evident that all the tax-payers would sooner or later claim to be voters. This question recurs from time to time in all its ramifications, and though long deferred, became at last the chief question of Rhode Island politics.

For more than two-thirds of a century she had lived under the Charter of Charles II., first as a Colony and lastly as a State. This Charter was framed in the broad and liberal spirit of Roger Williams and John Clarke, and left room for large developments in every department of legitimate thought and action.

Unfortunately what might have been brought about by peaceful discussion was gradually fanned into the fiercest flame. Providence had entirely outgrown her old rival, Newport, and yet Newport had a representation of six in the Assembly, and Providence of only four. In other towns the disproportion was equally great. The property qualification also, a freehold of a hundred and thirty-four dollars, was bitterly opposed by those who had no freehold. In 1840 seventy-two representatives were chosen. Thirty-eight were chosen from towns having only twenty-nine thousand and twenty inhabitants and two thousand eight hundred and forty-six voters, and the remaining thirty-four came from towns which had only seventy-nine thousand eight hundred and four inhabitants, and five thousand seven hundred and seventy-six voters.

Equally irritating to those who had no share in it was the right conferred by primogeniture.

For many years these questions were prominent subjects of discussion, and were even brought forward as the most important objects of legislative action. But no relief could be obtained from the Assembly, for the Assembly itself was chiefly composed of the privileged classes. From the Assembly there was but one appeal—the appeal to the people, and upon the form of this appeal lay the choice between reform and revolution.

This is the event known in Rhode Island history as the Dorr Rebellion.

The first step towards action was the formation of suffrage associations, by which the public mind was excited and the popular will roused to exertion. All through the last weeks of 1840 and the first weeks of 1841, these associations were busy in guiding, kindling and stimulating the popular mind, and preparing it for decisive action. All classes were roused, for the contest was at every door, and every citizen was equally interested in the result.

The suffrage associations did their work actively and well. By the 5th of July, 1841, a mass convention was held in Providence, and the State Committee was authorized to call a convention for the formation of a Constitution. Confident of their strength the committee set themselves to their task. On the 28th of August delegates were chosen, and on the 4th of October the convention met. In this convention a Constitution was framed, and in December sent out to the people as the People's Constitution. Fourteen thousand voters, a majority, it was claimed, of all the male adult voters in the State, cast their votes for it. It claimed to be the will of the people authoritatively expressed. There was one more step to take, the consequence and complement of all that had hitherto been done, to complete the organization by the election of officers. The 18th of April, 1842, was fixed upon for this gravest function of freemen, and Thomas Wilson Dorr, of Providence, was chosen Governor.

Votes had done all that the mere expression of opinion could do. But underlying every lawful vote was the law which gave it validity, and this law had prescribed the form and manner in which these votes became effective. It had said that while the source of all power was in the people, the people themselves in order to secure progress and guard against revolution had set limits to their authority, and told when, where and for what it should be employed.

And now it was seen that there was another government which claimed to be in sole possession of this power, and the moment that the new government attempted to perform its executive functions it found itself face to face with the old. It was evident that one of the two parties must give way or there must be a collision and bloodshed.

The first attempt of the Suffragists to organize was made at Providence on the 3d of May, and was repelled. The moral strength was with the charter government which had the chartered companies, the organized militia and a strong body of volunteers at its control. It had also the strong moral support of that clause in the Constitution of the United States which guarantees to every state a republican government and protection against internal violence. Should Federal intervention become necessary, the time and the form of it had been provided for. But it was not needed. We have seen that on the 3d of May the government of Governor Dorr had attempted to displace the government of Governor King, and failed. On the 18th an attempt was made to seize the Arsenal, which also failed. Men who had grown up side by side in peaceful intimacy, had seized their arms under a strong political excitement, but when the moment for using them came, shrank from the fearful responsibility. Hundreds would have fought gallantly, but no one was prepared to begin. And thus when on the 25th of June an attempt was made to make a stand at Chepachet, the Suffragists gave way at the approach of the State troops, and returned to their homes without shedding a drop of blood. By the 28th of June all was over. The great body of the insurgents went quietly back to their stores and their farms. Their leader was tried for treason and condemned to imprisonment for life. But Rhode Island was not a place where so severe a punishment could be meted out to such an offence. In 1847 an act of general amnesty set him free, and in 1851 he was restored to his political and civil rights. Forgiveness went still further, and his sentence was reversed as illegal and unjust. But the Supreme Court refused to sustain this reversal as an assumption of judicial authority by the Legislature. Dorr's early death left him no time for new aspirations.

Meanwhile a new convention for the framing of a new Constitution had been called by the regularly constituted authorities, and a new draft submitted to the people. But this also was rejected. Another attempt was made, another convention called. Argument and discussion were exhausted. The popular mind was prepared for decision. The popular will called for it. The last day of the old Charter was come. At an adjourned meeting of the convention, held at East Greenwich on the 5th of November, a final decision was reached and a Constitution unanimously agreed upon. On the first Tuesday in May, 1843, it went into operation.

And thus Rhode Island, while she adhered firmly to the principle of freedom of opinion, adhered no less firmly to the principle of law and order. The Dorr Rebellion was the resistance of law to revolution, of order to the arbitrary assumption of power. Rhode Island had begun her career by a practical profession of freedom of thought and freedom of speech. She had struggled long and hard to secure them both, and now the day of reward was at hand. Henceforth the industries of peace will bring her wealth from the land and the sea, the salubrity of her climate will raise up on her inland and on her shores a thriving and vigorous population, and while in some things she will take the lead of her sister states, in no thing will she fall far behind.

CHAPTER XXXII.

LIFE UNDER THE CONSTITUTION.—THE WAR OF THE REBELLION.—THE CENTENARY.

WITH the adoption of the new Constitution business returned to its natural channels. Party animosities lost somewhat of their bitterness as the various forms of industry revived, and old friends were again brought into daily communication under the healing influence of common interests and common pleasures. The story of these calm pursuits brings out in pleasant relief the every-day virtues of domestic life and the higher qualities of combination and invention, but it seldom addresses itself to the imagination, or excites and surprises by glowing appeals to the passions. The happiest periods of history are those which are the most barren of incident.

Meanwhile one of the great epochs of our history was at hand, and Rhode Island was again called upon to furnish the materials for battles which were to be fought at a distance from her own soil. The war of secession found her, like her sisters, unprepared for the great struggle in which humanity had so much at stake, and which soon made it manifest that industrious peace is the best of preparations for a war of principle. Within three days after President Lincoln issued his proclamation calling for troops for the defence of Washington, a body of Rhode Islanders, well armed and equipped, was on its way thither. As the war continued she still met its increasing demands, till the sum-total of her contributions amounted to twenty-four thousand and forty-two, upon a population of one hundred and eighty-four thousand nine hundred and sixty-five. Of these, two hundred and fifty-five were killed; one thousand two hundred and sixty-three died of wounds or disease; one thousand two hundred and forty-nine were wounded.

As some readers may wish for more detail, I give the following statement, for which I am indebted to the politeness of Adjutant-General Heber Le Favour:

"There went into the field from Rhode Island during the late rebellion, twenty-four thousand and forty-two men; of which the infantry numbered ten thousand three hundred and eighty-two; cavalry, four thousand three hundred and ninety-four; heavy artillery, five thousand six hundred and forty-four; light artillery, two thousand nine hundred and seventy-seven; navy, six hundred and forty-five. This number is in excess of the actual number of persons furnished by the State, as many of them appear several times on the record under the head of promotions or re-enlistments after discharge from their three months, nine months, or three years terms of service.

Two hundred and fifty-five were killed, one thousand two hundred and sixty-five died of wounds or disease, and one thousand two hundred and forty-nine were wounded. There were eight regiments of infantry, of which three were for three months and two for nine months. There were three regiments of cavalry for three years, and one squadron for three months. There were three regiments of heavy artillery. There was one regiment of light artillery, composed of eight light batteries, and there were also two light batteries for three months service. One company of infantry was stationed at Portsmouth Grove as Hospital Guards."

On the 4th of July, 1876, the United States of America ended the first century of their national existence; a century of marvellous experiences throughout the civilized world; of experiences in the science of government, which bear directly upon the moral development of man and experiences in the physical sciences which minister directly and indirectly both to his material wants and to the demands of his intellectual nature. Civilization had reached in those hundred years a height and a completeness which it had never reached before.

Proud of what they had done, confident of what they could do, they invited the other civilized nations, their elders by centuries, to bring the choicest productions of their art and industry and set them side by side with those of the young republic. In this comparison how well Rhode Island bore her part the following list will show:

Rhode Island was conspicuous at the Exposition for the excellence of her products in the following departments: *

First—Machinery, including new inventions.

Second—Cotton fabrics, including sheeting and shirting, calico, fine muslins, jeans, drillings, etc.

Third—Woolen fabrics, broad cloths, cassimeres, shawls, worsteds, etc.

Fourth—Wood screws. (American Screw Co., Providence.)

Fifth — Fire-arms, rifles, carabines chiefly. The Peabody-Martini rifle furnished the Turkish government an arm of great excellence. (Providence Tool Co.)

Sixth—Fabrics of India rubber. (The Bristol Works.)

Seventh—Silver and plated ware. (Gorham's.)

Eighth—Steam engines.

Ninth—Hair cloth. (Various companies in Pawtucket.

Tenth—Files and mechanics' tools.

Eleventh—Stoves and furnaces. (Chiefly the product of the Barstow Works.)

Twelfth—Chemical manufactures.

---

* For the above list I am indebted to my friend, Hon. J. R. Bartlett, to whom Rhode Island is indebted for the preservation and publication of her Colonial Records.

And here I stay my hand. I have spoken kindly of the State of my birth, but mindful of the historian's first duty, I have striven in every thing to speak truthfully. It is an unvarnished tale, and yet there is a moral grandeur in it far beyond the grandeur of battle-fields and thrones. By deep and earnest convictions, by unwavering faith and unshaken resolution, Rhode Island has worked out for herself and for mankind one of the grandest problems of civilization.

It is the privilege of history that it teaches by examples. It is good for man that such men as Roger Williams and John Clark, should have lived. It is for the glory of Rhode Island that men like these, searching for a spot whereon they might build and live with unfettered consciences, should have chosen her for their dwelling place.

Author's Notes.

(*Referring to page* 196.) This is not strictly accurate. It was in honor of Nicholas, not John Brown, and several years after its removal from Warren to Providence, that the name of Rhode Island College was changed to Brown University.

It was in July, 1777, during the occupation of Newport by the British, that William Barton, Lieutenant-Colonel in the Rhode Island militia, performed his brilliant exploit of the capture of the British General Prescott; passing three British frigates unobserved and carrying off the British General in his night-clothes. Congress rewarded him with a gift of a sword, and what was still more valuable, a commission as Colonel in the Continental army.

Appendix.

The Charter,

GRANTED BY KING CHARLES II.,

July 8, 1663, and in force until the adoption of the Constitution, November, 1842.

CHARLES the Second, by the Grace of God, King of England, Scotland, France and Ireland, Defender of the Faith, &c., to all to whom these presents shall come, greeting: Whereas, we have been informed, by the humble petition of our trusty and well-beloved subject, John Clarke, on the behalf of Benjamin Arnold, William Brenton, William Codington, Nicholas Easton, William Boulston, John Porter, John Smith, Samuel Gorton, John Weeks, Roger Williams, Thomas Olney, Gregory Dexter, John Coggeshall, Joseph Clarke, Randall Holden, John Greene, John Roome, Samuel Wildbore, William Field, James Barker, Richard Tew, Thomas Harris, and William Dyre, and the rest of the purchasers and free inhabitants of our island, called Rhode Island, and the rest of the Colony of Providence Plantations, in the Narragansett Bay, in New England, in America, that they, pursuing, with peaceable and loyal minds, their sober, serious, and religious intentions, of godly edifying themselves, and one another, in the holy Christian faith and worship, as they were persuaded; together with the gaining over and conversion of the poor ignorant Indian natives, in those parts of America to the sincere profession and obedience of the same faith and worship, did, not only by the consent and good encouragement of our royal progenitors, transport themselves out of this kingdom of England into America, but also, since their arrival there, after their first settlement amongst other our subjects in those parts, for the avoiding of discord, and those many evils which were likely to ensue upon some of those our subjects not being able to bear, in these remote parts, their different apprehensions in religious concernments, and in pursuance of the aforesaid ends, did once again leave their desirable stations and habitations, and with excessive labor and travel, hazard and charge did transplant themselves into the midst of the Indian natives, who, as we are informed, are the most potent princes and people of all that country; where, by the good Providence of God, from whom the Plantations have taken their name, upon their labor and industry, they have not only been preserved to admiration, but have increased and prospered, and are seized and possessed, by purchase and consent of the said natives, to their full content, of such lands, islands, rivers, harbors and roads, as are very convenient, both for plantations, and also for building of ships, supply of pipe-staves, and other merchandize; and which lie very commodious, in many respects, for commerce, and to accommodate our southern plantations, and may much advance the trade of this our realm, and greatly enlarge the the territories thereof; they having by near neighborhood to and friendly society with the great body of the Narragansett Indians, given them encouragement of their own accord, to subject themselves, their people and lands, unto us; whereby, as is hoped, there may, in time, by the blessing of God upon their endeavors be laid a sure foundation of happiness to all America: And whereas, in their humble address, they have freely declared, that it is much on their hearts (if they may be permitted) to hold forth a lively experiment, that a most flourishing civil state may stand and best be maintained, and that among our English subjects, with a full liberty in religious concernments; and that true piety rightly grounded upon gospel principles, will give the best and greatest security to sovereignty, and will lay in the hearts of men the strongest obligations to true loyalty: Now, know ye, that we, being willing to encourage the hopeful undertaking of our said loyal and loving subjects, and to secure them in the free exercise and enjoyment of all their civil and religious rights, appertaining to them, as our loving subjects; and to preserve unto them that liberty, in the true Christian faith and worship of God, which they have sought with so much travail, and with peaceable minds, and loyal subjection to our royal progenitors and ourselves, to enjoy; and because some of the people and inhabitants of the same colony cannot, in their private opinions, conform to the public exercise of religion, according to the liturgy, forms and ceremonies of the Church of England, or take or subscribe the oaths and articles made and established in that behalf; and for that the same, by reason of the remote distances of those places, will (as we hope) be no breach of the unity and uniformity established in this nation: Have therefore thought fit, and do hereby publish, grant, ordain and declare, That our royal will and pleasure is, that no person within the said Colony, at any time hereafter, shall be any wise molested, punished, disquieted, or called in question, for any differences in opinion in matters of religion, and do not actually disturb the civil peace of our said Colony; but that all and every person and persons may, from time to time, and at all times hereafter, freely and fully have and enjoy his and their own judgments and consciences, in matters of religious concernments, throughout the tract of land hereafter mentioned, they behaving themselves peaceably and quietly, and not using this liberty to licentiousness and profaneness, nor to the civil injury or outward disturbance of others, any law, statute, or clause therein contained, or to be contained, usage or custom of this realm, to the contrary hereof, in any wise, notwithstanding. And that they may be in the better capacity to defend themselves, in their just rights and liberties, against all the enemies of the Christian faith, and others, in all respects, we have further thought fit, and at the humble petition of the persons aforesaid are graciously pleased to declare, That they shall have and enjoy the benefit of our late act of indemnity and free pardon, as the rest of our subjects in other our dominions and territories have; and to create and make them a body politic or corporate, with the powers and privileges hereinafter mentioned. And accordingly our will and pleasure is, and of our especial grace, certain knowledge, and mere motion, we have ordained, constituted and declared, and by these presents, for us, our heirs and successors, do ordain, constitute and declare, That they, the said William Brenton, William Coddington, Nicholas Easton, Benedict Arnold, William Boulston, John Porter, Samuel Gorton, John Smith, John Weeks, Roger Williams, Thomas Olney, Gregory Dexter, John Coggeshall, Joseph Clarke, Randall Holden, John Greene, John Roome, William Dyre, Samuel Wildbore, Richard Tew, William Field, Thomas Harris, James Barker, —— Rainsborrow, —— Williams, and John Nickson, and all such others as now are, or hereafter shall be, admitted and made free of the company and society of our Colony of Providence Plantations, in the Narragansett Bay, in New England, shall be from time to time, and forever hereafter, a body corporate and politic, in fact and name, by the name of the Governor and Company of the English Colony of Rhode Island and Providence Plantations, in New England, in America; and that, by the same name, they and their successors shall and may have perpetual succession, and shall and may be persons able and capable, in the law, to sue and be sued, to plead and be impleaded, to answer, and be answered unto, to defend and to be defended, in all and singular suits, causes, quarrels, matters, actions, and things, of what kind or nature soever; and also to have, take, possess, acquire, and purchase lands, tenements or hereditaments, or any goods or chattels, and the same to lease, grant, demise, aliene, bargain, sell and dispose of, at their own will and pleasure, as other our liege people of this our realm of England, or any corporation or body politic, within the same, may lawfully do. And further, that they the said Governor and Company, and their successors, shall and may, forever hereafter, have a common seal, to serve and use for all matters, causes, things and affairs, whatsoever, of them, and their successors; and the same seal to alter, change, break, and make new, from time to time, at their will and pleasure, as they shall think fit. And further, we will and ordain, and by these presents, for us, our heirs, and successors, do declare and appoint that, for the better ordering and managing of the affairs and business of the said Company, and their successors, there shall be one Governor, one Deputy-Governor and ten Assistants, to be from time to time, constituted, elected and chosen, out of the freemen of the said Company, for the time being, in such manner and form as is hereafter in these presents expressed, which said officers shall apply themselves to take care for the best disposing and ordering of the general business and affairs of and concerning the lands, and hereditaments hereinafter mentioned to be granted, and the plantation thereof, and the government of the people there. And, for the better execution of our royal pleasure herein, we do, for us, our heirs and successors, assign, name, constitute, and appoint the aforesaid Benedict Arnold to be the first and present Governor of the said Company, and the said William Brenton to be the Deputy-Governor, and the said William Boulston, John Porter, Roger Williams, Thomas Olney, John Smith, John Greene, John Coggeshall, James Barker, William Field, and Joseph Clarke, to be the ten present Assistants of the said Company, to continue in the said several offices, respectively, until the first Wednesday which shall be in the month of May now next coming. And further, we will, and by these presents, for us, our heirs and successors, do ordain and grant that the Governor of the said Company, for the time being, or, in his absence, by occasion of sickness, or otherwise, by his leave and permission, the Deputy-Governor, for the time being, shall and may, from time to time, upon all occasions, give order for the assembling of the said Company, and calling them together, to consult and advise of the business and affairs of the said Company. And that forever hereafter, twice in every year, that is to say, on every first Wednesday in the month of May, and on every last Wednesday in October, or oftener, in case it shall be requisite, the Assistants and such of the freemen of the said Company, not exceeding six persons for Newport, four persons for each of the respective towns of Providence, Portsmouth, and Warwick, and two persons for each other place, town or city, who shall be, from time to time, thereunto elected or deputed by the major part of the freemen of the respective towns or places for which they shall be so elected or deputed, shall have a general meeting or assembly, then and there to consult, advise and determine, in and about the affairs and business of the said Company and Plantations. And, further, we do, of our especial grace, certain knowledge, and mere motion, give and grant unto the said Governor and Company of the English Colony of Rhode Island and Providence Plantations, in New England, in America, and their successors, that the Governor, or, in his absence, or, by his permission, the Deputy-Governor, of the said Company, for the time being, the Assistants, and such of the freemen of the said Company as shall be so as aforesaid elected or deputed, or so many of them as shall be present at such meeting or assembly, as aforesaid, shall be called the General Assembly; and that they, or the greatest part of them present, whereof the Governor or Deputy-Governor, and six of the Assistants, at least to be seven, shall have, and have hereby given and granted unto them, full power and authority, from time to time, and at all times hereafter, to appoint, alter and change such days, times and places of meeting and General Assembly, as they shall think fit; and to choose, nominate and appoint, such and so many other persons as they shall think fit, and shall be willing to accept the same, to be free of the said Company and body politic, and them into the same to admit; and to elect and constitute such offices and officers, and to grant such needful commissions, as they shall think fit and requisite, for the ordering, managing, and dispatching of the affairs of the said Governor and Company, and their successors; and from time to time, to make, ordain, constitute or repeal, such laws, statutes, orders and ordinances, forms and ceremonies of government and magistracy, as to them shall seem meet, for the good and welfare of the said Company, and for the government and ordering of the lands and hereditaments, hereinafter mentioned to be granted, and of the people that do, or at any time hereafter shall, inhabit or be within the same; so as such laws, ordinances and constitutions, so made, be not contrary and repugnant unto, but as near as may be, agreeable to the laws of this our realm of England, considering the nature and constitution of the place and people there; and also to appoint, order and direct, erect and settle, such places and courts of jurisdiction, for the hearing and determining of all actions, cases, matters and things, happening within the said Colony and Plantation, and which shall be in dispute, and depending there, as they shall think fit; and also to distinguish and set forth the several names and titles, duties, powers and limits, of each court, office and officer, superior and inferior; and also to contrive and appoint such forms of oaths and attestations, not repugnant, but as near as may be agreeable, as aforesaid, to the laws and statutes of this our realm, as are convenient and requisite, with respect to the due administration of justice, and due execution and discharge of all offices and places of trust by the persons that shall be therein concerned; and also to regulate and order the way and manner of all elections to offices and places of trust, and to prescribe, limit and distinguish the numbers and bounds of all places, towns or cities, within the limits and bounds hereinafter mentioned, and not herein particularly named, who have, or shall have, the power of electing and sending of freemen to the said General Assembly; and also to order, direct and authorize the imposing of lawful and reasonable fines, mulcts, imprisonments, and executing other punishments, pecuniary and corporal, upon offenders and delinquents, according to the course of other corporations within this our kingdom of England; and again to alter, revoke, annul or pardon, under their common seal, or otherwise, such fines, mulcts, imprisonments, sentences, judgments and condemnations, as shall be thought fit; and to direct, rule, order and dispose of, all other matters and things, and particularly that which relates to the making of purchases of the native Indians, as to them shall seem meet; whereby our said people and inhabitants in the said Plantations, may be so religiously, peaceably and civilly governed, as that by their good life and orderly conversation, they may win and invite the native Indians of the country to the knowledge and obedience of the only true God and Saviour of mankind; willing, commanding and requiring, and by these presents, for us, our heirs and successors, ordaining and appointing, that all such laws, statutes, orders and ordinances, instructions, impositions and directions, as shall be so made by the Governor, Deputy-Governor, Assistants and freemen, or such number of them as aforesaid, and published in writing, under their common seal, shall be carefully and duly observed, kept, performed and put in execution, according to the true intent and meaning of the same. And these our letters patent, or the duplicate or exemplification thereof, shall be to all and every such officer, superior or inferior, from time to time, for the putting of the same orders, laws, statutes, ordinances, instructions and directions in due execution, against us, our heirs and successors, a sufficient warrant and discharge. And further, our will and pleasure is, and we do hereby, for us, our heirs and successors, establish and ordain, that yearly, once in the year, forever hereafter, namely, the aforesaid Wednesday in May, and at the town of Newport, or elsewhere, if urgent occasion do require, the Governor, Deputy-Governor and Assistants of the said Company, and other officers of the said Company, or such of them as the General Assembly shall think fit, shall be, in the said General Court or Assembly to be held from that day or time, newly chosen for the year ensuing, by such greater part of the said Company, for the time being, as shall be then and there present; and if it shall happen that the present Governor, Deputy-Governor and Assistants, by these presents appointed, or any such as shall hereafter be newly chosen into their rooms, or any of them, or any other the officers of the said Company, shall die or be removed from his or their several offices or places, before the said general day of election, (whom we do hereby declare, for any misdemeanor or default, to be removable by the Governor, Assistants and Company, or such greater part of them, in any of the said public courts, to be assembled as aforesaid,) that then, and in every such case, it shall and may be lawful to and for the said Governor, Deputy-Governor, Assistants and Company aforesaid, or such greater part of them, so to be assembled as is aforesaid, in any their assemblies, to proceed to a new election of one or more of their Company, in the room or place, rooms or places, of such officer or officers, so dying or removed, according to their discretions ; and immediately upon and after such election or elections made of such Governor, Deputy-Governor, Assistant or Assistants, or any other officer of the said Company, in manner and form aforesaid, the authority, office and power, before given to the former Governor, Deputy-Governor, and other officer and officers, so removed, in whose stead and place new shall be chosen, shall, as to him and them, and every of them, respectively, cease and determine : *Provided always*, and our will and pleasure is, that as well such as are by these presents appointed to be the present Governor, Deputy-Governor and Assistants of the said Company, as those that shall succeed them, and all other officers to be appointed and chosen as aforesaid, shall, before the undertaking the execution of the said offices and places respectively, give their solemn engagement, by oath, or otherwise, for the due and faithful performance of their duties in their several offices and places, before such person or persons as are by these presents hereafter appointed to take and receive the same, that is to say : the said Benedict Arnold, who is hereinbefore nominated and appointed the present Governor of the said Company, shall give the aforesaid engagement before William Brenton, or any two of the said Assistants of the said Company ; unto whom we do by these presents give full power and authority to require and receive the same; and the said William Brenton, who is hereby before nominated and appointed the present Deputy-Governor of the said Company, shall give the aforesaid engagement before the said Benedict Arnold, or any two of the Assistants of the said Company; unto whom we do by these presents give full power and authority to require and receive the same; and the said William Boulston, John Porter, Roger Williams, Thomas Olney, John Smith, John Greene, John Coggeshall, James Barker, William Field, and Joseph Clarke who are herein before nominated and appointed the present Assistants of the said Company, shall give the said engagement to their offices and places respectively belonging, before the said Benedict Arnold and William Brenton, or one of them; to whom respectively we do hereby give full power and authority to require, administer or receive the same: and further, our will and pleasure is, that all and every other future Governor or Deputy-Governor, to be elected and chosen by virtue of these presents, shall give the said engagement before two or more of the said Assistants of the said Company for the time being; unto whom we do by these presents give full power and authority to require, administer or receive the same; and the said Assistants, and every of them, and all and every other officer or officers to be hereafter elected and chosen by virtue of these presents, from time to time, shall give the like engagements, to their offices and places respectively belonging, before the Governor or Deputy-Governor for the time being: unto which said Governor, or Deputy-Governor, we do by these presents give full power and authority to require, administer or receive the same accordingly. And we do likewise, for us, our heirs and successors, give and grant unto the said Governor and Company, and their successors, by these presents, that, for the more peaceable and orderly government of the said Plantations, it shall and may be lawful for the Governor, Deputy-Governor, Assistants and all other officers and ministers of the said Company, in the administration of justice, and exercise of government, in the said Plantations, to use, exercise, and put in execution, such methods, rules, orders and directions, not being contrary or repugnant to the laws and statutes of this our realm, as have been heretofore given, used and accustomed, in such cases respectively, to be put in practice, until at the next or some other General Assembly, special provision shall be made and ordained in the cases aforesaid. And we do further, for us, our heirs and successors, give and grant unto the said Governor and Company, and their successors, by these presents, that it shall and may be lawful to and for the said Governor, or, in his absence, the Deputy-Governor, and major part of the said Assistants, for the time being, at any time when the said General Assembly is not sitting, to nominate, appoint and constitute, such and so many commanders, governors and military officers, as to them shall seem requisite, for the leading, conducting and training up the inhabitants of the said Plantations in martial affairs, and for the defence and safeguard of the said Plantations: and that it shall and may be lawful to and for all and every such commander, governor and military officer, that shall be so as aforesaid, or by the Governor, or in his absence, the Deputy-Governor, and six of the said Assistants, and major part of the freemen of the said Company present at any General Assemblies, nominated, appointed and constituted, according to the tenor of his and their respective commissions and directions to assemble, exercise in arms, martial array, and put in warlike posture, the inhabitants of the said Colony, for their special defence and safety; and to lead and conduct the said inhabitants, and to encounter, expulse, expel and resist, by force of arms, as well by sea as by land, and also to kill, slay and destroy, by all fitting ways, enterprises and means, whatsoever, all and every such person or persons as shall, at any time hereafter, attempt or enterprise the destruction, invasion, detriment, or annoyance of the said inhabitants or Plantations; and to use and exercise the law martial in such cases only as occasion shall necessarily require; and to take or surprise, by all ways and means whatsoever, all and every such person and persons, with their ship or ships, armor, ammunition or other goods of such persons, as shall, in hostile manner, invade or attempt the defeating of the said Plantation, or the hurt of the said Company and inhabitants; and upon just causes, to invade and destroy the native Indians, or other enemies of the said Colony. Nevertheless, our will and pleasure is, and we do hereby declare to the rest of our Colonies in New England, that it shall not be lawful for this our said Colony of Rhode Island and Providence Plantations, in America, in New England, to invade the natives inhabiting within the bounds and limits of their said Colonies, without the knowledge and consent of the said other Colonies. And it is hereby declared, that it shall not be lawful to or for the rest of the Colonies to invade or molest the native Indians or any other inhabitants inhabiting within the bounds and limits hereafter mentioned, (they having subjected themselves unto us, and being by us taken into our special protection,) without the knowledge and consent of the Governor and Company of our Colony of Rhode Island and Providence Plantations. Also our will and pleasure is, and we do hereby declare unto all Christian Kings, Princes and States, that if any person, which shall hereafter be of the said Company or Plantations or any other, by appointment of the said Governor and Company for the time being shall at any time or times hereafter, rob or spoil, by sea or land, or do any hurt or unlawful hostility to any of the subjects of us, our heirs or successors, or any of the subjects of any Prince or State, being then in league with us, our heirs or successors, upon complaint of such injury done to any such Prince or State, or their subjects, we, our heirs and successors, will make open proclamation within any parts of our realm of England, fit for that purpose, that the person or persons committing any such robbery or spoil, shall, within the time limited by such proclamation, make full restitution, or satisfaction of all such injuries, done or committed, so as the said Prince, or others so complaining, may be fully satisfied and contented; and if the said person or persons who shall commit any such robbery or spoil shall not make satisfaction, accordingly, within such time, so to be limited, that then we, our heirs and successors, will put such person or persons out of our allegiance and protection; and that then it shall and may be lawful and free for all Princes or others to prosecute with hostility, such offenders, and every of them, their and every of their procurers, aiders, abettors, and counsellors, in that behalf: *Provided also*, and our express will and pleasure is, and we do, by these presents, for us, our heirs and successors, ordain and appoint that these presents, shall not, in any manner, hinder any of our loving subjects, whatsoever, from using and exercising the trade of fishing upon the coast of New England, in America; but that they, and every or any of them, shall have full and free power and liberty to continue and use the trade of fishing upon the said coast, in any of the seas thereunto adjoining, or any arms of the seas, or salt water, rivers and creeks, where they have been accustomed to fish: and to build and to set upon the waste land belonging to the said Colony and Plantations, such wharves, stages and work-houses as shall be necessary for the salting, drying and keeping of their fish, to be taken or gotten upon that coast. And further, for the encouragement of the inhabitants of our said Colony of Providence Plantations to set upon the business of taking whales, it shall be lawful for them, or any of them having struck whale, dubertus, or other great fish, it or them, to pursue unto and available in all things in the law, to all intents, contents, constructions and purposes whatsoever, according to our true intent and meaning hereinbefore declared; and shall be construed, reputed and adjudged in all cases most favorably on the behalf, and for the best benefit and behoof of the said Governor and Company, and their successors; although express mention of the true yearly value or certainty of the premises, or any of them, or of any other gifts or grants, by us, or by any of our progenitors or predecessors, heretofore made to the said Governor of the Company of the English Colony of Rhode Island and Providence Plantations, in the Narragansett Bay, New England, in America, in these presents is not made, or any statue, act, ordinance, provision, proclamation or restriction, heretofore had, made, enacted, ordained or provided, or any other matter, cause or thing whatsoever, to the contrary thereof in any wise notwithstanding. In witness, whereof, we have caused these our letters to be made patent. Witness ourself, at Westminister, the eighth day of July, in the fifteenth year of our reign.

By the King:

HOWARD.

CONSTITUTION

OF THE

State of Rhode Island,

AND

Providence Plantations.

ARTICLE I.—*Declaration of Rights.*

SECTION 1. Right of the people to make and alter their Constitution.
SEC. 2 Object of government—How laws should be made and burdens distributed.
SEC. 3. Religious freedom secured.
SEC. 4. Slavery prohibited.
SEC. 5. Laws should provide remedies—Justice shall be free, complete, prompt.
SEC. 6. Rights of search and seizure regulated.
SEC. 7. Provisions concerning criminal proceedings.
SEC. 8. Bail, fines and punishments.
SEC. 9. Bail and *habeas corpus.*
SEC. 10. Rights of the accused in criminal proceedings.
SEC. 11. Debtors entitled to relief.
SEC. 12. No *ex post facto* law, &c., to be passed.
SEC. 13. No man to criminate himself.
SEC. 14. Presumption of innocence—Accused to be secured without severity.
SEC. 15. Trial by jury.
SEC. 16. Private property secured.
SEC. 17. Rights of fishery.
SEC. 18. Military subordinate—Martial law.
SEC. 19. Of quartering soldiers.
SEC. 20. Liberty of the press secured—Truth as a defence to libel.
SEC. 21. Right of the people to assemble, and to petition.
SEC. 22. Right to bear arms.
SEC. 23. Rule of construction.

ARTICLE II.—*Electors.*

SEC. 1. Of electors owning real estate.
SEC. 2. Of electors qualified to vote on adoption of Constitution—Registered voters—Qualified by dollar tax—Military duty—Who to vote for City Council in Providence, to impose a tax, &c.

Sec. 3. Of assessment and payment of registry tax.
Sec. 4. Who shall not gain residence or be permitted to vote.
Sec. 5. Residents on lands ceded, &c., not electors.
Sec. 6. Power of General Assembly over elections.

ARTICLE III.—*Powers Distributed.*

Three Departments.

ARTICLE IV.—*Legislative Powers.*

Section 1. Constitution supreme law.
Sec. 2. Two houses—General Assembly—Style of laws.
Sec. 3. Sessions of General Assembly.
Sec. 4. Members not to take fees, &c.
Sec. 5. Members exempt from arrest, &c.
Sec. 6. Powers of each house—Organization.
Sec. 7. Powers to make rules, &c.
Sec. 8. Of the journal and yeas and nays.
Sec. 9. Of adjournments.
Sec. 10. Of powers not prohibited.
Sec. 11. Pay of members.
Sec. 12. Lotteries prohibited.
Sec. 13. Debts not to be incurred.
Sec. 14. Private or local appropriations.
Sec. 15. Of valuations of property and assessments.
Sec. 16. Officers may be continued until successors are qualified.
Sec. 17. Bills to create corporations to be continued, except, &c.
Sec. 18. Of election of senators to Congress.

ARTICLE V.—*House of Representatives.*

Section 1. House, how constituted—Ratio of representation.
Sec. 2. May elect its officers, &c.

ARTICLE VI.—*Senate.*

Section 1. How constituted.
Sec. 2. Governor to preside—when to vote in grand committee.
Sec. 3. May elect presiding officer in case of vacancy, &c.
Sec. 4. Secretary and other officers.

ARTICLE VII.—*Executive.*

Section 1. Of the governor and lieutenant-governor—How elected.
Sec. 2. Duty of governor.
Sec. 3. He shall command military and naval forces, except, &c.
Sec. 4. He may grant reprieves, &c.
Sec. 5. He may fill vacancies.
Sec. 6. He may adjourn assembly, in case, &c.
Sec. 7. He may convene assembly, when, &c.
Sec. 8. Commissions, how signed, &c.
Sec. 9. Lieutenant-governor, when to act as governor.
Sec. 10. Vacancies, how filled.
Sec. 11. Compensation of governor, &c.
Sec. 12. Duties of general officers.

ARTICLE VIII.—*Elections.*

SECTION. 1. Governor and general officers, when elected.
SEC. 2. General officers and members of assembly, how voted for.
SEC. 3. Same subject—How votes to be sealed up, transmitted and counted.
SEC. 4. List of voters to be kept. [Obsolete.]
SEC. 5. Ballots for members of Assembly, how counted—Adjournment of elections, when.
SEC. 6.—Of voting in the City of Providence.
SEC. 7.—If governor or lieutenant-governor not elected by the people grand committee to elect, how.
SEC. 8. In case general officers not elected by the people, how vacancies shall be filled.
SEC. 9. Vacancies in Assembly, how filled.
SEC. 10. Majority required to elect.

ARTICLE IX.—*Qualifications for Office.*

SECTION 1. Qualified electors only eligible.
SEC. 2. Conviction of bribery a disqualification.
SEC. 3. Oath of general officers.
SEC. 4. Officers, how engaged.
SEC. 5. How oath to be administered to governor, &c.
SEC. 6. Holding office under United States, or other governments, a disqualification for certain offices,—except, &c.

ARTICLE X.—*Judiciary.*

SECTION 1. One supreme court—Inferior courts how established.
SEC. 2. Jurisdiction of courts—Chancery powers.
SEC. 3. Judges of supreme court to instruct jury—To give opinions, &c.
SEC. 4. Of election and tenure of office of judges of supreme court.
SEC. 5.—Vacancies, how filled.
SEC. 6. Compensation of judges.
SEC. 7. Justices of the peace and wardens, how elected—Their jurisdiction.

ARTICLE XI.—*Impeachments.*

SECTION 1. Impeachments, how ordered.
SEC. 2. Impeachments, how tried.
SEC. 3. What officers liable to impeachment—Effect of conviction.

ARTICLE XII.—*Education.*

SECTION 1. Duty of General Assembly to promote schools, &c.
SEC. 2. The permanent school fund.
SEC. 3. Donations for support of schools.
SEC. 4. Powers of General Assembly under this article.

ARTICLE XIII.—*Amendments.*

SECTION 1. Amendments, how proposed,—how voted upon,—how adopted.

ARTICLE XIV.—*Adoption of the Constitution.*

SECTION 1. Constitution, when to go into operation—Its effect on existing laws. charters, &c.
SEC. 2. Former debts, &c., adopted.
SEC. 3. Jurisdiction of supreme court.
SEC. 4. Exemptions of New Shoreham and Jamestown from military duty, continued.

AMENDMENTS TO THE CONSTITUTION.

ARTICLE I.

Lists of voters for general officers no longer required to be kept, &c.

ARTICLE II.

The pardoning power, how exercised.

ARTICLE III.

Sessions of the General Assembly.

ARTICLE IV.

Electors absent from the state in the military service of the United States, allowed to vote.

WE, the people of the State of Rhode Island and Providence Plantations, grateful to Almighty God for the civil and religious liberty which He hath so long permitted us to enjoy, and looking to Him for a blessing upon our endeavors to secure and to transmit the same, unimpaired, to succeeding generations, do ordain and establish this Constitution of Government.

ARTICLE I.

DECLARATION OF CERTAIN CONSTITUTIONAL RIGHTS AND PRINCIPLES.

In order effectually to secure the religious and political freedom established by our venerated ancestors, and to preserve the same for our posterity, we do declare that the essential and unquestionable rights and principles hereinafter mentioned, shall be established, maintained and preserved, and shall be of paramount obligation in all legislative, judicial and executive proceedings.

SECTION 1. In the words of the Father of his Country, we declare, that, "the basis of our political systems is the right of the people to make and alter their constitutions of government: but that the constitution which at any time exists, till changed by an explicit and authentic act of the whole people, is sacredly obligatory upon all."

SEC. 2. All free governments are instituted for the protection, safety and happiness of the people. All laws, therefore, should be made for the good of the whole; and the burdens of the state ought to be fairly distributed among its citizens.

APPENDIX. 305

Sec. 3. Whereas, Almighty God hath created the mind free; and all attempts to influence it by temporal punishments, or burthens, or by civil incapacitations, tend to beget habits of hypocrisy and meanness; and whereas, a principal object of our venerable ancestors in their migration to this country and their settlement of this state, was, as they expressed it, to hold forth a lively experiment, that a flourishing civil state may stand and be best maintained with full liberty in religious concernments; we therefore declare that no man shall be compelled to frequent or to support any religious worship, place or ministry whatever, except in fulfillment of his own voluntary contract; nor enforced, restrained, molested or burthened in his body or goods; nor disqualified from holding any office; nor otherwise suffer on account of his religious belief; and that every man shall be free to worship God according to the dictates of his own conscience, and to profess and by argument to maintain his opinion in matters of religion; and that the same shall in no wise diminish, enlarge, or affect his civil capacity.

Sec. 4. Slavery shall not be permitted in this state.

Sec. 5. Every person within this state ought to find a certain remedy, by having recourse to the laws, for all injuries or wrongs which he may receive in his person, property or character. He ought to obtain right and justice freely, and without purchase, completely, and without denial; promptly and without delay; conformably to the laws.

Sec. 6. The right of the people to be secure in their persons, papers and possessions, against unreasonable searches and seizures, shall not be violated; and no warrants shall issue, but on complaint in writing, upon probable cause, supported by oath or affirmation, and describing as nearly as may be the place to be searched, and the persons or things to be seized.

Sec. 7. No person shall be held to answer for a capital or other infamous crime, unless on presentment or indictment by a grand jury, except in cases of impeachment, or of such offences as are cognizable by a justice of the peace; or in cases arising in the land or naval forces, or in the militia when in actual service in time of war or public danger. No person shall, after an acquittal, be tried for the same offence.

Sec. 8. Excessive bail shall not be required, nor excessive fines imposed, nor cruel punishments inflicted; and all punishments ought to be proportioned to the offence.

Sec. 9. All persons imprisoned ought to be bailed by sufficient surety, unless for offences punishable by death or by imprisonment for life, when the proof of guilt is evident, or the presumption great. The privilege of the writ of *habeas corpus* shall not be suspended, unless when in cases of rebellion or invasion the public service shall require it, nor ever without the authority of the General Assembly.

Sec. 10. In all criminal prosecutions, the accused shall enjoy the right to a speedy and public trial, by an impartial jury; to be informed of the nature and cause of the accusation, to be confronted with the witnesses against him, to have compulsory process for obtaining them in his favor, to have the assistance of counsel in his defence, and shall be at liberty to speak for himself; nor shall he be deprived of life, liberty, or property, unless by the judgment of his peers, or the law of the land.

Sec. 11. The person of a debtor, when there is not strong presumption of fraud, ought not to be continued in prison, after he shall have delivered up his property for the benefit of his creditors, in such manner as shall be prescribed by law.

Sec. 12. No *ex post facto* law, or law impairing the obligation of contracts, shall be passed.

Sec. 13. No man in a court of common law shall be compelled to give evidence criminating himself.

Sec. 14. Every man being presumed innocent, until he is pronounced guilty by the law, no act of severity which is not necessary to secure an accused person shall be permitted.

Sec. 15. The right of trial by jury shall remain inviolate.

Sec. 16. Private property shall not be taken for public uses, without just compensation.

Sec. 17. The people shall continue to enjoy and freely exercise, all the rights of fishery, and the privileges of the shore, to which they have been heretofore entitled, under the charter and usages of this state. But no new right is intended to be granted, nor any existing right impaired by this declaration.

Sec. 18. The military shall be held in strict subordination to the civil authority, and the law martial shall be used and exercised in such cases only as occasion shall necessarily require.

Sec. 19. No soldier shall be quartered in any house, in time of peace, without the consent of the owner; nor in time of war, but in manner to be prescribed by law.

Sec. 20. The liberty of the press being essential to the security of freedom in a state, any person may publish his sentiments on any subject, being responsible for the abuse of that liberty; and in all trials for libel, both civil and criminal, the truth, unless published from malicious motives, shall be sufficient defence to the person charged.

Sec. 21. The citizens have a right, in a peaceable manner, to assemble for their common good, and to apply to those invested with the powers of government, for redress of grievances, or for other purposes, by petition, address, or remonstrance.

Sec. 22. The right of the people to keep and bear arms shall not be infringed.

Sec. 23. The enumeration of the aforegoing rights shall not be construed to impair or deny others retained by the people.

ARTICLE II.

OF THE QUALIFICATIONS OF ELECTORS.

Section 1. Every male citizen of the United States, of the age of twenty-one years, who has had his residence and home in this state for one year, and in the town or city in which he may claim a right to vote, six months next preceding the time of voting, and who is really and truly possessed in his own right of real estate in such town or city, of the value of one hundred and thirty-four dollars, over and above all incumbrances, or which shall rent for seven dollars per annum, over and above any rent reserved, or the interest of any incumbrances thereon, being an estate in fee simple, fee tail, for the life of any person, or an estate in reversion or remainder, which qualifies no other person to vote, the conveyance of which estate, if by deed, shall have been recorded at least ninety days, shall thereafter have a right to vote in the election of all civil officers, and on all questions in all legal town or ward meetings, so long as he continues so qualified. And if any person hereinbefore described shall own any such estate within this state out of the town or city in which he resides, he shall have a right to vote in the election of all general officers and members of the General Assembly, in the town or city in which he shall have had his residence and home for the term of six months next preceding the election, upon producing a certificate from the clerk of the town or city in which his estate lies, bearing date within ten days of the time of his voting, setting forth that such person has a sufficient estate therein to qualify him as a voter; and that the deed, if any, has been recorded ninety days.

SEC. 2. Every male native citizen of the United States, of the age of twenty-one years, who has had his residence and home in this state two years, and in the town or city in which he may offer to vote, six months next preceding the time of voting, whose name is registered pursuant to the act calling the convention to frame this Constitution, or shall be registered in the office of the clerk of such town or city at least seven days before the time he shall offer to vote and before the last day of December in the present year; and who has paid or shall pay a tax or taxes, assessed upon his estate within this state, and within a year of the time of voting, to the amount of one dollar, or who shall voluntarily pay, at least seven days before the time he shall offer to vote, and before said last day of December, to the clerk or treasurer of the town or city where he resides, the sum of one dollar, or such sum as, with his other taxes, shall amount to one dollar, for the support of public schools therein, and shall make proof of the same, by the certificate of the clerk, treasurer or collector of any town or city where such payment is made; or who, being so registered has been enrolled in any military company in this state, and done military service or duty therein, within the present year, pursuant to law, and shall, (until other proof is required by law,) prove by the certificate of the officer legally commanding the regiment, or chartered or legally authorized volunteer company, in which he may have served or done duty, that he has been equipped and done duty according to law, or by the certificate of the commissioners upon military claims that he has performed military service shall have a right to vote in the election of all civil officers, and on all questions in all legally organized town or ward meetings, until the end of the first year after the adoption of this Constitution, or until the end of the year eighteen hundred and forty-three.

From and after that time, every such citizen, who has had the residence herein required, and whose name shall be registered in the town where he resides, on or before the last day of December, in the year next preceding the time of his voting, and who shall show by legal proof, that he has for and within the year next preceding the time he shall offer to vote, paid a tax or taxes assessed against him in any town or city in this state, to the amount of one dollar; or that he has been enrolled in a military company in this state, been equipped and done duty therein, according to law, and at least for one day during such year, shall have a right to vote in the election of all civil officers, and on all questions in all legally organized town or ward meetings: Provided, that no person shall at any time be allowed to vote in the election of the City Council of the City of Providence, or upon any proposition to impose a tax, or for the expenditure of money in any town or city, unless he shall, within the year next preceding have paid a tax assessed upon his property therein, valued at least at one hundred and thirty-four dollars.

SEC. 3. The assessors of each town or city shall annually assess upon every person whose name shall be registered, a tax of one dollar, or such sum as with his other taxes shall amount to one dollar, which registry tax shall be paid into the treasury of such town or city, and be applied to the support of public schools therein; but no compulsory process shall issue for the collection of any registry tax: Provided that the registry tax of every person who has performed military duty according to the provisions of the preceding section, shall be remitted for the year he shall perform such duty; and the registry tax assessed upon any mariner, for any year while he is at sea, shall, upon his application, be remitted; and no person shall be allowed to vote whose

ARTICLE V.

OF THE HOUSE OF REPRESENTATIVES.

SECTION 1. The house of representatives shall never exceed seventy-two members, and shall be constituted on the basis of population, always allowing one representative for a fraction exceeding half the ratio; but each town or city shall always be entitled to at least one member; and no town or city shall have more than one-sixth of the whole number of members to which the house is hereby limited. The present ratio shall be one representative to every fifteen hundred and thirty inhabitants, and the General Assembly may, after any new census taken by the authority of the United States, or of this state, reapportion the representation by altering the ratio; but no town or city shall be divided into districts for the choice of representatives.

SEC. 2. The house of representatives shall have authority to elect its speaker, clerks and other officers. The senior member from the town of Newport, if any be present, shall preside in the organization of the house.

ARTICLE VI.

OF THE SENATE.

SECTION 1. The senate shall consist of the lieutenant-governor and of one senator from each town or city in the state.

SEC. 2. The governor, and, in his absence the lieutenant-governor, shall preside in the senate and in grand committee. The presiding officer of the senate and grand committee shall have a right to vote in case of equal division, but not otherwise.

SEC. 3. If, by reason of death, resignation, absence or other cause, there be no governor or lieutenant-governor present, to preside in the senate, the senate shall elect one of their own members to preside during such absence or vacancy; and until such election is made by the senate the secretary of state shall preside.

SEC. 4. The secretary of state shall, by virtue of his office, be secretary of the senate, unless otherwise provided by law; and the senate may elect such other officers as they may deem necessary.

ARTICLE VII.

OF THE EXECUTIVE POWER.

SECTION 1. The chief executive power of this state shall be vested in a governor, who, together with a lieutenant-governor, shall be annually elected by the people.

SEC. 2. The governor shall take care that the laws be faithfully executed.

SEC. 3. He shall be captain-general and commander-in-chief of the military and naval forces of this state, except when they shall be called into the service of the United States.

SEC. 4. He shall have power to grant reprieves after conviction, in all cases except those of impeachment, until the the end of the next session of the General Assembly.

SEC. 5. He may fill vacancies in office not otherwise provided for by this constitution, or by law, until the same shall be filled by the General Assembly or by the people.

SEC. 6. In case of disagreement between the two houses of the General Assembly, respecting the time or place of adjournment certified to him by either, he may adjourn them to such time and place as he shall think proper: provided that the time of adjournment shall not be extended beyond the day of the next stated session.

SEC. 7. He may, on extraordinary occasions, convene the General Assembly at any town or city in this state, at any time not provided for by law; and in case of danger from the prevalence of epidemic or contagious disease, in the place in which the General Assembly are by law to meet, or to which they may have been adjourned, or for other urgent reasons, he may, by proclamation, convene said Assembly at any other place within this state.

SEC. 8. All commissions shall be in the name and by the authority of the State of Rhode Island and Providence Plantations; shall be sealed with the state seal, signed by the governor, and attested by the secretary.

SEC. 9. In case of vacancy in the office of governor, or of his inability to serve, impeachment, or absence from the state, the lieutenant-governor shall fill the office of governor, and exercise the powers and authority appertaining thereto, until a governor is qualified to act, or until the office is filled at the next annual election.

SEC. 10. If the offices of governor and lieutenant-governor be both vacant by reason of death, resignation, impeachment, absence, or otherwise, the person entitled to preside over the senate for the time being shall in like manner fill the office of governor during the absence or vacancy.

SEC. 11. The compensation of the governor and lieutenant-governor shall be established by law and shall not be diminished during the term for which they are elected.

SEC. 12. The duties and powers of the secretary, attorney-general, and general treasurer, shall be the same under this constitution as are now established, or as from time to time may be prescribed by law.

ARTICLE VIII.

OF ELECTIONS.

SECTION 1. The governor, lieutenant-governor, senators, representatives, secretary of state, attorney-general, and general treasurer, shall be elected at the town, city, or ward meetings, to be holden on the first Wednesday of April, annually; and shall severally hold their offices for one year, from the first Tuesday of May next succeeding, and until others are legally chosen, and duly qualified to fill their places. If elected or qualified after the said first Tuesday of May, they shall hold their offices for the remainder of the political year, and until their successors are qualified to act.

SEC. 2. The voting for governor, lieutenant-governor, secretary of state, attorney-general, general treasurer, and representatives to Congress shall be by ballot; senators and representatives to the General Assembly, and town or city officers shall be chosen by ballot, on demand of any seven persons entitled to vote for the same; and in all cases where an election is made by ballot or paper vote, the manner of balloting shall be the same as is now required in voting for general officers, until otherwise prescribed by law.

SEC. 3. The names of the persons voted for as governor, lieutenant-governor, secretary of state, attorney-general, and general treasurer, shall be placed upon one ticket; and all votes for these officers shall, in open town or ward meetings, be sealed up by the moderators and town clerks and by the wardens and ward clerks, who shall certify the same, and deliver or send them to the secretary of state; whose duty it shall be securely to keep and deliver the same to the grand committee, after the organization of the two houses at the annual May session; and it shall be the duty of the two houses at said session, after their organization, upon the request of either house, to join in grand committee, for the purpose of counting and declaring said votes, and of electing other officers.

Sec. 4. The town and ward clerks shall also keep a correct list or register of all persons voting for general officers, and shall transmit a copy thereof to the General Assembly, on or before the first day of said May session.

Sec. 5. The ballots for senators and representatives in the several towns shall, in each case, after the polls are declared to be closed, be counted by the moderator, who shall announce the result, and the clerk shall give certificates to the persons elected. If, in any case, there be no election, the polls may be reopened, and the like proceedings shall be had until an election shall take place: Provided, however, that an adjournment or adjournments of the election may be made to a time not exceeding seven days from the first meeting.

Sec. 6. In the city of Providence, the polls for senator and representatives shall be kept open during the whole time of voting for the day, and the votes in the several wards shall be sealed up at the close of the meeting by the wardens and ward clerks in open ward meeting, and afterwards delivered to the city clerk. The mayor and aldermen shall proceed to count said votes within two days from the day of election; and if no election of senator and representatives or if an election of only a portion of the representatives shall have taken place, the mayor and aldermen shall order a new election, to be held not more than ten days from the day of the first election, and so on until the election shall be completed. Certificates of election shall be furnished by the city clerk to the persons chosen.

Sec. 7. If no person shall have a majority of votes for governor, it shall be the duty of the grand committee to elect one by ballot from the two persons having the highest number of votes for the office, except when such a result is produced by rejecting the entire vote of any town, city or ward for informality or illegality, in which case a new election by the electors throughout the state shall be ordered; and in case no person shall have a majority of votes for lieutenant-governor, it shall be the duty of the grand committee to elect one by ballot from the two persons having the highest number of votes for the office.

Sec. 8. In case an election of the secretary of state, attorney-general, or general treasurer, should fail to be made by the electors at the annual election, the vacancy or vacancies shall be filled by the General Assembly in grand committee from the two candidates for such office having the greatest number of the votes of the electors. Or, in case of a vacancy in either of said offices, from other causes, between the sessions of the General Assembly, the governor shall appoint some person to fill the same, until a successor elected by the General Assembly is qualified to act; and in such case, and also in all other cases of vacancies, not otherwise provided for, the General Assembly may fill the same in any manner they may deem proper.

Sec. 9. Vacancies from any cause in the senate and house of representatives, may be filled by a new election.

Sec. 10. In all elections held by the people under this constitution, a majority of all the electors voting shall be necessary to the election of the persons voted for.

APPENDIX.

ARTICLE IX.

OF QUALIFICATIONS FOR OFFICE.

SECTION 1. No person shall be eligible to any civil office (except the office of school committee), unless he be a qualified elector for such office.

SEC. 2. Every person shall be disqualified from holding any office to which he may have been elected, if he be convicted of having offered, or procured any other person to offer, any bribe to secure his election, or the election of any other person.

SEC. 3. All general officers shall take the following engagement before they act in their respective offices, to wit: You . . . being by the free vote of the electors of this State of Rhode Island and Providence Plantations, elected unto the place of . . . . do solemnly swear, (or affirm,) to be true and faithful unto this state, and to support the constitution of this state and of the United States; that you will faithfully and impartially discharge all the duties of your aforesaid office to the best of your abilities, according to law: So help you God. Or, this affirmation you make and give upon the peril of the penalty of perjury.

SEC. 4. The members of the General Assembly, the judges of all the courts, and all other officers, both civil and military, shall be bound by oath or affirmation to support this constitution, and the constitution of the United States.

SEC. 5. The oath or affirmation shall be administered to the governor, lieutenant-governor, senators and representatives, by the secretary of state, or, in his absence, by the attorney-general. The secretary of state, attorney-general and general treasurer shall be engaged by the governor, or by a justice of the supreme court.

SEC. 6. No person holding any office under the government of the United States, or of any other state or country, shall act as a general officer, or as a member of the General Assembly, unless at the time of taking his engagement he shall have resigned his office under such government; and if any general officer, senator, representative, or judge, shall after his election and engagement, accept any appointment under any other government his office under this shall be immediately vacated; but this restriction shall not apply to any person appointed to take depositions or acknowledgment of deeds, or other legal instruments, by the authority of any other state or country.

ARTICLE X.

OF THE JUDICIAL POWER.

SECTION 1. The judicial power of this state shall be vested in one supreme court, and in such inferior courts as the General Assembly may, from time to time, ordain and establish.

SEC. 2. The several courts shall have such jurisdiction as may, from time to time, be prescribed by law. Chancery powers may be conferred on the supreme court, but on no other court to any greater extent than is now provided by law.

SEC. 3. The judges of the supreme court shall, in all trials, instruct the jury in the law. They shall also give their written opinion upon any question of law whenever requested by the governor, or by either house of the General Assembly.

SEC. 4. The judges of the supreme court shall be elected by the two houses in grand committee. Each judge shall hold his office until his place be declared vacant by a resolution of the General Assembly to that effect; which resolution shall be voted for by a majority of all the members elected to the house in which it may originate, and be concurred in by the same majority of the other house. Such resolutions shall not be entertained at any other than the annual session for the election of public officers; and in default of the passage thereof at said session, the judge shall hold his place as is herein provided. But a judge of any court shall be removed from office, if, upon impeachment, he shall be found guilty of any official misdemeanor.

SEC. 5. In case of vacancy by death, resignation, removal from the state or from office, refusal or inability to serve, of any judge of the supreme court, the office may be filled by the grand committee, until the next annual election, and the judge then elected shall hold his office as before provided. In cases of impeachment or temporary absence or inability, the governor may appoint a person to discharge the duties of the office during the vacancy caused thereby.

SEC. 6. The judges of the supreme court shall receive a compensation for their services, which shall not be diminished during their continuance in office.

SEC. 7. The towns of New Shoreham and Jamestown may continue to elect their wardens as heretofore. The other towns and the city of Providence may elect such number of justices of the peace, resident therein, as they may deem proper. The jurisdiction of said justices and wardens shall be regulated by law. The justices shall be commissioned by the governor.

ARTICLE XI.

OF IMPEACHMENTS.

SECTION 1. The house of representatives shall have the sole power of impeachment. A vote of two-thirds of all the members elected shall be required for an impeachment of the governor. Any officer impeached shall thereby be suspended from office until judgment in the case shall have been pronounced.

SEC. 2. All impeachments shall be tried by the senate; and, when sitting for that purpose, they shall be under oath or affirmation. No person shall be convicted, except by vote of two-thirds of the members elected. When the governor is impeached, the chief or presiding justice of the supreme court, for the time being, shall preside, with a casting vote in all preliminary questions.

SEC. 3. The governor and all other executive and judicial officers shall be liable to impeachment; but judgment in such cases shall not extend further than to removal from office. The person convicted shall, nevertheless, be liable to indictment, trial and punishment according to law.

ARTICLE XII.

OF EDUCATION.

SECTION 1. The diffusion of knowledge, as well as of virtue among the people, being essential to the preservation of their rights and liberties, it shall be the duty of the General Assembly to promote public schools, and to adopt all means which they may deem necessary and proper to secure to the people the advantages and opportunities of education.

SEC. 2. The money which now is, or which may hereafter be appropriated by law for the establishment of a permanent fund for the support of public schools shall be securely invested, and remain a perpetual fund for that purpose.

SEC. 3. All donations for the support of public schools, or for other purposes of education, which may be received by the General Assembly, shall be applied according to the terms prescribed by the donors.

SEC. 4. The General Assembly shall make all necessary provisions by law for carrying this article into effect. They shall not divert said money or fund from the aforesaid uses, nor borrow, appropriate, or use the same, or any part thereof, for any other purpose, under any pretence whatsoever.

ARTICLE XIII.

ON AMENDMENTS.

The General Assembly may propose amendments to this constitution by the votes of a majority of all the members elected to each house. Such propositions for amendment shall be published in the newspapers and printed copies of them shall be sent by the secretary of state, with the names of all the members who shall have voted thereon, with the yeas and nays, to all the town and city clerks in the state. The said propositions shall be, by said clerks, inserted in the warrants or notices by them issued, for warning the next annual town and ward meetings in April; and the clerks shall read said propositions to the electors when thus assembled, with the names of all the representatives and senators who shall have voted thereon, with the yeas and nays, before the election of senators and representatives shall be had. If a majority of all the members elected to each house, at said annual meeting, shall approve any proposition thus made, the same shall be published and submitted to the electors in the mode provided in the act of approval; and if then approved by three-fifths of the electors of the state present, and voting thereon in town and ward meetings, it shall become a part of the constitution of the state.

ARTICLE XIV.

ON THE ADOPTION OF THIS CONSTITUTION.

SECTION 1. This constitution, if adopted, shall go into operation on the first Tuesday of May, in the year one thousand eight hundred and forty-three. The first election of governor, lieutenant-governor, secretary of state, attorney-general and general treasurer, and of senators and representatives under said constitution, shall be had on the first Wednesday of April next preceding, by the electors qualified under said constitution. And the town and ward meetings therefor shall be warned and conducted as is now provided by law. All civil and military officers now elected, or who shall hereafter be elected, by the General Assembly, or other competent authority, before the said first Wednesday of April, shall hold their offices and may exercise their powers until the said first Tuesday of May, or until their successors shall be qualified to act. All statutes, public and private, not repugnant to this constitution, shall continue in force until they expire by their own limitation, or are repealed by the General Assembly. All charters, contracts, judgments, actions, and rights of action shall be as valid as if this constitution had not been made The present government shall exercise all the powers with which it is now clothed, until the said first Tuesday of May, one thousand eight hundred and forty-three, and until the government under this constitution is duly organized.

SEC. 2. All debts contracted and engagements entered into, before the adoption of this constitution, shall be as valid against the state as if this constitution had not been adopted.

SEC. 3. The supreme court, established by this constitution, shall have the same jurisdiction as the supreme judicial court at present established, and shall have jurisdiction of all causes which may be appealed to. or pending in the same; and shall be held at the same times and places, and in each county, as the present supreme judicial court, until otherwise prescribed by the General Assembly.

SEC. 4. The towns of New Shoreham and Jamestown shall continue to enjoy the exemptions from military duty which they now enjoy, until otherwise prescribed by law.

Done in convention, at East Greenwich, this fifth day of November, A. D. one thousand eight hundred and forty-two.

JAMES FENNER, *President.*
HENRY Y. CRANSTON, *Vice-Pres't.*

THOMAS A. JENCKES,
WALTER W. UPDIKE, } *Secretaries.*

ARTICLES OF AMENDMENT.

ADOPTED NOVEMBER, 1854.

ARTICLE I.

It shall not be necessary for the town or ward clerks to keep and transmit to the General Assembly a list or register of all persons voting for general officers; but the General Assembly shall have power to pass such laws on the subject as they may deem expedient.

ARTICLE II.

The governor, by and with the advice and consent of the senate, shall hereafter exclusively exercise the pardoning power, except in cases of impeachment, to the same extent as such power is now exercised by the General Assembly.

ARTICLE III.

There shall be one session of the General Assembly holden annually, commencing on the last Tuesday in May, at Newport, and an adjournment from the same shall be holden annually at Providence.

ADOPTED AUGUST, 1864.

ARTICLE IV.

Electors of this state who in time of war are absent from the state, in the actual military service of the United States, being otherwise qualified, shall have a right to vote in all elections in the state for electors of president and vice-president of the United States, representatives in Congress, and general officers of the state. The General Assembly shall have full power to provide by law for carrying this article into effect; and until such provision shall be made by law, every such absent elector on the day of such elections, may deliver a written or printed ballot, with the names of the persons voted for thereon, and his Christian and surname, and his voting residence in the state, written at length on the back thereof, to the officer commanding the regiment or company to which he belongs; and all such ballots, certified by such commanding officer to have been given by the elector whose name is written thereon, and returned by such commanding officer to the secretary of state within the time prescribed by law for counting the votes in such elections, shall be received and counted with the same effect as if given by such elector in open town, ward, or district meeting; and the clerk of each town or city, until otherwise provided by law, shall, within five days after any such election, transmit to the secretary of state a certified list of the names of all such electors on their respective voting lists.

[*Copy of the Dorr Constitution.*]

CONSTITUTION

OF THE

State of Rhode Island,

AND

Providence Plantations,

As finally adopted by the Convention of the People assembled at Providence, on the 18th day of November, 1841.

WE, the PEOPLE of the STATE of RHODE ISLAND and PROVIDENCE PLANTATIONS, grateful to Almighty God for His blessing vouchsafed to the "lively experiment" of Religious and Political Freedom here "held forth" by our venerated ancestors, and earnestly imploring the favor of His gracious Providence toward this our attempt to secure, upon a permanent foundation, the advantages of well ordered and rational Liberty, and to enlarge and transmit to our successors the inheritance that we have received, do ordain and establish the following CONSTITUTION of Government for this State:

ARTICLE I.

DECLARATIONS OF PRINCIPLES AND RIGHTS.

1. In the spirit of and in the words of ROGER WILLIAMS, the illustrious founder of this state, and of his venerated associates, WE DECLARE "that this government shall be a DEMOCRACY," or government of the PEOPLE, "by the major consent" of the same, "ONLY IN CIVIL THINGS." The will of the people shall be expressed by representatives freely chosen, and returning at fixed periods to their constituents. This state shall be and forever remain, as in the design of its founder, sacred to "SOUL LIBERTY," to the rights of conscience, to freedom of thought, of expression and of action, as hereinafter set forth and secured.

2. All men are created free and equal and are endowed by their Creator with certain natural, inherent and inalienable rights, among

ARTICLE II.

OF ELECTORS AND THE RIGHT OF SUFFRAGE.

1. Every white male citizen of the United States, of the age of twenty-one years, who has resided in this state for one year, and in any town, city or district of the same for six months next preceding the election at which he offers to vote, shall be an elector of all officers who are elected or may hereafter be made eligible by the people. But persons in the military, naval or marine service of the United States shall not be considered as having such established residence by being stationed in any garrison, barrack or military place in any town or city in this state.

2. Paupers and persons under guardianship, insane or lunatic are excluded from the electoral right; and the same shall be forfeited on conviction of bribery, forgery, perjury, theft, or other infamous crime; and shall not be restored unless by an act of the General Assembly.

3. No person who is excluded from voting for want of the qualification first named in section first of this article, shall be taxed or be liable to do military duty; provided that nothing in said first article shall be so construed as to exempt from taxation any property or persons now liable to be taxed.

4. No elector who is not possessed of and assessed for ratable property in his own right to the amount of one hundred and fifty dollars, or who shall have neglected or refused to pay any tax assessed upon him in any town, city or district for one year preceding the town, city, ward or district meeting at which he shall offer to vote, shall be entitled to vote on any question of taxation, or the expenditure of any public moneys in such town, city or district, until the same be paid.

5. In the city of Providence and other cities no person shall be eligible to the office of mayor, alderman or common councilman, who is not taxed or who shall have neglected or refused to pay his tax, as provided in the preceding section.

6. The voting for all officers chosen by the people, except town or city officers, shall be by ballot; that is to say, by depositing a written or printed ticket in the ballot box, without the name of the voter written thereon. Town or city officers shall be chosen by ballot, on the demand of any two persons entitled to vote for the same.

7. There shall be a strict registration of all qualified voters in the towns and cities of the state; and no person shall be permitted to vote whose name has not been entered upon the list of voters before the polls are opened.

8. The General Assembly shall pass all necessary laws for the prevention of fraudulent voting by persons not having an actual permanent residence or home in the state, or otherwise disqualified according to this constitution; for the careful registration of all voters, previously to the time of voting; for the prevention of frauds upon the ballot box; for the preservation of the purity of elections; and for the safe keeping and accurate counting of the votes; to the end that the will of the people may be freely and fully expressed, truly ascertained and effectually exerted, without intimidation, suppression or unnecessary delay.

9. The electors shall be exempted from arrest on days of election and one day before and one day after the same, except in cases of treason, felony or breach of the peace.

10. No person shall be eligible to any office by the votes of the people who does not possess the qualifications of an elector.

APPENDIX.

ARTICLE III.

OF THE DISTRIBUTION OF POWERS.

1. The powers of the government shall be distributed into three departments, the legislative, the executive and the judicial.
2. No person or persons connected with one of these departments shall exercise any of the powers belonging to either of the others, except in cases herein directed or permitted.

ARTICLE IV.

OF THE LEGISLATIVE DEPARTMENT.

1. The legislative power shall be vested in two distinct houses, the one to be called the house of representatives, the other the senate, and both together the General Assembly. The concurrent votes of the two houses shall be necessary to the enactment of laws; and the style of their laws shall be—*Be it enacted by the General Assembly as follows.*
2. No member of the General Assembly shall be eligible to any civil office under the authority of the state during the term for which he shall have been elected.
3. If any representative or senator in the General Assembly of this state shall be appointed to any office under the government of the United States, and shall accept the same after his election as such senator or representative, his seat shall thereby become vacant.
4. Any person who holds an office under the government of the United States may be elected a member of the General Assembly and may hold his seat therein if at the time of taking his seat he shall have resigned said office, and shall declare the same on oath or affirmation, if required.
5. No member of the General Assembly shall take any fees, be of counsel, or act as advocate in any case pending before either branch of the General Assembly, under penalty of forfeiting his seat upon due proof thereof.
6. Each house shall judge of the election and qualifications of its members; and a majority of all the members of each house, whom the towns and senatorial districts are entitled to elect, shall constitute a quorum to do business; but a smaller number may adjourn from day to day, and may compel the attendance of absent members in such manner and under such penalties as each house may have previously prescribed.
7. Each house may determine the rules of its proceedings, punish its members for disorderly behavior, and, with the concurrence of two-thirds of the members elected, expel a member; but not a second time for the same cause.
8. Each house shall keep a journal of its proceedings, and publish the same when required by one-fifth of its members. The yeas and nays of the members of either house shall, at the desire of any five members present, be entered on the journal.
9. Neither house shall, without the consent of the other, adjourn for more than two days, nor to any other place than that at which the General Assembly is holding its session.
10. The senators and representatives shall in all cases of civil process be privileged from arrest during the session of the General Assembly, and for two days before the commencement and two days after the termination of any session thereof. For any speech in debate in either house no member shall be called in question in any other place.

11. The civil and military officers heretofore elected in grand committee shall hereafter be elected annually by the General Assembly in joint committee, composed of the two houses of the General Assembly, excepting as is otherwise provided in this constitution, and excepting the captains and subalterns of the militia who shall be elected by the ballots of the members composing their respective companies, in such manner as the General Assembly may prescribe; and such officers so elected shall be approved of and commissioned by the governor, who shall determine their rank, and if said companies shall neglect or refuse to make such elections after being duly notified, then the governor shall appoint suitable persons to fill such offices.

12. Every bill and every resolution requiring the concurrence of the two houses (votes of adjournment accepted) which shall have passed both houses of the General Assembly, shall be presented to the governor for his revision. If he approve of it he shall sign and transmit the same to the secretary of state, but if not he shall return it to the house in which it shall have originated, with his objections thereto which shall be entered at large on their journal. The house shall then proceed to reconsider the bill; and if after such reconsideration that house shall pass it by a majority of all the members elected, it shall be sent with the objections to the other house which shall also reconsider it; and if approved by that house by a majority of all the members elected it shall become a law. If the bill shall not be returned by the governor within forty-eight hours (Sundays excepted) after it shall have been presented to him, the same shall become a law, in like manner as if he had signed it, unless the General Assembly by their adjournment prevent its return, in which case it shall not be a law.

13. There shall be two sessions of the General Assembly in every year; one session to be held at Newport, on the first Tuesday of June, for the organization of the government, the election of officers, and for other business; and one other session on the first Tuesday of January, to be held at Providence, in the first year after the adoption of this constitution and in every second year thereafter. In the intermediate years the January session shall be forever hereafter held in the counties of Washington, Kent, or Bristol, as the General Assembly may determine before their adjournment in June.

ARTICLE V.

OF THE HOUSE OF REPRESENTATIVES.

1. The house of representatives shall consist of members chosen by the electors in the several towns and cities in their respective town and ward meetings annually.

2. The towns and cities shall severally be entitled to elect members according to the apportionment which follows, viz: Newport to elect five; Warwick, four; Smithfield, five; Cumberland, North Providence and Scituate, three; Portsmouth, Westerly, New Shoreham, North Kingstown, South Kingstown, East Greenwich, Glocester, West Greenwich, Coventry, Exeter, Bristol, Tiverton, Little Compton, Warren, Richmond, Cranston, Charlestown, Hopkinton, Johnston, Foster and Burrillville to elect two; and Jamestown, Middletown and Barrington to elect one.

3. In the city of Providence there shall be six representative districts, which shall be the six wards of said city. And the electors resident in said districts for the term of three months next preceding the election at which they offer to vote, shall be entitled to elect two representatives for each district.

4. The General Assembly in case of great inequality in the population of the wards of the city of Providence, may cause the boundaries of the six representative districts therein to be so altered as to include in each district as nearly as may be, an equal number of inhabitants.

5. The house of representatives shall have authority to elect their own speaker, clerks and other officers. The oath of office shall be administered to the speaker by the secretary of state, or, in his absence, by the attorney-general.

6. Whenever the seat of a member of the house of representatives shall be vacated by death, resignation, or otherwise, the vacancy may be filled by a new election.

ARTICLE VI.

OF THE SENATE.

1. The state shall be divided into twelve senatorial districts; and each district shall be entitled to one senator, who shall be annually chosen by the electors in his district.

2. The first, second and third representative districts in the city of Providence shall constitute the first senatorial district; the fourth, fifth and sixth representative districts in said city the second district; the town of Smithfield the third district; the towns of North Providence and Cumberland the fourth district; the towns of Scituate, Glocester, Burrillville and Johnston the fifth district; the towns of Warwick and Cranston the sixth district; the towns of East Greenwich, West Greenwich, Coventry and Foster the seventh district; the towns of Newport, Jamestown and New Shoreham the eighth district; the towns of Portsmouth, Middletown, Tiverton and Little Compton the ninth district; the towns of North Kingstown and South Kingstown the tenth district; the towns of Westerly, Charlestown, Exeter, Richmond and Hopkinton the eleventh district; the towns of Bristol, Warren and Barrington the twelfth district.

3. The lieutenant-governor, shall be by virtue of his office, president of the senate; and shall have a right, in case of an equal division to vote in the same, and also to vote in joint committe of the two houses.

4. When the government shall be administered by the lieutenant-governor, or he shall be unable to attend as president of the senate, the senate shall elect one of their own members president of the same.

5. Vacancies in the senate occasioned by death, resignation or otherwise, may be filled by a new election.

6. The secretary of state shall be, by virtue of his office, secretary of the senate.

ARTICLE VII.

OF IMPEACHMENTS.

1. The house of representatives shall have the sole power of impeachment.

2. All impeachments shall be tried by the senate; and when sitting for that purpose they shall be on oath or affirmation. No person shall be convicted except by vote of two-thirds of the members elected. When the governor is impeached the chief-justice of the supreme court shall preside, with a casting vote in all preliminary questions.

3. The governor and all other executive and judicial officers shall be liable to impeachment, but judgments in such cases shall not

extend further than removal from office. The party convicted shall nevertheless be liable to indictment, trial and punishment, according to law.

ARTICLE VIII.

OF THE EXECUTIVE DEPARTMENT.

1. The chief executive power of this state, shall be vested in a governor who shall be chosen by the electors, and shall hold his office for one year and until his successor be duly qualified.

2. No person holding any office or place under the United States, this state, any other of the United States, or any foreign power, shall exercise the office of governor.

3. He shall take care that the laws are faithfully executed.

4. He shall be commander-in-chief of the military and naval forces of the state, except when called into the actual service of the United States ; but he shall not march nor convey any of the citizens out of the state without their consent, or that of the General Assembly, unless it shall become necessary in order to march or transport them from one part of the state to another, for the defence thereof.

5. He shall appoint all civil and military officers whose appointment is not by this constitution, or shall not, by law, be otherwise provided for.

6. He shall from time to time inform the General Assembly of the condition of the state, and recommend to their consideration such measures as he may deem expedient.

7. He may require from any military officer or any officer in the executive department, information upon any subject relating to the duties of his office.

8. He shall have power to remit forfeitures and penalties, and to grant reprieves, commutation of punishments and pardons after conviction, except in cases of impeachment.

9. The governor shall at stated times receive for his services a compensation, which shall not be increased nor diminished during his continuance in office.

10. There shall be elected in the same manner as is provided for the election of governor, a lieutenant-governor, who shall continue in office for the same term of time. Whenever the office of governor shall become vacant by death, resignation, removal from office or otherwise, the lieutenant-governor shall exercise the office of governor until another governor shall be duly qualified.

11. Whenever the offices of governor and lieutenant-governor shall both become vacant by death, resignation, removal from office, or otherwise, the president of the senate shall exercise the office of governor until a governor be duly qualified; and should such vacancies occur during a recess of the General Assembly, and there be no president of the senate, the secretary of state shall by proclamation convene the senate, that a president may be chosen to exercise the office of governor.

12. Whenever the lieutenant-governor or president of the senate shall exercise the office of governor, he shall receive the compensation of governor only; and his duties as president of the senate shall cease while he shall continue to act as governor; and the senate shall fill the vacancy by an election from their own body.

13. In case of a disagreement between the two houses of the General Assembly respecting the time or place of adjournment, the person exercising the office of governor may adjourn them to such time or place as he shall think proper; provided, that the time of adjournment shall not be extended beyond the first day of the next stated session.

14. The person exercising the office of governor may, in cases of special necessity convene the General Assembly at any town or city in this state, at any other time than herein before provided. And, in case of danger from the prevalence of epidemic or contagious diseases, or from other circumstances in the place in which the General Assembly are next to meet, he may by proclamation convene the Assembly at any other place within the state.

15. A secretary of state, a general treasurer and an attorney-general shall also be chosen annually, in the same manner and for the same time as is herein provided respecting the governor. The duties of these offices shall be the same as are now or may hereafter be prescribed by law. Should there be a failure to choose either of them, or should a vacancy occur in either of their offices, the General Assembly shall fill the place by an election in joint committee.

16. The electors in each county shall, at the annual elections, vote for an inhabitant of the county to be sheriff of said county for one year and until a successor be duly qualified. In case no person shall have a majority of the electoral votes of his county for sheriff, the General Assembly, in joint committee, shall elect a sheriff from the two candidates, who shall have the greatest number of votes in such county.

17. All commissions shall be in the name of the State of Rhode Island and Providence Plantations, sealed with the seal of the state, and attested by the secretary.

ARTICLE IX.

GENERAL PROVISIONS.

1. This constitution shall be the supreme law of the state, and all laws contrary to or inconsistent with the same which may be passed by the General Assembly shall be null and void.

2. The General Assembly shall pass all necessary laws for carrying this constitution into effect.

3. The judges of all the courts, and all other officers, both civil and military, shall be bound by oath or affirmation to the due observance of this constitution and of the constitution of the United States.

4. No jurisdiction shall hereafter be entertained by the General Assembly in cases of insolvency, divorce, sale of real estate of minors, or appeal from judicial decisions, nor in any other matters appertaining to the jurisdiction of judges and courts of law. But the General Assembly shall confer upon the courts of the state all necessary powers for affording relief in the cases herein named; and the General Assembly shall exercise all other jurisdiction and authority which they have heretofore entertained, and which is not prohibited by, or repugnant to this constitution.

5. The General Assembly shall from time to time cause estimates to be made of the ratable property of the state, in order to the equitable apportionment of state taxes.

6. Whenever a direct tax is laid by the state, one-sixth part thereof shall be assessed on the polls of the qualified electors, provided that the tax on a poll shall never exceed the sum of fifty cents, and that all persons who actually perform military duty, or duty in the fire department, shall be exempted from said poll tax.

7. The General Assembly shall have no power hereafter to incur state debts to an amount exceeding the sum of fifty thousand dollars, except in time of war, or in case of invasion, without the express consent of the people. Every proposition for such increase shall be

submitted to the electors at the next annual election, or on some day to be set apart for that purpose, and shall not be farther entertained by the General Assembly, unless it receive the votes of a majority of all the persons voting. This section shall not be construed to refer to any money that now is, or hereafter may be, deposited with this state by the general government.

8. The assent of two-thirds of the members elected to each house of the General Assembly shall be requisite to every bill appropriating the public moneys, or property for local or private purposes; or for creating, continuing, altering or renewing any body politic or corporate, banking corporations excepted.

9. Hereafter when any bill creating, continuing, altering or renewing any banking corporation, authorized to issue its promissory notes for circulation shall pass the two houses of the General Assembly, instead of being sent to the governor, it shall be referred to the electors for their consideration at the next annual election, or on some day to be set apart for that purpose, with printed tickets, containing the question, shall said bill (with a brief description thereof) be approved, or not; and if a majority of the electors voting shall vote to approve said bill it shall become a law, otherwise not.

10. All grants of incorporation shall be subject to future acts of the General Assembly, in amendment or repeal thereof, or in any wise affecting the same, and this provision shall be inserted in all acts of incorporation hereafter granted.

11. The General Assembly shall exercise as heretofore a visitorial power over corporations. Three bank commissioners shall be chosen at the June session for one year, to carry out the powers of the General Assembly in this respect. And commissioners for the visitation of other corporations, as the General Assembly may deem expedient, shall be chosen at the June session for the same term of office.

12. No city council or other government in any city shall have power to vote any tax upon the inhabitants thereof, excepting the amount necessary to meet the ordinary public expenses in the same, without first submitting the question of an additional tax or taxes to the electors of said city; and a majority of all who vote shall determine the question. But no elector shall be entitled to vote in any city upon any question of taxation thus submitted, unless he shall be qualified by the possession in his own right of ratable property to the amount of one hundred and fifty dollars, and shall have been assessed thereon to pay a city tax, and shall have paid the same as provided in section fourth of Article II. Nothing in that article shall be construed as to prevent any elector from voting for town officers, and in the city of Providence and other cities for mayor, aldermen, and members of the common council.

13. The General Assembly shall not pass any law nor cause any act or thing to be done in any way to disturb any of the owners or occupants of land in any territory now under the jurisdiction of any other state or states, the jurisdiction whereof may be ceded to, or decreed to belong to this state; and the inhabitants of such territory shall continue in the full, quiet and undisturbed enjoyment of their titles to the same, without interference in any way on the part of this state.

ARTICLE X.

OF ELECTIONS.

1. The election of the governor, lieutenant-governor, secretary of state, general treasurer, attorney-general, and also of senators and representatives to the General Assembly, and of sheriffs of the counties, shall be held on the third Wednesday of April, annually.

2. The names of the persons voted for as governor, lieutenant-governor, secretary of state, general treasurer, attorney-general and sheriffs of the respective counties, shall be put upon one ticket; and the tickets shall be deposited by the electors in a box by themselves. The names of the persons voted for as senators and as representatives shall be put upon separate tickets, and the tickets shall be deposited in separate boxes. The polls for all the officers named in this section shall be opened at the same time.

3. All the votes given for governor, lieutenant-governor, secretary of state, general treasurer, attorney-general, sheriffs, and also for senators shall remain in the ballot boxes till the polls be closed. These votes shall then, in open town and ward meetings, and in the presence of at least ten qualified voters, be taken out and sealed up in separate envelopes by the moderators and town clerks and by the wardens and ward clerks, who shall certify the same and forthwith deliver or send them to the secretary of state, whose duty it shall be securely to keep the same, and to deliver the votes for state officers and sheriffs to the speaker of the house of representatives after the house shall be organized at the June session of the General Assembly. The votes last named shall, without delay, be opened, counted and declared in such manner as the house of representatives shall direct, and the oath of office shall be administered to the persons who shall be declared to be elected by the speaker of the house of representatives, and in the presence of the house; provided that the sheriffs may take their engagement before a senator, judge or justice of the peace. The votes for senators shall be counted by the governor and secretary of state within seven days from the day of election; and the governor shall give certificates to the senators who are elected.

4. The boxes containing the votes for representatives to the General Assembly in the several towns shall not be opened till the polls for representatives are declared to be closed. The votes shall then be counted by the moderator and clerk, who shall announce the result and give certificates to the persons elected. If there be no election, or not an election of the whole number of representatives to which the town is entitled, the polls for representatives may be reopened, and the like proceedings shall be had until an election shall take place; provided, however, that an adjournment of the election may be made to a time not exceeding seven days from the first meeting.

5. In the city of Providence and other cities, the polls for representatives shall be kept open during the whole time of voting for the day; and the votes in the several wards shall be sealed up at the close of the meeting by the wardens and ward clerks, in the presence of at least ten qualified electors, and delivered to the city clerks. The mayor and aldermen of said city or cities shall proceed to count said votes within two days from the day of election; and if no election, or an election of only a portion of the representatives whom the representative districts are entitled to elect shall have taken place, the mayor and aldermen shall order a new election, to be held not more than ten days from the day of the first election; and so on till the election of representatives shall be completed. Certificates of election shall be furnished to the persons chosen by the city clerks.

6. If there be no choice of a senator or senators at the annual election, the governor shall issue his warrant to the town and ward clerks of the several towns and cities in the senatorial district or districts that may have failed to elect, requiring them to open town or ward meetings for another election, on a day not more than fifteen days beyond the time of counting the votes for senators. If, on the second trial there shall be no choice of a senator or senators the governor shall certify the result to the speaker of the house of representatives; and

the house of representatives, and as many senators as shall have been chosen, shall forthwith elect, in joint committee, a senator or senators from the two candidates who may receive the highest number of votes in each district.

7. If there be no choice of governor at the annual election, the speaker of the house of representatives shall issue his warrant to the clerks of the several towns and cities requiring them to notify town and ward meetings for another election, on a day to be named by him, not more than thirty nor less than twenty days beyond the time of receiving the report of the committee of the house of representatives, who shall count the votes for governor. If, on this second trial there shall be no choice of a governor, the two houses of the General Assembly, shall, at their next session, in joint committee elect a governor from the two candidates having the highest number of votes, to hold his office for the remainder of the political year, and until his successor be duly qualified.

8. If there be no choice of governor and lieutenant-governor at the annual election, the same proceedings for the choice of a lieutenant-governor shall be had as are directed in the preceding section; provided that the second trial for the election of governor and lieutenant-governor shall be on the same day; and also provided, that if the governor shall be chosen at the annual election and the lieutenant-governor shall not be chosen, then the last named officer shall be elected in joint committee of the two houses from the two candidates having the highest number of votes, without a further appeal to the electors. The lieutenant-governor, elected as is provided in this section, shall hold his office as is provided in the preceding section respecting the governor.

9. All town, city and ward meetings for the choice of representatives, justices of the peace, sheriffs, senators, state officers, representatives to Congress and electors of president and vice-president, shall be notified by the town, city and ward clerks at least seven days before the same are held.

10. In all elections held by the people under this constitution, a majority of all the electors voting shall be necessary to the choice of the person or persons voted for.

11. The oath or affirmation to be taken by all the officers named in this article shall be the following: You, being elected to the place of governor, lieutenant-governor, secretary of state, general treasurer, attorney-general, or to the places of senators or representatives, or to the office of sheriff or justice of the peace, do solemnly swear, or severally solemnly swear, or affirm, that you will be true and faithful to the State of Rhode Island and Providence Plantations, and that you will support the constitution thereof; that you will support the constitution of the United States, and that you will faithfully and impartially discharge the duties of your aforesaid office to the best of your abilities and understanding—So help you God! or, this affirmation you make and give upon the peril of the penalty of perjury.

ARTICLE XI.

OF THE JUDICIARY.

1. The judicial power of this state shall be vested in one supreme court, and in such other courts inferior to the supreme court as the legislature may, from time to time, ordain and establish; and the jurisdiction of the supreme and of all other courts, may, from time to time be regulated by the General Assembly.

2. Chancery powers may be conferred on the supreme court; but no other court exercising chancery powers shall be established in this state, except as is now provided by law.

3. The justices of the supreme court shall be elected in joint committee of the two houses, to hold their offices for one year, and until their places be declared vacant by a resolution to that effect, which shall be voted for by a majority of all the members elected to the house in which it may originate, and be concurred in by the same vote of the other house, without revision by the governor. Such resolution shall not be entertained at any other than the annual session for the election of public officers; and in default of the passage thereof at the said session, the judge or judges shall hold his or their place or places for another year. But a judge of any court shall be removable from office, if upon impeachment, he shall be found guilty of any official misdemeanor.

4. In case of vacancy by the death, resignation, refusal, or inability to serve, or removal from the state of a judge of any court, his place may be filled by the joint committee until the next annual election; when, if elected, he shall hold his office as herein provided.

5. The justices of the supreme court shall receive a compensation, which shall not be diminished during their continuance in office.

6. The judges of the courts inferior to the supreme court shall be annually elected in joint committee of the two houses, except as herein provided.

7. There shall be annually elected by each town and by the several wards in the city of Providence, a sufficient number of justices of the peace or wardens resident therein with such jurisdiction as the General Assembly may prescribe. And said justices or wardens, (except in the towns of New Shoreham and Jamestown) shall be commissioned by the governor.

8. The General Assembly may provide that justices of the peace who are not re-elected, may hold their offices for a time not exceeding ten days beyond the day of the annual election of these officers.

9. The courts of probate in this state, except the supreme court, shall remain as at present established by law, until the General Assembly shall otherwise prescribe.

ARTICLE XII.

OF EDUCATION.

1. All moneys which now are, or may hereafter be appropriated by the authority of the state to public education, shall be securely invested, and remain a perpetual fund for the maintenance of free schools in this state; and the General Assembly are prohibited from diverting said moneys or fund from this use, and from borrowing, appropriating or using the same or any part thereof for any other purpose, or under any pretence whatsoever. But the income derived from said moneys or fund, shall be annually paid over by the general treasurer to the towns and cities of the state, for the support of said schools in equitable proportions; provided, however, that a portion of said income may, in the discretion of the General Assembly, be added to the principal of said fund.

2. The several towns and cities shall faithfully devote their portions of said annual distribution to the support of free schools; and in default thereof shall forfeit their shares of the same to the increase of the fund.

3. All charitable donations for the support of free schools and other purposes of public education, shall be received by the General

Assembly and invested, and applied agreeably to the terms prescribed by the donors, provided the same be not inconsistent with the constitution, or with sound public policy; in which case the donation shall not be received.

ARTICLE XIII.

AMENDMENTS.

The General Assembly may propose amendments to this constitution by the vote of a majority of all the members elected to each house. Such propositions shall be published in the newspapers of the state; and printed copies of said propositions shall be sent by the secretary of state, with the names of all the members who shall have voted thereon, with the yeas and nays, to all the town and city clerks in the state; and the said propositions shall be by said clerks inserted in the notices by them issued for warning the next annual town and ward meetings in April; and the town and ward clerks shall read said propositions to the electors when thus assembled, with the names of all the representatives and senators who shall have voted thereon, with the yeas and nays, before the election of representatives and senators shall be had. If a majority of all the members elected at said annual meetings, present in each house, shall approve any proposition thus made, the same shall be published as before provided and then sent to the electors in the mode provided in the act of approval; and if then approved by a majority of the electors who shall vote in town and ward meetings to be specially convened for that purpose, it shall become a part of the constitution of the state.

ARTICLE XIV.

OF THE ADOPTION OF THE CONSTITUTION.

1. This constitution shall be submitted to the people for their adoption or rejection, on Monday, the 27th day of December next, and on the two succeeding days; and all persons voting are requested to deposit in the ballot-boxes printed or written tickets in the following form: I am an American citizen, of the age of twenty-one years, and have my permanent residence or home in this state. I am (or not) qualified to vote under the existing laws of this state. I vote for (or against) the constitution formed by the convention of the people, assembled at Providence, and which was proposed to the people by said convention, on the 18th day of November, 1841.

2. Every voter is requested to write his name on the face of his ticket; and every person entitled to vote as aforesaid, who from sickness or other causes may be unable to attend and vote in the town or ward meetings, assembled for voting upon said constitution on the days aforesaid, is requested to write his name upon a ticket, and to obtain the signature upon the back of the same of a person who has given his vote as a witness thereto. And the moderator or clerk of any town or ward meeting convened for the purpose aforesaid, shall receive such vote on either of the three days next succeeding the three days before named for voting on said constitution.

3. The citizens of the several towns in this state, and of the several wards in the city of Providence, are requested to hold town and ward meetings on the days appointed and for the purpose aforesaid; and also to choose in each town and ward a moderator and clerk to conduct said meetings and receive the votes.

4. The moderators and clerks are required to receive and carefully to keep the votes of all persons qualified to vote as aforesaid, and to make registers of all the persons voting; which, together with the tickets given in by the voters shall be sealed up and returned by said

moderators and clerks, with certificates signed and sealed by them, to the clerks of the convention of the people, to be by them safely deposited and kept, and laid before said convention to be counted and declared at their next adjourned meeting on the 12th day of January, 1842.

5. This constitution, except so much thereof as relates to the election of the officers named in the sixth section of this article, shall, if adopted, go into operation on the first Tuesday in May, in the year one thousand eight hundred and forty-two.

6. So much of the constitution as relates to the election of officers named in this section, shall go into operation on the Monday before the third Wednesday of April next preceding. The first election under this constitution of governor, lieutenant-governor, secretary of state, general treasurer and attorney-general, of senators and representatives, of sheriffs for the several counties, and of justices of the peace for the several towns and the wards of the city of Providence, shall take place on the Monday aforesaid

7. The electors of the several towns and wards are authorized to assemble on the day aforesaid, without being notified as is provided in section ninth of Article X., and without the registration required in section seventh of Article II., and to choose moderators and clerks, and proceed in the election of the officers named in the preceding section.

8. The votes given in at the first election for representatives to the General Assembly and for justices of the peace, shall be counted by the moderators and clerks of the towns and wards chosen as aforesaid; and certificates of election shall be furnished by them to the representatives and justices of the peace elected.

9. Said moderators and clerks shall seal up, certify, and transmit to the house of representatives all the votes that may be given in at said first election for governor and state officers, and for senators and sheriffs; and the votes shall be counted as the house of representatives may direct.

10. The speaker of the house of representatives shall, at the first session of the same, qualify himself to administer the oath of office to the members of the house and to other officers, by taking and subscribing the same oath in presence of the house.

11. The first session of the General Assembly shall be held in the city of Providence, on the first Tuesday of May, in the year one thousand eight hundred and forty-two, with such adjournments as may be necessary; but all other sessions shall be held as is provided in Article IV. of this Constitution.

12. If any of the representatives whom the towns or districts are entitled to choose, at the first annual election aforesaid, shall not be then elected, or if their places shall become vacant during the year, the same proceedings may be had to complete the election, or to supply vacancies as are directed concerning elections in the preceding sections of this article.

13. If there shall be no election of governor or lieutenant-governor, or of both of these officers, or of a senator or senators at the first annual election, the house of representatives and as many senators as are chosen, shall forthwith elect, in joint committee, a governor or lieutenant-governor, or both, or a senator or senators, to hold their offices for the remainder of the political year, and, in the case of the two officers first named, until their successors shall be duly qualified.

14. If the number of the justices of the peace determined by the several towns and wards on the day of the first annual election shall not be then chosen, or if vacancies shall occur, the same proceedings shall be had as are provided for in this article in the case of a non-election of representatives and senators, or of vacancies in their offices.

The justices of the peace thus elected shall hold office for the remainder of the political year, or until the second annual election of justices of the peace to be held on such day as may be prescribed by the General Assembly.

15. The justices of the peace elected in pursuance of the provisions of this article may be engaged by the persons acting as moderators of the town and ward meetings as herein provided; and said justices after obtaining their certificates of election, may discharge the duties of their office for a time not exceeding twenty days, without a commission from the governor.

16. Nothing contained in this article, inconsistent with any of the provisions of other articles of the constitution shall continue in force for a longer period than the first political year under the same.

17. The present government shall exercise all the powers with which it is now clothed, until the said first Tuesday in May, one thousand eight hundred and forty-two, and until their successors under this constitution shall be duly elected and qualified.

18. All civil, judicial and military officers now elected, or who shall hereafter be elected by the General Assembly or other competent authority, before the said first Tuesday of May, shall hold their offices and may exercise their powers until that time.

19. All laws and statutes, public and private, now in force and not repugnant to this constitution, shall continue in force until they expire by their own limitation, or are repealed by the General Assembly. All contracts, judgments, actions, and rights of action, shall be as valid as if this constitution had not been made. All debts contracted, and engagements entered into before the adoption of this constitution, shall be as valid against the state as if this constitution had not been made.

20. The supreme court established by this constitution shall have the same jurisdiction as the supreme judicial court at present established; and shall have jurisdiction of all causes which may be appealed to or pending in the same; and shall be held in the same times and places in each county as the present supreme judicial court until the General Assembly shall otherwise prescribe.

21. The citizens of the town of New Shoreham shall be hereafter exempted from military duty and the duty of serving as jurors in the courts of this state. The citizens of the town of Jamestown shall be forever hereafter exempted from military field duty.

22. The General Assembly shall, at their first session after the adoption of this constitution, propose to the electors the question, whether the word "white," in the first line of the first section of Article II. of the constitution shall be stricken out. The question shall be voted upon at the succeeding annual election; and if a majority of the electors voting shall vote to strike out the word aforesaid, it shall be stricken from the constitution; otherwise not. If the word aforesaid shall be stricken out, section third of Article II. shall cease to be a part of the constitution.

23. The president, vice-president and secretaries shall certify and sign this constitution, and cause the same to be published.

Done in convention at Providence, on the eighteenth day of November, in the year one thousand eight hundred and forty-one, and of American Independence the sixty-sixth.

JOSEPH JOSLIN, *President of the Convention.*

WAGER WEEDEN, } *Vice Presidents.*
SAMUEL H. WALES,

Attest:

WILLIAM H. SMITH, } *Secretaries.*
JOHN S. HARRIS,

The State Seal.

The coat of arms of the State is familiar to every citizen, for it is impressed on public documents and meets the eye on monuments and in newspapers. Its simplicity and its significance, as well as its correct heraldry render it superior to that of any of the other states; and the words by which it is described in our statute book, have a singular force and beauty. "There shall continue to be one seal for the public use of the State; the form of an anchor shall be engraven thereon, and the motto thereof shall be the word Hope."

This has been the seal of the State ever since the adoption of the charter, in May, 1664. Previous to that time the seal consisted of an anchor only, on a shield, without the motto "Hope." At the first meeting of the General Assembly under the "parliamentary patent," in 1647, it was "ordered that the seal of the province shall be an anchor," and on the margin of the original manuscript, now preserved in the office of the secretary of state, is simply an anchor upon a shield, drawn by the pen of the writer.

But this was not the first seal the State may claim to have possessed. At a meeting of the Newport Colony at Portsmouth, in 1641, six years before the establishment of the anchor as the seal, it was "ordered, that a manual seale shall be provided for the State, and that the signett or engraving thereof, shall be a sheaf of arrows bound up, and on the liass or band, this motto: *Amor omnia vincit.*"

The seal of the anchor with the motto "Hope," was surrounded by a circle, in which was inscribed the words COLONIE OF RHODE ISLAND AND PROVIDENCE PLANTATIONS, and several impressions of it may be found among the old records of the State. This seal Andros broke, at the time of his usurpation in 1686-7. But after his expulsion, and on the reorganization of the General Assembly, 1689-90, a new seal was ordered, precisely like the old seal, except that the words "Colonie of Rhode Island and Providence Plantations" were omitted; nor did these words ever again form a part of the seal until this year, (1875), when they were restored by an act of the General Assembly, in January last, and the date 1636 added. Of course the word "Colonie" was altered to the word "State."

No impression of the Newport seal—the sheaf of arrows; nor of the seal under the parliamentary patent—the anchor alone—exists among the archives of the State. Perhaps some of the antiquarian readers of the *Journal* may know where such impressions may be found. And perhaps also some one may know why the anchor originally came to be chosen as the device of the seal. Was this the "bearing" of the shield of the family of Roger Williams, or of any of the families who accompanied him? Did the idea arise from the depressing circumstances of the time? If so, why was the word Hope not added until seventeen years afterwards, and in comparatively prosperous times? Was there any reason why the legend "Colonie of Rhode Island and Providence Plantations" was omitted after the expulsion of Andros? Whence came the cable now surrounding the shank, and thus converting the anchor into a "foul anchor"? And whence the rock and the waves, with light-house and ship in the distance, as is now frequently seen? And how came the shield altered into unmeaning scroll-work? Is there any more authority for these changes than the ill-informed fancy of the seal-engravers from time to time?

NOTE.—For this excellent dissertation on the seal of Rhode Island, I am indebted to my friend, the Hon. T. P. Shepard.

Governors of Rhode Island.

The State originally consisted of four towns: Providence, settled in 1636; Portsmouth, in 1638; Newport, in 1639; and Warwick, in 1642. Each town was governed independently until 1647. Providence and Warwick had no executive head till 1647.

PORTSMOUTH.
JUDGES.

William Coddington,	March 7, 1638 to April 30, 1639.
William Hutchinson,	April 30, 1639 to March 12, 1640.

NEWPORT.
JUDGE.

William Coddington,	April 28, 1639 to March 12, 1640.

PORTSMOUTH AND NEWPORT.*
GOVERNOR.

William Coddington,	March 12, 1640 to May 19, 1647.

In 1647 the four towns were united under a charter or patent, granted in 1643, by Parliament.

PRESIDENTS UNDER THE PATENT.

John Coggeshall,	May, 1647 to May, 1648.
William Coddington,	May, 1648 to May, 1649.
John Smith,	May, 1649 to May, 1650.
Nicholas Easton,	May, 1650 to Aug., 1651.

In 1651 a separation occurred between the towns of Providence and Warwick on the one side, and Portsmouth and Newport on the other.

PROVIDENCE AND WARWICK.
PRESIDENTS.

Samuel Gorton,	Oct., 1651 to May, 1652.
John Smith,	May, 1652 to May, 1653.
Gregory Dexter,	May, 1653 to May, 1654.

PORTSMOUTH AND NEWPORT.
PRESIDENT.

John Sandford, Senior.	May, 1653 to May, 1654.

In 1654 the union of the four towns was reëstablished.

---

* United in 1640.

PRESIDENTS.

Nicholas Easton,	May, 1654 to Sept. 12, 1654.
Roger Williams,	Sept., 1654 to May, 1657.
Benedict Arnold,	May, 1657 to May, 1660.
William Brenton,	May, 1660 to May, 1662.
Benedict Arnold,	May, 1662 to Nov. 25, 1663.

ROYAL CHARTER.

GOVERNORS.

Benedict Arnold,	Nov., 1663 to May, 1666.
William Brenton,	May, 1666 to May, 1669.
Benedict Arnold,	May, 1669 to May, 1672.
Nicholas Easton,	May, 1672 to May, 1674.
William Coddington,	May, 1674 to May, 1676.
Walter Clarke,	May, 1676 to May, 1677.
Benedict Arnold,	1677 to June 20, 1678. Died.
William Coddington,	Aug. 28, 1678 to Nov. 1, 1678. Died.
John Cranston,	Nov., 1678 to March 12, 1680. Died.
Peleg Sandford,	March 16, 1680 to May, 1683.
William Coddington, Jr.,	May, 1683 to May, 1685.
Henry Bull,	May, 1685 to May, 1686.
Walter Clarke,*	May, 1686 to June 29, 1686.
Henry Bull,	Feb. 27, to May 7, 1690.
John Easton,	May, 1690 to May, 1695.
Caleb Carr,	May, 1695 to Dec. 17, 1695. Died.
Walter Clarke,	Jan., 1696 to March, 1698.
Samuel Cranston,	., 1698 to April 26, 1727. Died.
Joseph Jenckes,	May, 1727 to May, 1732.
William Wanton,	May, 1732 to Dec., 1733. Died.
John Wanton,	May, 1734 to July 5, 1740. Died.
Richard Ward,	July 15, 1740 to May, 1743.
William Greene,	May, 1743 to May, 1745.
Gideon Wanton,	May, 1745 to May, 1746.
William Greene,	May, 1746 to May, 1747.
Gideon Wanton,	May, 1747 to May, 1748.
William Greene,	May, 1748 to May, 1755.
Stephen Hopkins,	May, 1755 to May, 1757.
William Greene,	May, 1757 to Feb. 22, 1758. Died.
Stephen Hopkins,	March 14, 1758 to May, 1762.
Samuel Ward,	May, 1762 to May, 1763.
Stephen Hopkins,	May, 1763 to May, 1765.
Samuel Ward,	May, 1765 to May, 1767.
Stephen Hopkins,	May, 1767 to May, 1768.
Josias Lyndon,	May, 1768 to May, 1769.
Joseph Wanton,	1769 to Nov. 7, 1775. Deposed.
Nicholas Cooke,	Nov., 1775 to May, 1778.

---

* The charter was suspended till 1689. The Deputy-Governor, John Coggeshall, acted as Governor during the interval, Governor Clarke refusing to serve.

William Greene,	May, 1778 to 1786.
John Collins,	May, 1786 to 1790.
Arthur Fenner,*	1790 to 1805. Died.
James Fenner,	May, 1807 to 1811.
William Jones,	May, 1811 to 1817.
Nehemiah R. Knight,†	May, 1817 to Jan. 9, 1821.
William C. Gibbs,	May, 1821 to 1824.
James Fenner,	May, 1824 to 1831.
Lemuel H. Arnold,	1831 to 1833.
John Brown Francis,	1833 to 1838.
William Sprague,‡	1838 to 1839.
Samuel Ward King,	1840 to 1843.

UNDER THE CONSTITUTION.

(Adopted in 1842.)

James Fenner,	1843 to 1845.
Charles Jackson,	1845 to 1846.
Byron Diman,	1846 to 1847.
Elisha Harris,	1847 to 1849.
Henry B. Anthony,	1849 to 1851.
Philip Allen,§	1851 to 1853.
William Warner Hoppin,	1854 to 1857.
Elisha Dyer,	1857 to 1859.
Thomas G. Turner,	1859 to 1860.
William Sprague,	1860 to March 3, 1863. Resigned.
William C. Cozzens,‖	March 3, 1863 to May, 1863.
James Y. Smith,	1863 to 1866.
Ambrose E. Burnside,	1866 to 1869.
Seth Padelford,	1869 to 1873.
Henry Howard,	1873 to 1875.
Henry Lippitt,	1875 to ———

* Paul Mumford, Deputy-Governor, died. Henry Smith, First Senator, officiated as Governor. In 1806, no election; Isaac Wilbour, Lieutenant-Governor, officiated.

† Elected United States Senator January 9, 1821, for unexpired term of James Burrill, Jr., deceased.

‡ In 1839 no choice; Samuel Ward King was First Senator and Acting-Governor.

§ Resigned July 20, 1853, having been elected United States Senator May 4, 1853. Lieutenant-Governor, F. M. Dimond, officiated.

‖ Governor Sprague resigned March 3, 1863, and Lieutenant-Governor Arnold having been elected to the Senate Mr. Cozzens became Governor by virtue of his office as President of the Senate.

Deputy Governors.

William Brenton, ... March 12, 1640 to May 19, 1647.

From 1647 to 1663 the Colony was governed by a president, with four assistants.

William Brenton,	1663 to 1666.
Nicholas Easton,	1666 to 1669.
John Clarke,	1669 to 1670.
Nicholas Easton,	1670 to 1671.
John Clarke,	1671 to 1672.
John Cranston,	1672 to 1673.
William Coddington,	1673 to 1674.
John Easton,	1674 to 1676.
John Cranston,	1676 to 1678.
James Barker.	1678 to 1679.
Walter Clarke,	1679 to 1686.
John Coggeshall,	May to June, 1686.

(Charter suspended, 1686 to 1690.)

John Coggeshall,	1690.
John Greene,	1690 to 1700.
Walter Clarke,	1700 to 1714. Died.
Henry Tew,	1714 to 1715.
Joseph Jencks,	1715 to 1721.
John Wanton,	1721 to 1722.
Joseph Jencks,	1722 to 1727.
Jonathan Nicholls,	May to August, 1727. Died.
Thomas Frye,	1727 to 1729.
John Wanton,	1729 to 1734.
George Hassard,	1734 to 1738. Died.
Daniel Abbott,	1738 to 1740.
Richard Ward,	May to July, 1740.
William Greene,	1740 to 1743.
Joseph Whipple,	1743 to 1745.
William Robinson,	1745 to 1746.
Joseph Whipple,	1746 to 1747.
William Robinson,	1747 to 1748.
William Ellery,	1748 to 1750.
Robert Haszard,	1750 to 1751.
Joseph Whipple,	1751 to 1753.
Jonathan Nichols,	1753 to 1754.
John Gardner,	1754 to 1755.
Jonathan Nichols,	1755 to 1756.
John Gardner,	1756 to 1764.
Joseph Wanton, Jr.,	1764 to 1765.
Elisha Brown,	1765 to 1767.
Joseph Wanton, Jr.,	1767 to 1768.
Nicholas Cooke,	1768 to 1769.
Darius Sessions,	1769 to 1775.
Nicholas Cooke,	May to November, 1775.
William Bradford,	1775 to 1778.

338 HISTORY OF RHODE ISLAND.

Jabez Bowen,	1778 to 1780.
William West,	1780 to 1781.
Jabez Bowen,	1781 to 1786.
Daniel Owen,	1786 to 1790.
Samuel J. Potter,	1790 to 1799.

The title was now changed to lieutenant-governor.

LIEUTENANT-GOVERNORS.

Samuel J. Potter,	Feb., 1799 to May, 1799.
George Brown,	1799 to 1800.
Samuel J. Potter,	1800 to 1803.
Paul Mumford,	1803 to 1806.
Isaac Wilbour,	1806 to 1807.
Constant Taber,	1807 to 1808.
Simeon Martin,	1808 to 1810.
Isaac Wilbour,	1810 to 1811.
Simeon Martin,	1811 to 1816.
Jeremiah Thurston,	1816 to 1817.
Edward Wilcox,	1817 to 1821.
Caleb Earle,	1821 to 1824.
Charles Collins,	1824 to 1833.
Jeffrey Hazard.	1833 to 1835.
George Engs,	1835 to 1836.
Jeffrey Hazard,	1836 to 1837.
Benjamin B. Thurston,	1837 to 1838.
Joseph Childs,	1838 to 1840.
Byron Diman,	1840 to 1842.
Nathaniel Bullock,	1842 to 1843.
Byron Diman,	1843 to 1846.
Elisha Harris,*	1846 to 1847.
Edward W. Lawton,	1847 to 1849.
Thomas Whipple,	1849 to 1851.
William Beach Lawrence,	1851 to 1852.
Samuel G. Arnold,	1852 to 1853.
Francis M. Dimond,	1853 to 1854.
John J. Reynolds,	1854 to 1855.
Anderson C. Rose,	1855 to 1856.
Nicholas Brown,	1856 to 1857.
Thomas G. Turner,	1857 to 1859.
Isaac Saunders,	1859 to 1860.
J. Russell Bullock,	1860 to 1861.
Samuel G. Arnold.	1861 to 1863.
Seth Padelford,	1863 to 1865.
Duncan C. Pell,	1865 to 1866.
William Greene,	1866 to 1868.
Pardon W. Stevens,	1868 to 1872.
Charles R. Cutler,	1872 to 1873.
Charles C. Van Zandt,*	1873 to 1875.
Henry T. Sisson,*	1875 to ——

* Elected by the Assembly: no choice by the people.

MEMBERS

OF THE

Continental Congress

FROM RHODE ISLAND.

Jonathan Arnold,	1782 to 1783.
Peleg Arnold,	1787 to 1789.
John Collins,	1778 to 1782.
Ezekiel Cornell,	1780 to 1782.
William Ellery,	1776 to 1784.
Jonathan J. Hazard.	1787 to 1789.
Stephen Hopkins,	1774 to 1779.
David Howell,	1782 to 1784.
James Manning,	Feb., 1786.
Henry Marchant,	Feb., 1777 to 1784.
Nathan Miller,	Feb., 1786.
Daniel Mowry,	1780 to 1781.
James M. Varnum,	1780, '81, '86.
Samuel Ward,	1774 to 1775.
John Gardner,	1788 to 1789.
William Bradford,*	Oct., 1776.
John Brown,*	1785.
George Champlin,*	1785 to 1786.
Paul Mumford,*	1785.
Peter Phillips,*	1785.
Sylvester Gardner,*	1787.
Thomas Holden,*	1788 to 1789.

* Duly elected, but their names are not in the Journals of Congress.

Towns in Rhode Island,

DATE OF INCORPORATION, ETC.

COUNTIES AND TOWNS.	DATE OF INCORPORATION.	FROM WHAT TAKEN, ORIGINAL NAMES, CHANGES OF BOUNDARIES, &c.
BRISTOL Co........	Feb'y 17, 1746–47...	Incorporated with same county limits as at present. Originally the county consisted of two towns, Bristol and Warren. Afterwards, June, 1770, Warren was divided, and the Town of Barrington was incorporated.
Barrington	June 16, 1770.......	Taken from Warren, which see.
Bristol	Jan'y 27, 1746–47...	Five towns received from Massachusetts this date. A portion of Bristol annexed to Warren, May 30, 1873.
Warren.............	Jan'y 27, 1746–47...	See Bristol. The territory of the Town of Warren, when admitted to the State, included the Town of Barrington, and a portion of the towns of Swanzey and Rehoboth, in Massachusetts. In 1770 Warren was divided. and one of the original names (Barrington) was given to the new town.
KENT Co...........	June 15, 1750.......	Taken from Providence County. Incorporated with the same county limits as at present, and same towns.
Coventry	August 21, 1741.....	Taken from Warwick.
East Greenwich.....	October 31. 1677	Incorporated as the Town of East Greenwich. Name changed to Dedford, June 23, 1686. The original name restored in 1689. The town divided in 1741.
West Greenwich....	April 6, 1741........	Taken from East Greenwich, which see.

APPENDIX. 341

Counties and Towns.	Date of Incorporation.	From what Taken, Original Names, Changes of Boundaries, &c.
Warwick	Original town	First settled January, 1642–43. Named from Earl of Warwick, who signed the Patent of Providence Plantations, March 14, 1643. The first action of the inhabitants as a town was August 8, 1647. Indian name, Shawomet.
Newport Co.	June 22, 1703.	Originally incorporated as Rhode Island County, June 16, 1729, incorporated as Newport County, and included Newport, Portsmouth, Jamestown and New Shoreham.
Fall River	October 6, 1856	Taken from Tiverton. Ceded to Massachusetts in the settlement of the boundary question, March 1, 1862. See Pawtucket and East Providence.
Jamestown	November 4, 1678.	Named in honor of King James. Indian name Quononoqutt (Conanicut).
Little Compton	Jan'y 27, 1746–47	One of the five towns received from Massachusetts. Annexed to Newport County February 17, 1746–47. Indian name, Seaconnet.
Middletown	June 16, 1743.	Town in the "middle" of the island. Taken from Newport.
Newport	Original town	Settled in 1639. Line between Newport and Portsmouth established September 14, 1640. Incorporated as a city June 1, 1784. City charter given up March 27, 1787. City incorporated the second time at the May session, 1853, and the charter accepted May 20, 1853.
New Shoreham	November 6, 1672.	Admitted to Colony as Block Island, May 4, 1664. When incorporated in 1672, name changed to New Shoreham "as signes of our unity and likeness to many parts of our native country." Indian name Mannasses or Manisses.
Portsmouth	Original town	Settled in 1638. Indian name Pocasset. "At a quarter meeting of the first of ye 5th month 1639, it is agreed upon to call this town Portsmouth." At the "Generall Courte" at "Nieuport" 12th of 1st month, 1640, the name of Portsmouth was confirmed.
Tiverton	Jan'y 27, 1746–47.	One of the five towns received this date from Massachusetts. See Bristol, Warren, &c. Indian name Pocasset. Annexed to Newport County, February 17, 1746–47.

Counties and Towns.	Date of Incorporation.	From what Taken, Original Names, Changes of Boundaries, &c.
Providence Co...	June 22, 1703.......	Originally incorporated as the County of Providence Plantations, and included the present territory of Providence, Kent and Washington counties, excepting the present towns of Cumberland, Pawtucket and East Providence. The name was changed to Providence County June 16, 1729. See Kent and Washington counties.
Burrillville	October 29, 1806	Taken from Glocester. The town was first authorized to meet to elect officers, Nov. 17, 1806. Named from Hon. James Burrill.
Cranston	June 14, 1754.......	Taken from Providence. Probably named from Samuel Cranston, who was Governor of Rhode Island from March, 1698, to April 26, 1727, when he died. A portion re-united to Providence, June 10, 1868, and March 28, 1873.
Cumberland........	Jan'y 27, 1746-47...	One of the five towns received this date See Tiverton, Bristol, &c. Until incorporated in Rhode Island it was known as Attleboro Gore. Named from Cumberland, England. Annexed to Providence County, February 17, 1746-47. A portion of Cumberland was incorporated as the Town of Woonsocket, January 31, 1867.
East Providence	March 1, 1862.......	The westerly part of Rehoboth, Massachusetts, was incorporated as Seekonk, February 26, 1812. The westerly part of Seekonk was annexed to Rhode Island, incorporated as a town, and named East Providence in the settlement of the boundary question in 1862. See Pawtucket and Fall River.
Foster..............	August 24, 1781	Taken from Scituate. Named probably from Hon. Theodore Foster.
Glocester..........	Feb'y 20, 1730-31...	Taken from Providence. At this date an act was passed "for erecting and incorporating the outlands of the Town of Providence into three towns." These towns were Scituate, Glocester and Smithfield.
Johnston	March 6, 1759.......	Taken from Providence, and named in honor of Augustus Johnston, Esq., the attorney-general of the Colony at that time.
Lincoln.............	March 8, 1871.......	Taken from Smithfield, and named in honor of Abraham Lincoln, late President of the United States.

APPENDIX. 343.

COUNTIES AND TOWNS.	DATE OF INCORPORATION.	FROM WHAT TAKEN, ORIGINAL NAMES, CHANGES OF BOUNDARIES, &c.
North Providence	June 13, 1765.	Taken from Providence. A small portion reunited to Providence June 29; 1767, and March 28, 1873. The town was divided March 27, 1874, a portion was annexed to the City of Providence and a portion to the Town of Pawtucket. The act went into effect May 1, 1874.
North Smithfield	March 8, 1871.	Taken from Smithfield, and incorporated as the Town of Slater. Name changed to North Smithfield, March 24, 1871.
Pawtucket	March 1, 1862.	Name of Indian origin. Part of Seekonk, Mass., was incorporated as the Town of Pawtucket, March 1, 1828. The whole Town of Pawtucket except a small portion lying easterly of Seven Mile River was annexed to Rhode Island, with East Providence, which see. A portion of the Town of North Providence annexed to Pawtucket, May 1, 1874.
Providence	Original town	Settled in 1636. Named Providence by Roger Williams, "in gratitude to his supreme deliverer." Originally comprised the whole county. City incorporated in 1832. Portions of the Town of Cranston were re-annexed to Providence June 10, 1768, and March 28, 1873. Portions of North Providence were re-annexed June 29, 1767, March 28, 1873, and May 1, 1874.
Scituate	Feb'y 20, 1730-31	Taken from Providence. See Glocester
Smithfield	Feb'y 20, 1730-31	Taken from Providence. See Glocester. The town was divided March 8, 1871, a portion being annexed to Woonsocket, and the remainder divided into three towns. See Lincoln and North Smithfield.
Woonsocket	Jan'y 31, 1867	Name of Indian origin. Taken from Cumberland. A portion of Smithfield was annexed to Woonsocket March 8, 1871.
WASHINGTON CO.	June 16, 1729.	Originally called the "Narragansett country." Named King's Province, March 20, 1654. Boundaries established May 21, 1669. Incorporated June, 1729, as King's County, with three towns and same territory as at present. Name changed to Washington County, October 29, 1781.
Charlestown	August 22, 1738.	Taken from Westerly.
Exeter	March 8, 1742-43	Taken from North Kingstown.

Counties and Towns.	Date of Incorporation.	From what Taken, Original Names, Changes of Boundaries, &c.
Hopkinton	March 19, 1757	Taken from Westerly.
North Kingstown	October 28, 1674	First settlement, 1641. Incorporated in 1674, under the name of King's Towne, as the seventh town in the Colony. Incorporation reaffirmed in 1679. Name changed to Rochester June 23, 1686. Name restored in 1689; see East Greenwich. Kingstown, divided into North and South Kingstown, February, 1722. The act provided that North Kingstown should be the oldest town.
South Kingstown	Feb'y 26, 1722-23	See North Kingstown. Pettiquamscut settled January 20, 1657-58.
Richmond	August 18, 1747	Taken from Charlestown.
Westerly	May 14, 1669	Original name Misquamicut. Incorporated in May, 1669, under the name of Westerly, as the fifth town in the Colony. Name of Westerly changed to Haversham, June 23, 1686, but soon restored.

NOTE.—In several cases the exact date of the passage of the act of incorporation of towns cannot be ascertained. In such cases the date of the meeting of the General Assembly at which the act was passed is given.

Total Population of Rhode Island,
From 1708 to 1875.

Towns and Divisions of the State.	Settled or Incorp'td.	1708.	1730.	1748.	1755.	1774.	1776.
Barrington,	1770	—	—	—	—	601	538
Bristol,	1747	—	—	1,069	1,080	1,209	1,067
Warren,	1747	—	—	680	925	979	1,005
Bristol Co.,	1747	—	—	1,749	2,005	2,789	2,610
Coventry,	1741	—	—	792	1,178	3,023	2,300
East Greenwich,	1677	240	1,223	1,044	1,167	1,663	1,664
West Greenwich,	1741	—	—	766	1,246	1,764	1,653
Warwick,	1643	480	1,178	1,782	1,911	2,438	2,376
Kent Co.,	1750	720	2,401	4,384	5,502	7,888	7,993
Fall River,	1856	—	—	—	—	—	—
Jamestown,	1678	206	321	420	517	563	322
Little Compton,	1747	—	—	1,152	1,170	1,232	1,302
Middletown,	1743	—	—	680	778	881	860
Newport,	1639	2,203	4,640	6,508	6,753	9,209	5,299
New Shoreham,	1672	208	290	300	378	575	478
Portsmouth,	1638	628	813	992	1,363	1,512	1,347
Tiverton,	1747	—	—	1,040	1,325	1,956	2,091
Newport Co.,	1703	3,245	6,064	11,092	12,284	15,928	11,699
Burrillville,	1806	—	—	—	—	—	—
Cranston,	1754	—	—	—	1,460	1,861	1,701
Cumberland,	1747	—	—	806	1,083	1,756	1,686
East Providence,	1862	—	—	—	—	—	—
Foster,	1781	—	—	—	—	—	—
Glocester,	1731	—	—	1,202	1,511	2,945	2,832
Johnston,	1759	—	—	—	—	1,031	1,022
North Providence,	1765	—	—	—	—	830	813
Pawtucket,	1862	—	—	—	—	—	—
Scituate,	1731	—	—	1,232	1,813	3,601	3,289
Smithfield,	1731	—	—	450	1,921	2,888	2,781
Towns, Prov. Co.,	1703	—	—	3,690	7,788	14,912	14,124
Providence City,	1636	1,446	3,916	3,452	3,159	4,321	4,355
Charlestown,	1738	—	—	1,002	1,130	1,821	1,835
Exeter,	1743	—	—	1,174	1,404	1,864	1,982
Hopkinton,	1757	—	—	—	—	1,808	1,845
North Kingstown,	1674	1,200	2,105	1,935	2,109	2,472	2,761
South Kingstown,	1723	—	1,523	1,978	1,913	2,835	2,779
Richmond,	1747	—	—	508	829	1,257	1,204
Westerly,	1669	570	1,926	1,809	2,291	1,812	1,824
Washington Co.,	1724	1,770	5,554	8,406	9,676	13,869	14,230
Whole State,	1636	7,181	17,935	32,773	40,414	59,707	55,011

Note.—The permission to use these valuable tables I owe to Hon. J. M. Addeman, Secretary of State.

TOWNS AND DIVISIONS OF THE STATE.	1782.	1790.	1800.	1810.	1820.	1830.
Barrington,	534	683	650	604	634	612
Bristol,	1,032	1,406	1,678	2,693	3,197	3,034
Warren,	905	1,122	1,473	1,775	1,806	1,800
BRISTOL CO.,	2,471	3,211	3,801	5,072	5,637	5,446
Coventry,	2,107	2,477	2,423	2,928	3,139	3,851
East Greenwich,	1,609	1,824	1,775	1,530	1,519	1,591
West Greenwich,	1,698	2,054	1,757	1,619	1,927	1,817
Warwick,	2,112	2,493	2,532	3,757	3,643	5,529
KENT CO.,	7,526	8,848	8,487	9,834	10,228	12,788
Fall River,	—	—	—	—	—	—
Jamestown,	345	507	501	504	448	415
Little Compton,	1,341	1,542	1,577	1,553	1,580	1,378
Middletown,	674	840	913	976	949	915
Newport,	5,530	6,716	6,739	7,907	7,319	8,010
New Shoreham,	478	682	714	722	955	1,185
Portsmouth,	1,350	1,560	1,684	1,795	1,645	1,727
Tiverton,	1,959	2,453	2,717	2,837	2,875	2,905
NEWPORT CO.,	11,677	14,300	14,845	16,294	15,771	16,535
Burrillville,	—	—	—	1,834	2,164	2,196
Cranston,	1,589	1,877	1,644	2,161	2,274	2,652
Cumberland,	1,548	1,964	2,056	2,210	2,653	3,675
East Providence,	—	—	—	—	—	—
Foster,	1,763	2,268	2,457	2,613	2,900	2,672
Glocester,	2,791	4,025	4,009	2,310	2,504	2,521
Johnston,	996	1,320	1,364	1,516	1,542	2,115
North Providence,	698	1,071	1,067	1,758	2,420	3,503
Pawtucket,	—	—	—	—	—	—
Scituate,	1,628	2,315	2,523	2,568	2,834	3,993
Smithfield,	2,217	3,171	3,120	3,828	4,678	6,857
TOWNS, PROV. CO.,	13,230	18,011	18,240	20,796	23,069	30,184
PROVIDENCE CITY,	4,310	6,380	7,614	10,071	11,767	16,836
Charlestown,	1,523	2,022	1,454	1,174	1,160	1,284
Exeter,	2,058	2,495	2,476	2,256	2,581	2,383
Hopkinton,	1,735	2,462	2,276	1,774	1,821	1,777
North Kingstown,	2,328	2,907	2,794	2,957	3,007	3,036
South Kingstown,	2,675	4,131	3,438	3,560	3,723	3,663
Richmond,	1,094	1,760	1,368	1,330	1,423	1,363
Westerly,	1,720	2,298	2,329	1,911	1,972	1,915
WASHINGTON CO.,	13,133	18,075	16,135	14,962	15,687	15,421
WHOLE STATE,	52,347	68,825	69,122	77,031	83,059	97,210

APPENDIX. 347

TOWNS AND DIVISIONS OF THE STATE.	1840.	1850.	1860.	1865.	1870.	1875.
Barrington,	549	795	1,000	1,028	1,111	1,185
Bristol,	3,490	4,616	5,271	4,649	5,302	5,829
Warren,	2,437	3,103	2,636	2,792	3,008	4,005
BRISTOL Co.,	6,476	8,514	8,907	8,469	9,421	11,019
Coventry,	3,433	3,620	4,247	3,995	4,349	4,580
East Greenwich,	1,509	2,358	2,882	2,400	2,660	3,120
West Greenwich,	1,415	1,350	1,258	1,228	1,133	1,034
Warwick,	6,726	7,740	8,916	7,696	10,453	11,614
KENT Co.,	13,083	15,068	17,303	15,319	18,595	20,348
Fall River,	—	—	3,337	—	—	—
Jamestown,	365	358	400	349	378	488
Little Compton,	1,327	1,462	1,304	1,197	1,166	1,156
Middletown,	891	830	1,012	1,019	971	1,074
New Shoreham,	1,069	1,262	1,320	1,308	1,113	1,147
Portsmouth,	1,706	1,833	2,048	2,153	2,003	1,893
Tiverton,	3,183	4,699	1,927	1,973	1,898	2,101
TOWNS, NEWPORT Co.	8,541	10,444	11,388	7,999	7,529	7,859
NEWPORT CITY,	8,333	9,563	10,508	12,688	12,521	14,028
Burrillville,	1,982	3,538	4,140	4,861	4,674	5,249
Cranston,	2,901	4,311	7,500	9,177	4,822	5,688
Cumberland,	5,225	6,661	8,339	8,216	3,882	5,673
East Providence,	—	—	—	2,172	2,668	4,336
Foster,	2,181	1,932	1,935	1,873	1,630	1,543
Glocester,	2,304	2,872	2,427	2,286	2,385	2,098
Johnston,	2,477	2,937	3,440	3,436	4,192	4,999
Lincoln,	—	—	—	—	7,889	11,565
North Providence,	4,207	7,680	11,818	14,553	20,495	1,303
North Smithfield,	—	—	—	—	3,052	2,797
Pawtucket,	—	—	—	5,000	6,619	18,464
Scituate,	4,090	4,582	4,251	3,538	3,846	4,101
Smithfield,	9,534	11,500	13,283	12,315	2,605	2,857
Woonsocket,	—	—	—	—	11,527	13,576
TOWNS, PROV. Co.,	34,901	46,013	57,133	67,427	80,286	84,249
PROVIDENCE CITY,	23,172	41,513	50,666	54,595	68,904	100,675
Charlestown,	923	994	981	1,134	1,119	1,054
Exeter,	1,776	1,634	1,741	1,498	1,462	1,355
Hopkinton,	1,726	2,477	2,738	2,512	2,682	2,760
North Kingstown,	2,909	2,971	3,104	3,166	3,568	3,505
South Kingstown,	3,717	3,807	4,717	4,513	4,493	4,240
Richmond,	1,361	1,784	1,964	1,830	2,064	1,739
Westerly,	1,912	2,763	3,470	3,815	4,709	5,408
WASHINGTON Co.,	14,324	16,430	18,715	18,468	20,097	20,061
WHOLE STATE,	108,830	147,545	174,620	184,965	217,353	258,239

State Valuation.

Valuation of the several towns and cities in the State as returned by the town and city clerks to the Secretary of State, October, 1875.

TOWN OR CITY.*	Real Estate.	Personal Estate.	Total.	Rate of Tax on each $100.*
Barrington,	$985,505	$509,300	$1,494,805	$0.55
Bristol,	3,210,700	1,900,400	5,111,100	.78
Warren,	2,052,950	2,115,150	4,168,100	.64
BRISTOL COUNTY,	**$6,249,155**	**$4,524,850**	**$10,774,005**	
Coventry,	$2,616,300	$1,437,100	$4,053,400	.40
East Greenwich,	1,465,402	372,550	1,837,952	.50
West Greenwich,	362,030	143,140	505,170	.90
Warwick,	7,577,500	2,840,900	10,418,400	.50
KENT COUNTY,	**$12,021,232**	**$4,793,690**	**$16,814,922**	
Jamestown,	$785,300	$273,400	$1,058,700	.50
Little Compton,	830,950	435,600	1,266,550	.50
Middletown,	1,596,000	398,200	1,994,200	.60
Newport,	20,831,000	8,040,200	28,871,200	.77
New Shoreham,	287,384	45,304	332,688	2.25
Portsmouth,	1,556,400	674,500	2,230,900	.58
Tiverton,	1,262,913	484,285	1,747,198	.60
NEWPORT COUNTY,	**$27,149,947**	**$10,351,489**	**$37,501,436**	
Burrillville,	$1,853,600	$896,800	$2,750,400	.74
Cranston,	5,864,550	934,200	6,798,750	.50
Cumberland,	3,671,250	2,084,050	5,755,300	.65
East Providence,	4,565,700	817,800	5,383,500	.70
Foster,	535,300	148,900	684,200	.94
Glocester,	824,555	450,550	1,275,105	.80
Johnston,	3,686,600	784,900	3,871,500	.80
Lincoln,	5,474,350	1,732,800	7,207,150	.80
North Providence,	803,705	199,500	1,003,205	.80
North Smithfield,	1,270,550	966,400	2,236,950	.70
Pawtucket,	12,648,774	3,603,656	16,252,430	1.25
Providence,	82,862,900	39,091,800	121,954,700	1.45
Scituate,	1,571,300	776,600	2,347,900	.85
Smithfield,	1,366,600	728,900	2,095,500	.85
Woonsocket,	6,979,900	2,533,370	9,513,270	1.20
PROVIDENCE CO.,	**$133,379,634**	**$55,750,226**	**$189,129,860**	
Charlestown,	$612,800	$88,450	$701,250	.70
Exeter,	546,860	123,580	670,440	.50
Hopkinton,	1,326,850	438,450	1,765,300	.65
North Kingstown,	1,869,905	969,630	2,839,535	.52
South Kingstown,	3,002,490	1,458,610	4,461,100	.60
Richmond,	1,006,800	257,400	1,264,200	.65
Westerly,	3,113,800	1,379,175	4,492,975	.60
WASHINGTON CO.,	**$11,479,505**	**$4,715,295**	**$16,194,800**	
WHOLE STATE,	**$190,279,473**	**$80,135,550**	**$270,415,023**	

* Including highway tax.

The Corliss Engine

AT THE INTERNATIONAL EXPOSITION.

THIS engine was furnished by George H. Corliss, of Providence, Rhode Island, and was especially designed for supplying motive power at the International Exposition of 1876. This engine is of fourteen hundred horse-power, but is capable of doing the work of twenty-five hundred horses if necessary. With its appurtenances it weighs over seven hundred tons, and furnishes power to all the machinery in the building. Miles of shafting lead away from it along the aisles from end to end. Of these are eight main lines of shafting, four on each side of the central transept where the engine stands, extending lengthwise. Seven have a speed of one hundred and twenty revolutions, and one a speed of two hundred and forty revolutions a minute. A line of shafting is also provided for carrying power into the pump *annex*, and counter shafts are introduced into the aisles at different points. The power is transmitted by the *spur-gear* fly-wheel, thirty feet in diameter, weighing fifty-six tons; the jack-wheel ten feet in diameter on the main shafting, which being run under the floors to the pulleys, the power is transmitted thence to the eight main lines of shafting above the floor, aggregating more than a mile in length, from which the machinery of the Exposition derives its power. The engine makes thirty-six revolutions per minute, and for driving them there are twenty Corliss boilers capable of developing fourteen hundred horse-power, and of standing a pressure of one hundred pounds to the square inch. The platform on which the engine stands is breast high. From this, on either side, a long iron staircase mounts to the top of the A frames, where narrow walks with brass railings lead about among the moving masses aloft in the air. It is five times a man's height from the platform to the top of the walking-beam.

It is a tamed monster with unresistable power. To see a man walk calmly around among the great beams and cranks is a sight to make one shiver. He caresses a polished crank of steel that would crush him to bits if he should stop in its path. He pats the ends of the beams as they fly up and down past him, and touches the joints with his oiler. Aside from the fact that the engine is one of the largest of its kind, it is so unique in construction and form that it is all new to beholders. It is a model of simplicity and picturesqueness.

www.ingramcontent.com/pod-product-compliance
Lightning Source LLC
Chambersburg PA
CBHW030408230426
43664CB00007BB/792